A FALCON GUIDE®

Hiking Utah

Third Edition

Bill Schneider

Edited by Ann Seifert

D0967498

FALCON GUIDE®

GUILFORD, CONNECTICUT
HELENA, MONTANA
AN IMPRINT OF THE GLOBE PEQUOT PRESS

To buy books in quantity for corporate use
or incentives, call **(800) 962–0973, ext. 4551,**
or e-mail **premiums@GlobePequot.com.**

The author and The Globe Pequot Press assume no liability for accidents happening to, or
injuries sustained by, readers who engage in the activities described in this book.

WILDERNESS is . . .

The FREEDOM to experience true wildness . . .
to hear only nature's music . . .
to study the little secrets of the natural world . . .
and to enjoy the essence of quiet and solitude
so rare in the stressful lives we now live . . .

The CHALLENGE to respect and treasure wild, roadless land . . .
to be self-reliant . . . to take your time . . .
to test your physical abilities . . .
to courteously share the last blank spots on the map with others . . .
and to fully enjoy your Wilderness experience
but leave no trace of your passing . . .

The OPPORTUNITY to discover why Wilderness is priceless . . .
to see the threats to your Wilderness . . .
to decide to devote part of yourself to preserving it . . .
and to encourage others to do so.

—Bill Schneider

Contents

Preface ix
Hiking the Desert 1
Following Faint Trails 2
Archaeological Resources, the Law, and You 3
How to Use This Book 4
Map Legend 6

The Hikes

Northern Utah: The Wasatch, Uinta, and Stansbury Ranges, and Dinosaur National Monument

1. Wellsville Mountains 8
2. Malans Peak 11
3. Deseret Peak 14
4. Gobblers Knob 17
5. Mount Raymond 21
6. Lake Blanche 24
7. Lone Peak Area via Lake Hardy 27
8. Red Pine Lakes 32
9. The Pfeifferhorn 35
10. Mount Timpanogos via Aspen Grove Trail 39
11. Santaquin Peak 43
12. Mount Nebo 46
13. Daniels Canyon Nature Trails 49
14. Dry Canyon and Clegg Canyon 51
15. Center Canyon 53
16. Thornton Hollow 55
17. Log Hollow 57
18. Round, Sand, and Fish Lakes 60
19. Three Divide Lakes 64
20. Four Lakes Basin 67
21. Stillwater Drainage 72
22. West Fork Blacks Fork 75
23. Kings Peak 78
24. Rock Creek 82
25. Yellowstone Drainage 86
26. Eastern Uintas Highline Trail 89
27. Jones Hole Creek 92

Honorable Mentions, Northern Utah

A. Smithfield Dry Canyon Trail 96
B. Alexander Basin 96
C. Lone Peak via Draper Ridge 97

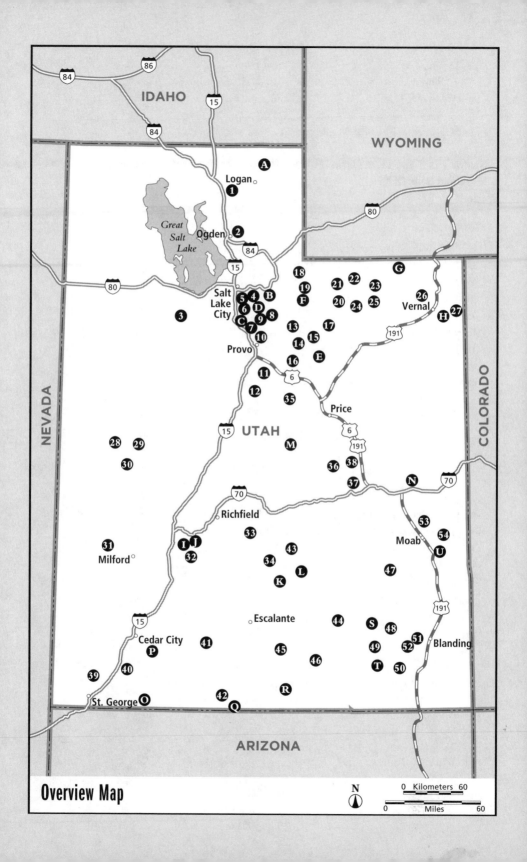

Overview Map

    D. Great Western Trail—Uinta National Forest 98
    E. Row Bench 98
    F. Hidden Lake 99
    G. Burnt Fork 99
    H. Dinosaur National Monument 100

Central Utah: The Great Basin, Fishlake National Forest, Wasatch Plateau, San Rafael River, and Book Cliffs

28. Tule Valley 102
29. Swasey Peak 105
30. Notch Peak 107
31. Wah Wah Mountains 110
32. Skyline National Recreation Trail 113
33. Fish Lake Mountains 115
34. Fish Creek Lake 118
35. Fish Creek 120
36. San Rafael River 123
37. Lower Black Box 126
38. Upper Black Box 129

Honorable Mentions, Central Utah

    I. Delano Peak 132
    J. Bullion Canyon Trail System 132
    K. Boulder Top Trails 133
    L. Slickrock Trail 134
    M. Left Fork of Huntington Creek 134
    N. Thompson Canyon 135

Southern Utah: The National Parks, Pine Valley Mountains, BLM Wilderness, Escalante River, Henry Mountains, and Grand Gulch Area

39. Pine Valley Mountains 138
40. Kolob Arch 141
41. Under-the-Rim Trail 145
42. Hackberry Canyon 148
43. Lower Muley Twist Canyon 152
44. Swett Canyon 155
45. Egypt–Twentyfive Mile Wash 158
46. Main Moody Canyon 161
47. Upheaval Dome 164
48. Dark Canyon 167
49. Bridges Loop 172
50. Fish Creek and Owl Creek Loop 176
51. Arch Canyon 179
52. Mule Canyon 182

53. Marching Men and Tower Arch 185

54. Negro Bill Canyon 188

Honorable Mentions, Southern Utah

    O. Canaan Mountain 192

    P. Rattlesnake Creek and Ashdown Gorge 193

    Q. Paria Canyon 193

    R. Navajo Point 194

    S. Fable Valley 195

    T. Grand Gulch 195

    U. Behind the Rocks 196

The Art of Hiking 197

Appendix A: Trail Finder 218

Appendix B: Local Conservation Organizations 222

Appendix C: Federal and State Agencies 223

Appendix D: Finding Maps 228

About the Author 229

Help Us Keep This Guide Up to Date

Every effort has been made by the author and editors to make this guide as accurate and useful as possible. However, many things can change after a guide is published—trails are rerouted, regulations change, techniques evolve, facilities come under new management, etc.

We would love to hear from you concerning your experiences with this guide and how you feel it could be improved and kept up to date. While we may not be able to respond to all comments and suggestions, we'll take them to heart, and we'll also make certain to share them with the author. Please send your comments and suggestions to the following address:

The Globe Pequot Press
Reader Response/Editorial Department
P.O. Box 480
Guilford, CT 06437

Or you may e-mail us at:

editorial@GlobePequot.com

Thanks for your input, and happy trails!

Preface

Hiking Is for Everybody

Although we occasionally hear claims that only the young, rich, and elite use wilderness, quite the reverse is true. Families spend many pleasurable nights camping far from vehicles. And day hiking (or "walking for pleasure," as agencies sometimes call it) is undoubtedly one of the most popular forms of outdoor recreation.

The people who make such statements must do little, if any, hiking, or they surely would see young, old, large, small, rich, and poor—all thoroughly enjoying the backcountry trails. Hiking and backpacking are available to all ages, sexes, and sizes. They only require a small amount of physical conditioning and a minimal amount of equipment.

That's right—a minimal investment. Yes, hiking and backpacking can be as expensive as any other pastime if you choose to make them so. On the other hand, they can be among the most economical forms of outdoor recreation—especially day hiking, which requires nothing except a pair of hiking shoes that may already be sitting in your closet.

For overnight trips, more expense is required. But even this can be a small investment. The cost of a two-week vacation, staying in motels and eating in restaurants, would be sufficient to outfit an entire family for backpacking. And this equipment can be used year after year. Once you've made the small initial investment, you can see millions of acres of spectacular, roadless country without spending another penny on equipment. You need only a few dollars for food and for transportation to the trailhead. After the trailhead, it's free.

Not only is hiking free in the economic sense, but it is also free of the stress and regulation of modern America. Once you're on the trail, you can forget (albeit only temporarily) the tension of your work, the Internal Revenue Service, the unpaid bills, the noise, and the pollution—it's all behind you for a few hours or days. You can't even hear the bad news on the radio.

Hiking provides an escape—a chance to inhale the pungent aroma of a wildflower meadow, to hear a bugling elk or the wind whistling through mature pines, to hook a native trout instead of a hatchery-raised catchable, to see the sunset across a mountain lake or a mountain goat race over cliffs that a person would need climbing gear to negotiate, and to study vegetation that evolved without human influence.

All this is here for the taking. Fortunately Utah offers plenty of opportunity to do so.

You can, of course, plan your own trips by talking to local hikers or agency personnel and searching through topographic maps. But to make the process easier, we published this guide. It contains enough hikes for a lifetime of backcountry thrills.

We've included hikes from almost every roadless portion of Utah—from the alpine splendor of the Uintas to the deep canyons of the slickrock country and the ranges and valleys of the Great Basin.

We've also included hikes for all kinds of hikers—beginners, families, experienced backpackers. In fact, most of the hikes are short day hikes, usually well suited for families or inexperienced hikers. Since we've picked hikes from throughout Utah, one of the trailheads is likely only a short drive away.

Also, we feel the way this guide is written makes it particularly valuable. Instead of relying on the experience of one or a small group of hikers, we've listed the favorite hikes of veteran Utah hikers—people who wish to share their experience with others, hoping new users will also come to appreciate these areas and fight to preserve them.

The maps included with each hike add a final touch to the descriptions. In addition, there are several chapters of interest to all hikers on subjects from backcountry ethics to hiking in the desert. With this guide, you should have no trouble discovering and enjoying wild Utah.

Writing a hiking guide for any state is a challenge. But for Utah—with thousands of hikes in the Wasatch, Uintas, Great Basin, Book Cliffs, canyon country, national parks, and elsewhere—the challenge becomes more difficult. Utah is unique among western states in that it offers exciting alpine hiking typical of the northern Rockies as well as some of the most breathtaking canyon hiking in the world.

Obviously, this guide does not cover every hike from every backcountry area of the state. Rather, our philosophy in assembling *Hiking Utah* has been to offer beginning and veteran hikers, longtime residents and newcomers alike an introduction to Utah's spectacular wildlands. There are hikers who know every peak and lake in the Uintas, yet know nothing of the Pine Valley Mountains, Mount Naomi, the San Rafael River, the Wah Wahs, and Grand Gulch.

In addition to getting you to the trailhead, it is also our intention to relate the importance of responsible wilderness use. With more people in the backcountry and increasing demands on public lands each year, some of our "pristine" areas are beginning to look like city parks. Hikers, along with other backcountry users and land management agencies, will have to assume the responsibility of maintaining the opportunity for quality outdoor experiences in the future.

Hence, this guide stresses outdoor ethics. You will find sections on walking softly, the preservation of archaeological resources, and wilderness in Utah. The names and addresses of state and federal land management agencies and local conservation organizations are provided in the appendices in the event you wish to ask a question, voice an opinion, or take a more active role in management issues. And, where appropriate, suggestions are made throughout *Hiking Utah* to make your trip a safe one and lessen your impact on the land.

Happy hiking.

Hiking the Desert

Many beginning hikers and newcomers to Utah are awed—indeed, perplexed—by the prospects of hiking the desert. Undoubtedly they are envisioning unending salt flats, heat waves dancing on the horizon, and a lone cactus breaking the monotony. Why would anyone want to hike here?

Actually the "desert," as Utah hikers like to call it—possibly to weed out the tenderfeet—is a diverse country of deep canyons, shady, often lush river bottoms, high plateaus, bizarre rock formations, and rich archaeological history. Hiking here inspires superlatives.

Conditions can be harsh, but the desert does not have to be an inhospitable place to travel. Follow the general advice below and you can have a safe and enjoyable trip.

- Before you come, get a general idea of the kind of hiking you will be doing. Call the appropriate management agency or a person familiar with the hike.

- Also get a report on road conditions leading to the trailhead.

- Avoid midsummer hikes. In most cases spring and fall hikes are preferable.

- Know what the water conditions are. If water quality is poor or if no water exists along the trail, you must carry all water in with you. Generally, one gallon per day per person is required.

- Do not drink untreated water.

- Some river water may be too silty to filter. Carrying in a collapsible plastic container permits the water to settle out while you are making camp.

- Prepare for the sun. Use a good sunscreen. A cap with a visor is also recommended. Legs can be particularly susceptible when hiking along rivers.

- Deerflies can be bothersome in some areas. A good brand of insect repellent helps to solve the problem.

- Watch the weather carefully. Flash flooding can be very dangerous. When hiking long distances in deep canyons, be sure to get a reliable long-term forecast. Remember that it does not have to be raining where you are hiking for danger to exist. A storm miles up the canyon can mean trouble.

- Canyon hiking does not require the heavy boots necessary elsewhere. In fact, they become a burden when hiking long distances through water. Light canvas boots or old running shoes are recommended.

- When river crossings are required, line your pack with heavy-duty plastic bags. Seal the bags well, and the pack will float across. Some hikers bring along an inflatable air mattress to use for ferrying packs.

- Above all, prepare for your trip and use common sense.

Following Faint Trails

Trails that receive infrequent use often fade away in grassy meadows, on ridges, in dry washes, or through rocky sections. If a trail fades away before you, don't panic. These sections are usually short, and you can often look ahead to see where the trail goes. If so, focus on the trail ahead and don't worry about being off it for a short distance. Also watch for other indicators that you are indeed on the right route, even if the trail isn't clearly visible. These might include cairns, blazes, downfall cut with saws, paths cleared through thick timber, and trees with the branches whacked off on one side. Nowadays land managers discourage the use of blazes, and rangers use small metal reflective markers instead. However, you can still see old blazes along many trails. If you rely on blazes to follow a faint trail, make sure you follow only official blazes—which are shaped like an upside-down exclamation point—instead of blazes made by hunters, outfitters, or other hikers.

Archaeological Resources, the Law, and You

Of approximately 25,000 recorded archaeological sites in Utah, over ninety percent of them show effects of vandalism.
— Richard Fike, archaeologist, Bureau of Land Management

While hiking in almost any part of Utah, it is common to find archaeological sites and artifacts—dwellings, pottery, arrowheads, grinding stones, and woven sandals. These discoveries are an intriguing, exciting part of Utah hiking. They give us a glimpse of former cultures, of farming, architecture, recreation, food gathering, art, and religion many hundreds of years old.

Unfortunately, artifacts are becoming less common, dwellings are crumbling under the weight of hikers scrambling over them, and rock art is being crowded by the likes of JIM LOVES SUE.

The largest wholesale removal of artifacts occurred during the nineteenth century, when scientific parties shipped thousands of pieces to eastern and foreign museums. Federal and state laws have since put controls on these activities. However, unauthorized pilfering continues.

Pocketing an arrowhead on federal or state land is illegal, and it leaves one less treasure for tomorrow's hiker to see. Artifacts should be left in place. They're of much more value where they are than they possibly could be in your bureau drawer.

Two federal laws, the Antiquities Act of 1906 and the Archaeological Resources Protection Act of 1979, forbid removal or destruction of archaeological resources on Utah's federal lands. These acts are intended to protect and preserve the resources for the future—for the scientific community *and* for other hikers who follow after you. Stiff fines and imprisonment can result from failure to follow these guidelines. The Utah State Antiquities Act, enacted in 1973, provides similar protection on state lands.

Seemingly innocent actions can contribute to irreparable damage. Ancient painted pigments can be altered by the oil from fingerprints. Sitting or climbing on rock walls can turn culturally priceless ruins into rubble. Walking across middens, the ancient trash heaps below ruins, can damage sites.

What can you do to help protect our state's splendid resources? First, recognize that you and several other hikers bringing home "just one small arrowhead" can over time be just as damaging as large-scale and purposeful vandalism. It takes a little longer, but the result is the same. So enjoy and study what you find, but leave all sites and artifacts undisturbed. Admire rock art from a distance and never touch it. When approaching a cultural site, avoid walking on soft soils to reduce the chance of erosion. Stay out of ruins. Report any vandalism to the nearest federal or state resource office. In some cases rewards are offered.

How to Use This Book

This guidebook won't answer every question you have concerning your planned hiking route—but then most people don't want to know everything before they go, lest they miss the thrill of making their own discoveries while exploring Utah's wild country. This book does provide the basic information needed to plan a successful trip, however. Here are some tips on using this book to help you have a more pleasant trip.

Types of Hikes

Suggested hikes have been split into the following categories:

Loop: Starts and finishes at the same trailhead, with no (or very little) retracing of your steps. Sometimes the definition of *loop* is stretched to include "lollipops" and trips that involve a short walk on a road at the end of the hike to get back to your vehicle.

Point to point: A hike that requires either two vehicles (leave one at the end of the trail) or a prearranged pickup at a designated time and place. One good way to manage the logistical problems of such shuttles is to arrange for another party to start at the other end of the trail. The two parties meet at a predetermined point and then trade car keys. When finished, they drive each other's vehicles to a designated rendezvous.

Out and back: Traveling to a specific destination, then retracing your steps to the trailhead.

Difficulty Ratings

We've tried to standardize the difficulty ratings as much as possible, as follows:

Easy trails are suitable for any hiker, including children and elderly persons. They feature little or no elevation gain, no serious trail hazards, and no off-trail or faint-trail route finding.

Moderate trails are suitable for most hikers who have some experience and at least an average fitness level. They might also be suitable for children or elderly folks with above-average fitness levels. The hikes may include some short sections where the trail is difficult to follow and may include up to 1,500 feet in elevation gain.

Strenuous trails are suitable for experienced hikers with above-average fitness levels. These trails may be difficult to follow or feature off-trail routes requiring serious map-and-compass skills. These hikes almost all feature serious elevation gain and possibly hazardous river fords or other risks.

Distances

It's almost impossible to determine precise distances for most trails. The distances used in this guidebook are based on a combination of actual experience hiking the trails, distances stated on Forest Service signs, and estimates from topo maps. In some cases distances may be slightly off; keep this in mind when planning a trip. Also remember that distance is often less important than difficulty—a rough, 2-mile cross-country trek can take longer than 5 or 6 miles on a good trail. Keep mileage estimates in perspective, too, because they are all at least slightly off. Almost all trail signs use estimates in whole miles. You've probably seen a sign saying it's 5 miles to a lake, but what's the chance that it's exactly 5 miles? Should we really worry about it?

Special Regulations and Permits

Land management agencies have special regulations for hikers and backcountry equestrians on many trails. In some cases the regulations apply throughout a large area, but in others they apply to specific trails or ranger districts. Check with the appropriate agency before you leave on your trip, and be sure to read and follow any special regulations posted on the information board at the trailhead. Agencies don't come up with regulations to inconvenience backcountry visitors. Instead, the regs are designed to promote sharing and preservation of the wilderness, and to make your trip as safe as possible.

Getting to the Trailhead

Some trailheads are located along major state highways, and others are found in remote backcountry. Make sure your vehicle is in good condition and appropriate for the roads to the trailhead. Have a full tank and carry basic emergency equipment, such as a shovel, ax, saw, extra water, emergency food, and warm clothing. If you're unsure about road conditions, check ahead with the appropriate agency. In this book we've made a point of noting when to expect a rough road on the way to the trailhead and if you'll need a high-clearance vehicle to get there.

About the Maps

The maps in this book that depict a detailed close-up of an area use elevation tints, called hypsometry, to portray relief. Each gray tone represents a range of equal elevation, as shown in the scale key with the map. These maps will give you a good idea of elevation gain and loss. The darker tones are lower elevations and the lighter grays are higher elevations. The lighter the tone, the higher the elevation. Narrow bands of different gray tones spaced closely together indicate steep terrain, whereas wider bands indicate areas of more gradual slope.

Maps that show larger geographic areas use shaded, or shadow, relief. Shadow relief does not represent elevation; it demonstrates slope or relative steepness. This gives an almost 3-D perspective of the physiography of a region and will help you see where ranges and valleys are.

Map Legend

══⟨15⟩══	Interstate
══⟨62⟩══	U.S. highway
──⟨137⟩──	State highway
──[410]──	Other road
= = = = =	Unimproved road
▬▬▬▬▬	Featured trail
---------	Other trail
··········	Off-trail hiking
∧	Arch
⋈	Bridge
♠	Cabin/lodge
⚑	Campground
≈	Falls
●—●	Gate
◌	Marsh
⚒	Mine
🅿	Parking
‿	Pass
▲+	Peak/elevation
⊼	Picnic area
▪	Point of interest
⬚	Ruin/other site
⚲	Spring
🚶	Trailhead
❓	Visitor information
👁	View Point
○	Water tank

Northern Utah: The Wasatch, Uinta, and Stansbury Ranges, and Dinosaur National Monument

1 Wellsville Mountains

A point-to-point hike to the crest of the Wellsville Mountains Wilderness. Enjoy views of Cache Valley extending north into Idaho, west past the Promontory and Raft River Ranges, and south to the Great Salt Lake. Fall raptor migrations offer exciting hawk-watching. Numerous trails ascend the eastern slopes of the Wellsvilles from Cache Valley.

Start: Deep Canyon Trailhead or Coldwater Canyon Trailhead.
Distance: 7.5 miles point to point.
Difficulty: Moderate.
Trail surface: Forest trail.
Seasons: Late spring through fall.
Land status: Wilderness area.
Nearest town: Logan.

Fees and permits: No fees or permits required.
Maps: USGS Honeyville and Wellsville quads; USFS Wasatch-Cache (North) Forest visitor's map.
Trail contacts: Logan Ranger District, Wasatch-Cache National Forest, 1500 East Highway 89, Logan, UT 84321; (435) 755-3620; www.fs.fed.us/r4/wcnf.

Finding the trailhead: To reach the Deep Canyon Trailhead (the recommended starting point), turn off Highway 23 in Mendon and drive west for 2 miles on Third North to the trailhead/parking area. Please stay on the road. This trailhead was built on private property with the landowner's permission.

To reach the Coldwater Canyon Trailhead, drive south on Main Street in Mendon as it diagonally crosses Highway 23, then follow the TO NATIONAL FOREST signs as the road zigzags west and south. This is a very rough road and requires a high-clearance four-wheel-drive vehicle. The distance from Mendon to the trailhead is about 3.5 miles. *DeLorme: Utah Atlas & Gazetteer:* Page 60 A3.

The Hike

The Wellsville Mountains have been called the steepest mountains in the world. After climbing the precipitous east side and gazing down the rugged west side to the oxbow bends of the Bear River, you'll agree. The hike is worth it, however, because this northern Utah range offers some splendid views from the ridge.

A point-to-point hike over the Deep Canyon and Coldwater Canyon Trails necessitates a car shuttle. Both trailheads offer good access to the ridge if you choose an out-and-back hike rather than the shuttle, though.

Expect a strenuous 2,700-foot climb to the ridge and more elevation gain as you continue along the ridgeline. Distances are not excessive, however, so an early start and a leisurely pace make the trip possible. Overnight camping is not recommended due to a lack of water and protected campsites on the ridge. The windchill factor on the exposed ridge may be substantial, so be prepared. Don't be misled by warm temperatures in the valley.

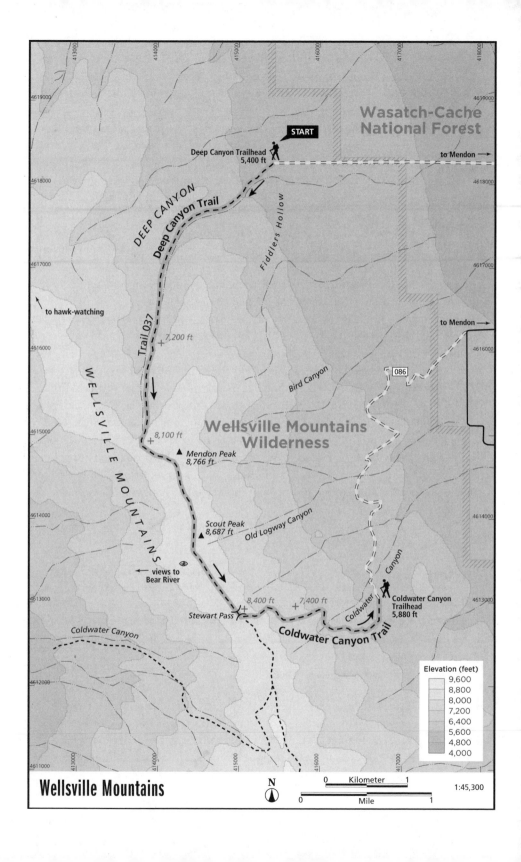

START

Deep Canyon Trailhead
5,400 ft

Wasatch-Cache
National Forest

to Mendon

DEEP CANYON

Deep Canyon Trail

Fiddlers Hollow

to Mendon →

Trail 037

to hawk-watching

7,200 ft

Bird Canyon

086

WELLSVILLE MOUNTAINS

Wellsville Mountains
Wilderness

8,100 ft

▲ Mendon Peak
8,766 ft

Scout Peak
8,687 ft

Old Logway Canyon

views to
Bear River

Coldwater Canyon

Coldwater Canyon
Trailhead
5,880 ft

8,400 ft   7,400 ft

Stewart Pass

Coldwater Canyon Trail

Coldwater Canyon

Wellsville Mountains

N

0   Kilometer   1

0   Mile   1

1:45,300

Elevation (feet)

9,600
8,800
8,000
7,200
6,400
5,600
4,800
4,000

The Deep Canyon Trail begins at 5,400 feet in scrub maple and continues through aspen and mountain ash for 3.2 miles before reaching Wellsville Ridge in a saddle at 8,100 feet. You get a good workout; this section of the hike travels steadily uphill.

From the saddle at the top of Deep Canyon, turn left (southeast) along the ridge. Stay directly atop the ridge as the trail ascends 8,766-foot Mendon Peak. As you approach the summit, the trail skirts it and continues south.

Half a mile south is Scout Peak (8,687 feet). Continue contouring near the ridge another mile to Stewart Pass at 8,400 feet. Watch carefully for the Coldwater Canyon Trail descending to the left (east). This is your route off the ridge. The ridge trail, incidentally, continues south to other attractions, among them 9,372-foot Box Elder Peak—the highest point in the range. Box Elder Peak is about 2 miles from Stewart Pass.

The descent from Stewart Pass is steep, dropping about 2,100 feet in a little more than 1.75 miles to tiny Coldwater Lake. Avoid the temptation to use the shortcuts between switchbacks. It is easier to stay on the established trail, preventing destructive erosion. You can then make a gentle 0.75-mile hike from the lake down to the Coldwater Canyon Trailhead.

Early in the twentieth century, overgrazing and uncontrolled burning left the Wellsvilles vulnerable to erosion. Although conditions were not as serious as they were farther south along the Wasatch Front, floods did pour out of the range onto the Wellsville-Mendon Road and into the Beaver Dam and Petersboro areas. Concerned citizens, hoping to return the mountain range to its original condition, formed the Wellsville Area Project Corporation in 1941. They obtained contributions, bought land, and deeded it to the Forest Service for protection. The Wellsville Mountains have now recovered to the point that the only readily visible evidence of past abuse is a few gullies.

The 23,556-acre Wellsville Mountains Wilderness was designated under the Utah Wilderness Act of 1984.

Key Points

0.0   Start at the Deep Canyon Trailhead.

3.2   Arrive at a saddle on the ridge of the Wellsville Mountains. Continue southeast.

4.9   Arrive at Stewart Pass. Take the Coldwater Lake Trail descending to the left (east).

6.75   Reach Coldwater Lake.

7.5   Arrive at the Coldwater Canyon Trailhead.

Option: From the saddle at Wellsville Ridge, you may continue along the ridge 0.75 mile to the northwest. The tallest peak (8,585 feet) is a popular hawk-watching spot during fall raptor migrations. It's one of the better places in the state to view raptors "face to face" as they ride updrafts along the mountain. No other location has as many birds passing this close to the ridge. The Logan Ranger District or the Division of Wildlife Resources can give you more information.

The views in all directions are spectacular. Of particular interest are the oxbow bends of the Bear River nearly 4,000 feet below. Not only does Wellsville Ridge offer an outstanding view of the northern portion of the state, but it also has a showy display of wildflowers. Old and determined stands of limber pine are scattered along the ridge, interspersed with clumps of Indian paintbrush. In spring and early summer, leopard and glacier lilies, bluebells, spring beauty, stinging nettle, and mountain-lover are visible along the trail. —*Originally contributed by Steve Flint and Eric Rechel*

2 Malans Peak

A moderately demanding hike and scramble located east of Ogden in the Wasatch Mountains, featuring spectacular views of Ogden, the Salt Lake Valley, and a 400-foot waterfall.

Start: Near the east end of 29th Street in Ogden.
Distance: 5.5-mile loop.
Difficulty: Moderate.
Trail surface: Dirt road and forest trail.
Seasons: Late spring through fall.
Land status: Currently the entire Malans Peak loop trail system is on private land and not maintained for public use by the Forest Service. Hikers should obtain permission from the private landowner prior to hiking. Contact the Ogden Ranger District (below) for more information on the status of this area.
Nearest town: Ogden.
Fees and permits: No fees or permits required.
Maps: USGS Ogden quad; Northern Utah Multipurpose Map.
Trail contacts: Ogden Ranger District, Wasatch-Cache National Forest, 507 25th Street, Ogden, UT 84403; (801) 625-5112; www.fs.fed.us/r4/wcnf.

Finding the trailhead: Drive to the east end of 29th Street in Ogden and turn right onto a dirt road. Park in a large parking area just east of a high-rise apartment building. *DeLorme: Utah Atlas & Gazetteer:* Page 60 C3.

The Hike

Beginning just east of Ogden, this 5.5-mile loop hike follows Waterfall Canyon to the Malans Basin high country. A gradual climb from there brings you to Malans Peak overlooking Ogden and the Great Salt Lake. Finally, a well-developed trail on the north side of the peak leads to within a few blocks of the trailhead. You gain plenty of elevation—more than 2,300 feet from the trailhead to Malans Peak.

The loop is an ideal day hike, but it's a good choice for an overnighter also. Campsites abound in the Malans Basin area. The best direction to hike this loop is

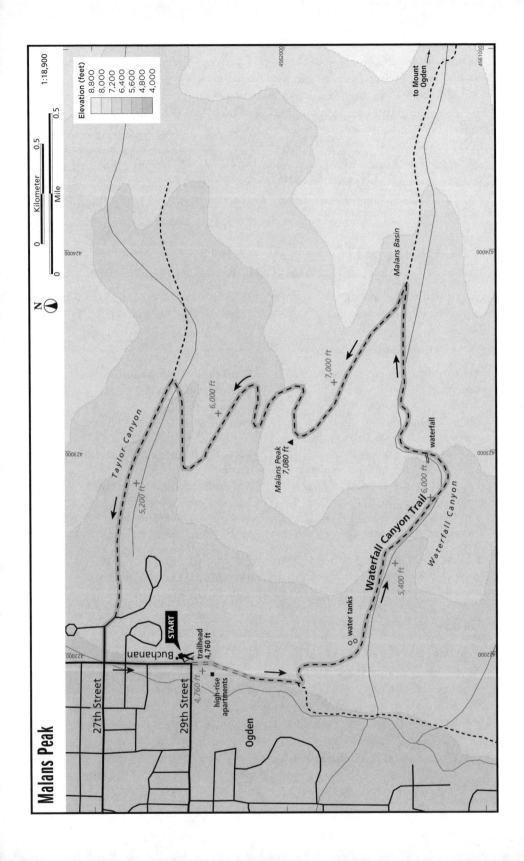

Malans Peak

N

1:18,900

Elevation (feet)
8,800
8,000
7,200
6,400
5,600
4,800
4,000

Kilometer 0.5
0 0.5 Mile

Taylor Canyon

5,200 ft

6,000 ft

7,000 ft

Malans Peak
7,080 ft

Malans Basin

to Mount
Ogden

waterfall

6,000 ft

Waterfall Canyon

Waterfall Canyon Trail

5,400 ft

water tanks

START

Buchanan

trailhead
4,760 ft

4,760 ft

high-rise
apartments

27th Street

29th Street

Ogden

4524000
4523000
4522000
4562000
4524000
4523000
4522000
4561000

counterclockwise—up Waterfall Canyon, over Malans Peak, and down Taylor Canyon. A steep scree slope at the top of Waterfall Canyon can make the hike dangerous and more difficult in the other direction.

Water is plentiful in Waterfall Canyon. But Taylor Canyon is dry in midsummer, so plan accordingly.

Start by hiking south on a dirt road just east of the apartment building. Take the first road heading to the left (east) up through the oak brush. It is easy to get side-tracked on one of the many roads not shown on maps, but if you continue generally to the south for 0.5 mile toward the obvious mouth of Waterfall Canyon, you will have no trouble. Just before entering the canyon, the road swings left (east) above two large water tanks and becomes a trail.

Entering the canyon is a relief after the short but dusty hike up from your car. Water flows year-round in Waterfall Canyon, and the overhanging vegetation offers plenty of shade on a hot summer day.

Hike and occasionally scramble along the trail beside the tumbling stream. White arrows placed strategically on rocks indicate the way. After a 0.5-mile, 800-foot climb past the mouth of the canyon, you arrive at a spectacular cascade. Not much water falls by midsummer, but you'll want to pause in the amphitheater. There are some nice lunch rocks here, and the spray of the falls keeps the temperature very comfortable.

When you are ready to continue to Malans Basin, look for the canyon continuing east up the gulch to the right of the falls. A few ledges warrant caution, but they are not dangerous, and no technical equipment is required.

Above the ledges is a fairly steep scree slope, and rocks are easily jarred loose and can tumble down the slope. For safety keep your group together in this area. Views behind you along this section are worth the pause.

After a few hundred yards, the gorge curves to the left (north). Follow the slope north above the waterfall. The trail becomes indistinct here, but if you contour northeast for 0.25 mile and drop into the stream drainage, the pathway appears again.

Malans Basin is 0.5 mile upstream to the east. There are campsites and relics of an old hotel. Signs of wildlife abound, and eagles and deer are commonly sighted.

From Malans Basin, the terrain to the east toward 9,572-foot Mount Ogden can be explored before beginning the gently rising traverse for 0.75 mile to Malans Peak. A well-beaten trail heads northwest from Malans Basin. Malans Peak presents a splendid panoramic view of Ogden and the Great Salt Lake.

The route down the north side of Malans Peak switches back several times in 1.25 miles before meeting the trail and streambed in Taylor Canyon—about 1,600 feet below. An excellent example of cutting off switchbacks can be observed on this slope. Hikers have made an unsightly shortcut straight up the slope. The cut is susceptible to erosion in several areas. Stay on the hiking trail.

Turning left (west) in Taylor Canyon, follow the trail about 0.75 mile to the top of 27th Street, 2 blocks north of your starting point. Turn left (south) onto Buchanan and follow this paved road to your car. —*Originally contributed by Jock Glidden*

Key Points

0.0 Trailhead at the large parking area east of the high-rise apartment building.

1.2 Reach the waterfall in Waterfall Canyon.

3.0 Enjoy the views from Malans Peak. Hike down the north side of the peak.

4.25 Junction with the trail in Taylor Canyon.

5.5 Arrive back at the parking area.

3 Deseret Peak

A demanding day hike or overnighter to the highest point in the Stansbury Mountains. Deseret Peak, located in the 25,500-acre Deseret Peak Wilderness, 42 miles southwest of Salt Lake City, offers outstanding views of northwest Utah—from the Wasatch Mountains on the east to the Nevada border on the west.

Start: Mill Fork Trailhead at the end of South Willow Canyon Road.
Distance: 8-mile loop.
Difficulty: Strenuous.
Trail surface: Forest trail.
Seasons: Late June through October.
Land status: Wilderness area.
Nearest town: Grantsville.
Fees and permits: No fees or permits required.

Maps: USGS Deseret Peak West and Deseret Peak East quads; Northern Utah Multipurpose Map.
Trail contacts: Public Lands Information Center, 3285 East 3300 S., Salt Lake City, UT 84109; (801) 466-6411. The land management agency is the Salt Lake Ranger District, Wasatch-Cache National Forest, 6944 South 3000 E., Salt Lake City, UT 84121; (801) 733-2660; www.fs.fed.us/r4/wcnf.

Finding the trailhead: Follow Interstate 80 west from Salt Lake City for about 20 miles. Take the Tooele exit onto Highway 36, turning right (southwest) after about 4 miles onto Highway 138. Continue another 10 miles to Grantsville. In the center of town, find the Forest Service sign on the right side of the street indicating South Willow Canyon. Turn left and drive about 5 miles to a fork signed SOUTH WILLOW CANYON. Take the right fork and follow the road into South Willow Canyon, past numerous campgrounds, about 7 miles to the trailhead at the south end of the Loop Campground. *DeLorme: Utah Atlas & Gazetteer:* Page 52 C2.

The Hike

While most Salt Lakers crowd into the nearby Wasatch Mountains on weekends, the Stansbury Mountains offer exceptional hiking in a less popular area but within easy

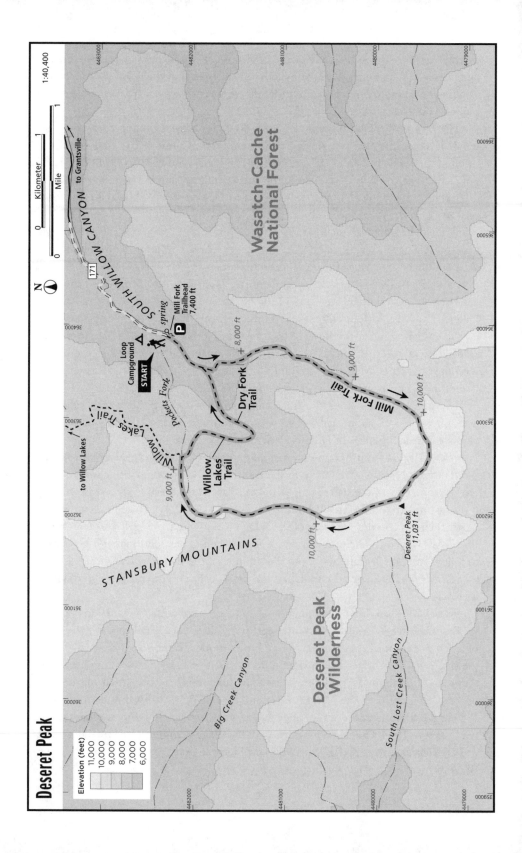

Deseret Peak

Elevation (feet)
11,000
10,000
9,000
8,000
7,000
6,000

1:40,400

N

Kilometer

Mile

SOUTH WILLOW CANYON

171

to Grantsville

spring

Mill Fork Trailhead
7,400 ft

P

Loop Campground

START

Pockets Fork

to Willow Lakes

Willow Lakes Trail

Willow Lakes Trail

Dry Fork Trail

Mill Fork Trail

9,000 ft

8,000 ft

9,000 ft

10,000 ft

10,000 ft

STANSBURY MOUNTAINS

Deseret Peak
11,031 ft

Wasatch-Cache National Forest

Deseret Peak Wilderness

Big Creek Canyon

South Lost Creek Canyon

driving distance of Salt Lake City. One of a number of isolated Great Basin mountain ranges, the Stansbury Mountains are two ranges west of the Wasatch Mountains. You'll need a little more than an hour by car from downtown Salt Lake to reach the trailhead for Deseret Peak.

The Deseret Peak loop begins its 3,600-foot climb by ascending through a lush stand of aspen. Streams run during spring and early summer. The trail continues through the forest for about 0.7 mile, where it crosses a perennial stream, Dry Lake Fork, and jogs to the left, back along the streambank. Within 50 feet the trail splits; the left fork, signed MILL FORK TRAIL, heads to Deseret Peak, while the right fork, DRY FORK TRAIL, continues to North and South Willow Lakes.

The left fork to Deseret Peak continues along Mill Fork and wanders through grass-filled meadows with occasional avalanche debris, reminding you how deeply these mountains are buried in snow during winter.

From 7,840 feet at the fork, you climb to 9,600 feet in 1.5 miles. As the trail approaches the upper cirque, views of the Great Salt Lake appear to the north, and Deseret Peak's 1,500-foot cliff looms to the southwest. Eventually the trail cuts back up the glacial cirque at the head of the canyon to a ridge at 10,000 feet. From the saddle, heavily forested, 10,305-foot Victory Mountain fills your view to the south, with the Sheeprock Mountains behind. To the north, the Great Salt Lake, Stansbury Island, and accompanying mudflats are visible.

The trail continues along the ridge, then switches back up the treeless ridgeline through patches of snow that last into early summer. After a 0.5-mile, 1,000-foot climb, you reach the top of Deseret Peak at 11,031 feet.

On a clear day you have a commanding view of 11,928-foot Mount Nebo to the southeast, Nevada's Pilot Peak to the northwest, the Wasatch Range on the eastern horizon, and all the desert ranges and salt flats to the west.

To complete the Deseret Peak loop, follow the trail down the mountain to the north, then traverse the west side of the ridge overlooking the South Lost Creek and Big Creek Canyons. The trail is not as well maintained here and may not be as easy to follow. After a 1.6-mile hike from the summit (and 1,200-foot elevation loss), the trail drops over the ridge and heads east into Pockets Fork. The trail is obvious where it crosses the ridge.

From here, head down the upper bowl and then parallel the streambed, dropping to the east. After 0.7 mile, you'll intersect the Willow Lakes Trail near a lone stand of aspen. A perennial stream flows through the meadow here, giving welcome relief (be sure to treat all water). Turn right onto the Willow Lakes Trail, hiking back into the trees. After about 1.5 miles you reach the junction that you passed on the way up. Stay left (north) on the Mill Fork Trail for an easy 0.7-mile walk back to the car.

The southern portion of the range, where you have been hiking, was designated wilderness in 1984. The northern portion of the range is administered by the Bureau of Land Management and is currently a wilderness study area with the Salt Lake BLM district. —*Originally contributed by Jim Kay*

Key Points

0.0 Start at Mill Fork Trailhead at end of South Willow Canyon Road.

0.7 Junction with the Dry Fork Trail. Turn left (south).

3.5 Arrive at Deseret Peak at 11,031 feet.

5.8 Junction with the Willow Lakes Trail. Turn right (south).

7.3 Junction with the Mill Fork Trail. Stay left (north).

8.0 Arrive back at the trailhead.

4 Gobblers Knob

A day hike or overnighter of intermediate difficulty, located just southeast of Salt Lake City in Mill Creek Canyon. The hike is point to point, so a car or bicycle shuttle is required unless you don't mind the 3.5-mile walk down Mill Creek Canyon Road at the end of your trek. Along the way you'll enjoy spectacular scenery, diverse vegetation, and abundant wildflowers in season.

Start: Bowman Fork Trailhead at Terrace Picnic Ground.

Distance: 7 miles point to point.

Difficulty: Moderate.

Trail surface: Forest trail and cross-country.

Seasons: Late spring through fall.

Land status: National forest, wilderness area.

Nearest town: Salt Lake City.

Fees and permits: No fees or permits required.

Maps: USGS Mount Aire quad; Northern Utah Multipurpose Map.

Trail contacts: Public Lands Information Center, 3285 East 3300 S., Salt Lake City, UT 84109; (801) 466-6411. The land management agency is the Salt Lake Ranger District, Wasatch-Cache National Forest, 6944 South 3000 E., Salt Lake City, UT 84121; (801) 733-2660; www.fs.fed.us/r4/wcnf.

Finding the trailhead: Take Interstate 215 south in Salt Lake City and exit onto the 39th South off-ramp. Turn left under the interstate and then left again at the light onto Wasatch Boulevard. Drive north for 1 block and turn right onto Mill Creek Canyon Road. Continue about 4.5 miles to the Terrace Picnic Ground, identified by a large Forest Service sign on the south side of the road. Depending on the time of year, you may need to park along the road opposite the picnic area, since the Forest Service seasonally locks the gate (open May 1 through October 1, 7:00 A.M. to 8:00 P.M.). If you plan to leave a car or bicycle at the Alexander Basin Trailhead, drive about 3.5 miles farther up Mill Creek Canyon, about a mile past the Fircrest and Clover Springs Picnic Grounds. The trailhead is on the right side of the road as it crosses the creek. *DeLorme: Utah Atlas & Gazetteer:* Page 53 B6.

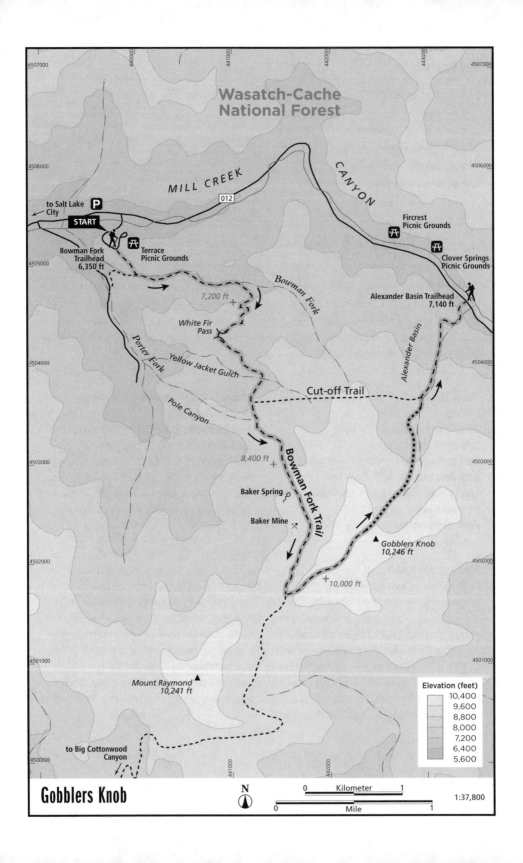

Wasatch-Cache
National Forest

MILL CREEK   CANYON

012

to Salt Lake City

START

P

Bowman Fork
Trailhead
6,350 ft

Terrace
Picnic Grounds

Fircrest
Picnic Grounds

Clover Springs
Picnic Grounds

Alexander Basin Trailhead
7,140 ft

Bowman Fork

7,200 ft

White Fir
Pass

Porter Fork

Yellow Jacket Gulch

Pole Canyon

Alexander Basin

Cut-off Trail

8,400 ft

Baker Spring

Baker Mine

Bowman Fork Trail

Gobblers Knob
10,246 ft

10,000 ft

Mount Raymond
10,241 ft

to Big Cottonwood
Canyon

Elevation (feet)

10,400
9,600
8,800
8,000
7,200
6,400
5,600

Gobblers Knob

N

0   Kilometer   1

0   Mile   1

1:37,800

The Hike

You'll ascend Bowman Fork in Mill Creek Canyon and head down Alexander Basin, so there will be no backtracking. This is a hefty day hike, but you could spend a night or two along the way. Camping is permitted in Mill Creek Canyon, and you may also cross the divide and camp in Big Cottonwood Canyon. The area is permanently closed to campfires, so carry a backpacking stove. No dogs or horses are permitted. If you decide to camp, please observe the backcountry camping regulations, which the Forest Service does enforce. Make your camp at least 200 feet from a trail, lake, stream, or spring. Practice zero-impact camping.

The trail gains about 3,900 feet in elevation over 5.25 miles, but there are only a few bothersome, steep sections. From Gobblers Knob, the route drops another 1.75 miles (3,100 feet) to the Alexander Basin Trailhead.

To start your hike, go up the paved Forest Service road through the picnic area. The trailhead is on the right side of the road, about half a mile from Mill Creek Canyon Road.

From 6,350 feet, the trail winds through dense canyon bottom vegetation alongside Bowman Fork, then leaves the stream to the south, enters a mature coniferous forest, and switches back up a steep hillside. You emerge from the forest at White Fir Pass—0.5 mile and more than 600 vertical feet after leaving the stream.

From White Fir Pass, the trail contours to the south and southeast around the head of Yellow Jacket Gulch, forested mostly with aspen and mature conifers. About 0.75 mile from White Fir Pass, Bowman Fork Trail passes a trail to Alexander Basin on the left, crosses a ridge, and enters Pole Canyon. Continue another 0.5 mile to Baker Spring, a small but perpetual spring. This is the last reliable source of water before the end of the hike, but it must be treated before drinking.

Baker Spring was once the site of an old mining camp. A mine dump on the hillside to the southeast and other remnants of mining activity are visible from here. The Baker Mine itself, however, is over the ridge to the south and not visible from the trail.

From Baker Spring, the trail contours about a mile around the head of Porter Fork to Baker Pass (about 9,400 feet) between Mount Raymond (to the west) and Gobblers Knob (to the east). You'll pass the junction with the Desolation Trail, leading to the south, to Big Cottonwood Canyon.

Wildflowers cover the slope here in spring. The slope is also the starting point for some of the most spectacular and fatal avalanches in the Wasatch Mountains. In the winter of 1979–1980, an avalanche that began on this slope continued about 2 miles to the northwest down Porter Fork, stopping just short of the summer homes at the bottom of the canyon.

At the saddle between Mount Raymond and Gobblers Knob, stop to enjoy the view of these two peaks and the Twin Peaks Wilderness south of Big Cottonwood Canyon. This is probably the best place for lunch. Then follow the ridgeline (no official Forest Service trail) to the northeast for 0.75 mile to the summit of 10,246-foot

Gobblers Knob. The path appears and disappears along the ridgeline, but the ridge itself is obvious and open. Reach the summit just a few feet before the ridge drops off abruptly into Alexander Basin.

After enjoying the views, scramble around the south side of Gobblers Knob to a saddle that lies about 400 yards east of the summit and down the ridge to a point where you can safely enter Alexander Basin—the huge basin to the north of the knob. No trail exists here, either, but the basin is quite open, and you'll have no trouble finding your way. The upper part of the basin is a rockfall. Descending the rockfall, you will find that the basin becomes broad and open, and you will discover many possible routes. Pick an easy one bearing toward the right (east) side of the canyon, and head down in that direction.

As you descend farther, bear more to the right. You'll come to a hillock that distinctly divides the possible routes into left and right branches. Keep to the right of this hillock and follow the streambed that becomes visible at about this point. Continue along the east slope of the canyon. Watch for a distinct trail (Alexander Basin Trail) entering the forest. Do not head into the trees until you have found it. It's on the east side of the canyon and is quite clear when you get close to it.

Follow the Alexander Basin Trail north down the slope another mile to the Alexander Basin Trailhead.

Key Points

0.0 Start at the Bowman Fork Trailhead.

5.25 Reach the summit of Gobblers Knob.

7.0 Arrive at the Alexander Basin Trailhead.

Option: You could backtrack from Gobblers Knob, eliminating the necessity for a shuttle, or continue into Big Cottonwood Canyon via several routes to the south.
—*Originally contributed by Walt Haas*

5 Mount Raymond

A challenging day hike or overnighter to the top of the Big Cottonwood Canyon–Mill Creek Canyon divide, featuring spectacular views of Dromedary, Sunrise, and Twin Peaks to the south.

Start: Mill B North Fork Trailhead.
Distance: 8 miles out and back.
Difficulty: Moderately strenuous.
Trail surface: Forest trail.
Seasons: Late spring through fall.
Land status: National forest, wilderness area.
Nearest town: Salt Lake City.
Fees and permits: No fees or permits required.

Maps: USGS Mount Aire quad; Northern Utah Multipurpose Map.
Trail contacts: Public Lands Information Center, 3285 East 3300 S., Salt Lake City, UT 84109; (801) 466-6411. The land management agency is the Salt Lake Ranger District, Wasatch-Cache National Forest, 6944 South 3000 E., Salt Lake City, UT 84121; (801) 733-2660; www.fs.fed.us/r4/wcnf.

Finding the trailhead: Take Interstate 215 south in Salt Lake City and exit at 6200 South. Turn left and continue 1.5 miles to the light at the mouth of Big Cottonwood Canyon. Turn left here and drive about 4.5 miles. Here you enter an S-turn. As you finish the second turn back to your right, the signed trailhead for the Mill B North Fork Trail is on your left. There is a turnout for limited parking. *DeLorme: Utah Atlas & Gazetteer:* Page 53 B6.

The Hike

The Mill B North Fork Trail is an easy way to get a good view of the most spectacular peaks of the Wasatch Range. This hike goes up a good trail on the north side of Big Cottonwood Canyon, climbing quickly to high-elevation vegetation and scenery. The hike is somewhat difficult, with an elevation gain of 4,000 feet from the road to the summit, but since it goes up and back by the same route, you can turn around before the summit.

Big Cottonwood Canyon is open to backcountry camping, so you may opt to camp along the trail to Mount Raymond. Remember that camping closer than 200 feet to a stream, spring, or trail is not permitted. Water quality is at stake, and the Forest Service is enforcing the regulation. A Forest Service sign marks the route to the Desolation Trail and Mill A Basin.

You may want to take a quick look at Hidden Falls, just a few hundred feet upstream, before starting your hike.

The trail starts at 6,200 feet and climbs quickly above the canyon, switching back several times. After reaching the top of the first rise in about 0.25 mile, the trail leaves the scrub oak and drops down along Mill B North Fork. You parallel the creek for another 0.25 mile before entering a mature Douglas fir stand. Several campsites here show overuse. There are cut trees, fire rings, and litter. At the end of

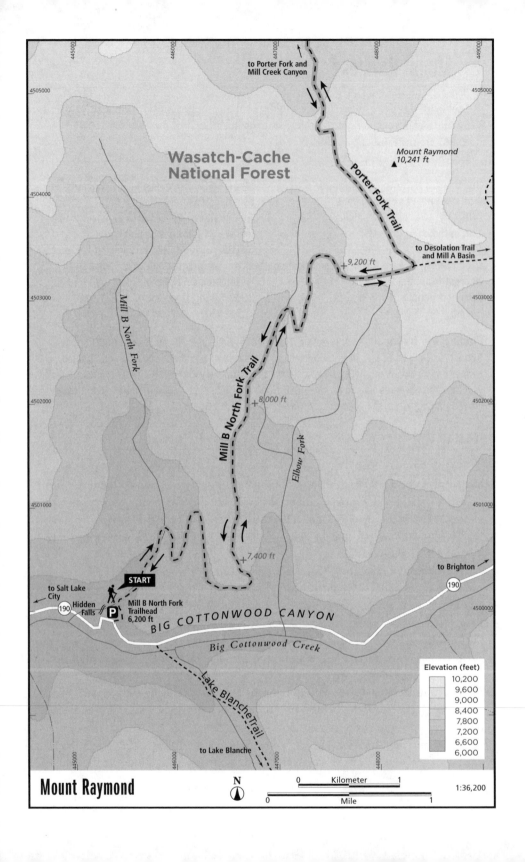

the stand, a jumble of rocks marks the spot where the trail cuts back sharply to your right and heads up the hillside.

The trail is obvious the rest of the way. You hike through a scrub oak forest, then climb through aspen and spruce-fir. The trail winds continuously uphill; you'll get plenty of exercise. Wildlife uses the trail regularly, avoiding the thick underbrush, and sign is abundant. You hike among rugged outcrops and steep canyons, and the many overlooks across Big Cottonwood Canyon to the south offer ideal lunch spots. At several locations along the trail, Mount Raymond is visible to the northeast.

At a point when you are nearly due south of Mount Raymond, about 3.5 miles from the trailhead, turn left (northwest) onto the Porter Fork Trail. Mount Raymond lies ahead to the northeast. You approach the 10,241-foot peak on this trail, which contours around on its west side. Since no actual trail goes to the top, your best bet is to make your way from a point due west of the peak to a small ridge on the northwest side of the summit. From here, a short scramble takes you to the top.

Like many of the Wasatch peaks, Mount Raymond offers wonderful views in all directions. Take a few minutes to study the Great Salt Lake and Antelope Island to the northwest, the Wasatch peaks to the north, the Uintas to the east, and the peaks of the Big Cottonwood–Little Cottonwood divide to the south.

There is interesting reading in the box at the top, and you may want to enter your thoughts while perched there. Among the many gems is "The Ballad of Mount Raymond." Says the author, "This was many years before us/Pre Mayor Teddy and Mormon Chorus/Pre MX and CUP/When the Ford was Model T."

You'll have to make the climb to read the rest.

Key Points

0.0 Start at the Mill B North Fork Trailhead.

3.5 Junction with the Porter Fork Trail. Turn left (northwest).

4.0 Arrive at the summit of Mount Raymond at 10,241 feet.

8.0 Arrive back at the trailhead.

Options: An alternative to summiting Mount Raymond would be to continue to skirt the west side of the peak on the Porter Fork Trail, heading north down Porter Fork into Mill Creek Canyon. Also check your topo for the loop option from Mount Raymond, down the Butler Fork Trail. —*Originally contributed by Walt Haas*

6 Lake Blanche

A popular day hike into a rugged, glaciated canyon in the 11,300-acre Twin Peaks Wilderness in the Wasatch Mountains. Only 10 miles southeast of Salt Lake City in Big Cottonwood Canyon, this hike features huge glacial cirques, several lakes, jagged 11,000-foot peaks, and waterfalls.

Start: Lake Blanche Trailhead.
Distance: 7 miles out and back.
Difficulty: Moderate.
Trail surface: Forest trail.
Seasons: Late spring through fall.
Land status: Wilderness area and national forest.
Nearest town: Salt Lake City.
Fees and permits: No fees or permits required.

Maps: USGS Mount Aire and Dromedary Peak quads; Northern Utah Multipurpose Map.
Trail contacts: Public Lands Information Center, 3285 East 3300 S., Salt Lake City, UT 84109; (801) 466-6411. The land management agency is the Salt Lake Ranger District, Wasatch-Cache National Forest, 6944 South 3000 E., Salt Lake City, UT 84121; (801) 733-2660; www.fs.fed.us/r4/wcnf.

Finding the trailhead: Drive south from Salt Lake City on Interstate 215 and exit at 6200 South. Turn left under the highway overpass and continue 1.5 miles to the traffic light at the mouth of Big Cottonwood Canyon. Turn left here and drive about 4.5 miles to the trailhead at the beginning of an S-turn in the road. *DeLorme: Utah Atlas & Gazetteer: Page 53 B6.*

The Hike

From the trailhead, you hike about 3.5 miles and gain 2,600 feet of elevation to get to Lake Blanche. The well-marked trail parallels Big Cottonwood Creek east and then turns southeast to follow the west side of Mill B South Fork. Within 0.25 mile the trail crosses a footbridge and cuts back to the left, remaining on the east side of the stream the rest of the way to Lake Blanche.

The trail passes through aspen stands along the glacially carved canyon bottom. About 1.9 miles along, your route begins to climb more abruptly along the east side of the canyon, away from the stream. You'll occasionally cross rockslides and other avalanche debris left from previous winter snows.

After 0.75 mile of steep climbing, the trail levels off onto an ancient, smooth rock outcropping. Notice how it was polished and etched by the most recent flow of glaciers in this region. The scratches left in the rock by debris carried along in the ice indicate the direction and force of the glacial flow. Follow the trail through these rock outcroppings a few hundred feet to the south. Lake Blanche is in a bowl with the cathedral spire of Sundial Peak beyond.

At Lake Blanche you are about 2,000 feet below the peaks of the Big and Little Cottonwood divides—Dromedary Peak (11,107 feet) to the southwest and Superior

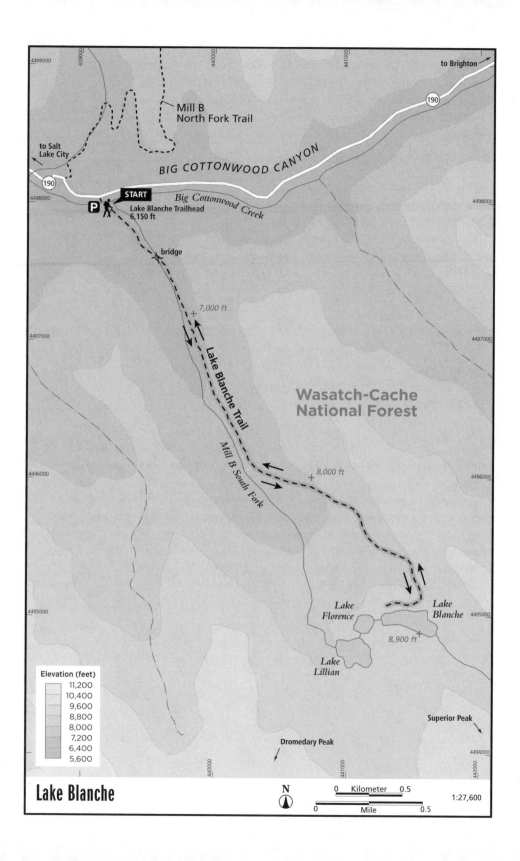

to Brighton

190

Mill B
North Fork Trail

BIG COTTONWOOD CANYON

to Salt
Lake City

190

START
P
Lake Blanche Trailhead
6,150 ft

Big Cottonwood Creek

bridge

7,000 ft

Lake Blanche Trail

Wasatch-Cache
National Forest

Mill B South Fork

8,000 ft

Lake
Florence

Lake
Blanche

8,900 ft

Lake
Lillian

Elevation (feet)

	11,200
	10,400
	9,600
	8,800
	8,000
	7,200
	6,400
	5,600

Superior Peak

Dromedary Peak

Lake Blanche

N

0   Kilometer   0.5

0   Mile   0.5

1:27,600

Peak (11,132 feet) to the southeast. Lake Blanche shares the area with Lake Lillian and Lake Florence; both are just to the west and a bit below Lake Blanche. All three lakes have fair to good fishing, as long as you don't mind small rewards. A large waterfall spills over a ledge just downstream from Lake Lillian, and during spring runoff another 75-foot waterfall drops over a cliff just west of Sundial Peak.

Because of its popularity, this area has received its share of human abuse—cans, bottles, trash-filled fire pits, and other garbage. Always carry out everything you bring in. The area is permanently closed to campfires, so carry a backpacker stove. If you decide to camp, please observe the backcountry camping regulations, which the Forest Service does enforce. Camping is permitted (and is popular on weekends) in Big Cottonwood Canyon, but you must make your camp at least 200 feet from a trail, lake, stream, or spring. Practice zero-impact camping.

After lunch at any of the three lakes (Lake Florence and Lake Lillian offer more solitude than Lake Blanche) and a little exploration, retrace your steps to the trail-head.

Key Points

- **0.0** Start at the Lake Blanche Trailhead.
- **3.5** Arrive at Lake Blanche.
- **7.0** Arrive back at the trailhead.

Option: If you're still feeling ambitious when you arrive at Lake Blanche, continue another mile to the southeast, without benefit of a trail, into the large glacial cirque below Superior Peak. You'll scramble more than 1,000 feet in the process, but the trip is worth it.

To reach this canyon, follow the stream that enters Lake Blanche on the east, staying to the northeast side of the Sundial Peak ridge. Several small lakes dot the area, and you certainly will see more marmots and pikas than people. (A reputable source has even made note of an occasional lurking moose in the general vicinity.) The high-alpine scenery is superb, with huge walls and jagged peaks all around you.

—*Originally contributed by Jim Kay*

7 Lone Peak Area via Lake Hardy

An overnight backpack through the heart of Utah's first congressionally designated wilderness, featuring spectacular geologic formations, alpine ridges and valleys, and panoramic views of northern Utah.

Start: Schoolhouse Springs Trailhead or Dry Creek Trailhead.
Distance: 12 miles point to point.
Difficulty: Extremely difficult.
Trail surface: Forest trail.
Seasons: Early summer through fall.
Land status: Wilderness area, national forest, city, private.
Nearest town: Alpine.
Fees and permits: No fees or permits required.
Maps: USGS Lehi, Draper, Dromedary Peak, and Timpanogos Cave quads; National Geographic Trails Illustrated Uinta National Forest Map.
Trail contacts: Pleasant Grove Ranger District, Uinta National Forest, 390 North 100 E., Pleasant Grove, UT 84062; (801) 785-3563; www.fs.fed.us/r4/uinta. Also, for information on the Little Cottonwood Canyon side, contact Salt Lake Ranger District, Wasatch-Cache National Forest, 6944 South 3000 E., Salt Lake City, UT 84121; (801) 733-2660; www.fs.fed.us/r4/wcnf.

Finding the trailhead: To reach the Schoolhouse Springs Trailhead in Alpine, drive south on Interstate 15 to exit 287, Alpine-Highland, and turn east onto Highway 92 (Alpine Scenic Highway). Travel east on Highway 92 about 5 miles to its junction with Highway 74. Here turn left onto Highway 74 and travel north into the city of Alpine. In Alpine, Highway 74 becomes Main Street. Continue north on Main to the four-way stop at 200 North. Turn east onto 200 North and go 2 blocks to 200 East. At this four-way stop, turn left onto Grove Drive and continue north past the cemetery. Follow Grove approximately 1 mile to a ninety-degree turn to the right. For the Schoolhouse Springs Trailhead, turn left here onto Alpine Cove Drive and continue north to Aspen Drive. At the end of Aspen Drive are two gates. If the gate on the right is locked, you must park on the street and begin your hike at this point. (Note: There is no designated parking at this point, so be sure your vehicle doesn't restrict local traffic.) If this gate is open, you may travel farther north to a second gate with LEHI CITY as a logo. There are several parking spots near this gate. Beyond the Lehi gate a jeep road crosses and ascends about 1.5 miles of city property (respect it) before reaching the Uinta National Forest boundary and the meadow area known as First Hamongog.

To leave a car at Bells Canyon, turn south off Little Cottonwood Canyon Road (9555 South, Highway 209) at 3100 East. Pass the Granite Elementary School on your right after 0.25 mile, then cross 9800 South. In another 0.25 mile the road makes a ninety-degree turn to the right; almost immediately after this, Dimple Dell Road (3050 East) turns to the left. Turn here, drive a few hundred yards down the hill, and turn left onto Bells Canyon Road (10025 South). In 0.25 mile turn left onto Wasatch Boulevard and park at the dead end. This is the bottom of Bells Canyon. *DeLorme: Utah Atlas & Gazetteer:* Page 53 C5.

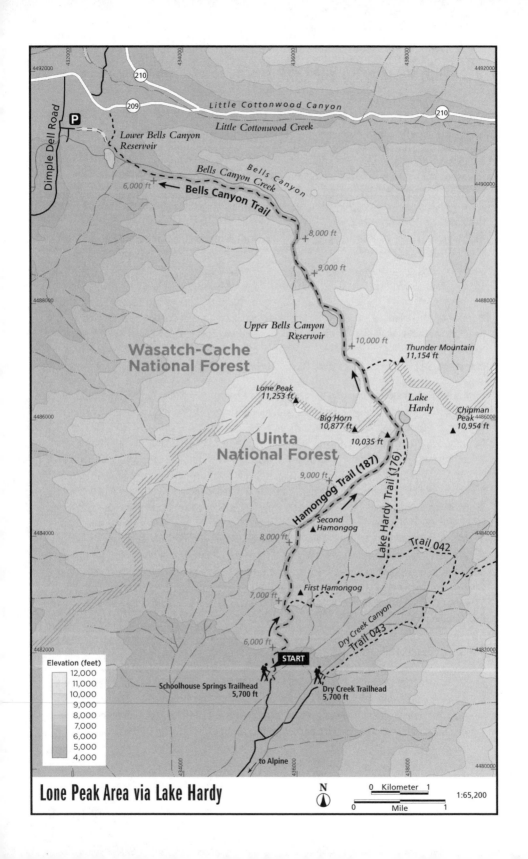

210
209
Little Cottonwood Canyon
210

Little Cottonwood Creek

Dimple Dell Road

P

Lower Bells Canyon
Reservoir

Bells Canyon

Bells Canyon Creek

6,000 ft

Bells Canyon Trail

8,000 ft

9,000 ft

Upper Bells Canyon
Reservoir

10,000 ft

Thunder Mountain
11,154 ft

Wasatch-Cache
National Forest

Lone Peak
11,253 ft

Lake
Hardy

Big Horn
10,877 ft

Chipman
Peak
10,954 ft

10,035 ft

Uinta
National Forest

Hamongog Trail (187)

Lake Hardy Trail (176)

9,000 ft

Trail 042

Second
Hamongog

8,000 ft

First Hamongog

7,000 ft

Dry Creek Canyon
Trail 043

6,000 ft

START

Schoolhouse Springs Trailhead
5,700 ft

Dry Creek Trailhead
5,700 ft

Elevation (feet)

| 12,000 |
| 11,000 |
| 10,000 |
| 9,000 |
| 8,000 |
| 7,000 |
| 6,000 |
| 5,000 |
| 4,000 |

to Alpine

Lone Peak Area via Lake Hardy

N

0   Kilometer   1

0   Mile   1

1:65,200

The Hike

The rocky cirques, wooded canyons, and alpine meadows and ridges of the Wasatch are nowhere more plentiful than in the Lone Peak Wilderness southeast of Salt Lake City. A demanding but spectacular ascent to this area is from the town of Alpine in Utah County, climbing past Lake Hardy and descending through Bells Canyon on the Little Cottonwood Canyon side.

Bells Canyon, a major drainage under 11,253-foot Lone Peak, has long been a favorite, if somewhat secret, three-season hiking area. Day trips into Bells Canyon are popular, but you must hike nearly 7 miles and 5,000 feet in elevation to the top. After crossing the ridge from Lake Hardy, you may thus prefer to spend a night on the Little Cottonwood side.

Keep in mind that wilderness regulations require you to make camp at least 200 feet from the nearest water source. Forest Service personnel do enforce this regulation.

A car shuttle is necessary if you choose this hike over the ridge. Of course, you could ascend from Alpine, spend a night or two, explore the area, and return to your car along the same route.

As you look north from the trailhead at about 5,700 feet, Lone Peak forms the sharp summit on the extreme left of the skyline. The peak's east ridge slopes gradually to the right—the horizon broken by a rocky outcropping—before climbing to the more rounded summit of 10,877-foot Big Horn. Lake Hardy, your destination for the first night, is behind and to the right of the Big Horn summit.

There are a couple of routes to Lake Hardy, either up the main drainage below the lake or along the slopes nearby. The more popular route starts from the Schoolhouse Springs Trailhead and then switches back up 1,300 vertical feet over the next 1.5 miles to the First Hamongog at the wilderness boundary. (*Hamongog* is a biblical term for "meadow.")

Two signed trails leave the First Hamongog. One heads north to the Second Hamongog (Trail 187); the other takes a steeper and more direct route (see the option at the end of this hike) to Lake Hardy.

Take Trail 187 to the Second Hamongog, situated beneath Big Horn. Notice the prominent ridge that drops south from this peak, with tree and brush cover ending about two-thirds of the way up the ridge at granite cliffs. From the Second Hamongog, the trail climbs northeast along the west side of this ridge (about a mile) before crossing to the east side. It then traverses northeast into the bowl (at just under 10,000 feet) framed by Big Horn, Thunder Mountain (11,154 feet), and Chipman Peak (10,954 feet).

Picturesque islands of conifers and wildflowers dot the granite slopes above timberline. The slopes allow fairly unrestricted cross-country travel.

Lake Hardy sits in a bowl north of an imaginary line between Big Horn and Chipman Peak. As you hike toward the lake, notice that the bowl is divided by a north–south ridge, indicated by a 10,035-foot location on the topo map. The route climbs along the side of this ridge, through beautiful secluded pockets, finally topping the crest of the ridge and dropping northeast to the lake.

As you approach Lake Hardy, stay midway up the granite slopes to the west of the lake. A cairned route winds through draws and granite boulders, among wildflowers, grasses, and stunted shrubs. Lightning-struck and weathered conifers attest to the harsh conditions and provide endless photographic and sketchbook compositions.

While there are springs at lower elevations, Lake Hardy offers the only reliable water near the crest. Be sure to treat all water before drinking.

The Lake Hardy area has good campsites, rewarding beauty, and opportunities for after-dinner exploration. The lake doesn't get the pounding from visitors that some areas across the ridge in Little Cottonwood Canyon receive, but that is no reason not to observe common sanitation and backcountry rules. A backpacker stove is recommended here, and remember to carry out all trash. Check with the Forest Service for current fire regulations.

The easiest and most scenic route to Bells Canyon is to return to the ridge, 0.25 mile west of Lake Hardy. Another 0.25 mile to the northwest, a grassy meadow just south of the saddle makes a good high campsite. Along this route, as well as elsewhere on the trail, you may see grouse, woodpeckers, and many passerine species. Also look for red-tailed hawks and golden eagles soaring above the ridges.

From here, you could traverse the high ridge west and northwest to the summit of 11,253-foot Lone Peak. You might also climb a mile due east from Lake Hardy to the saddle north of Chipman Peak. Here you get a magnificent view of upper Hogum Fork before traversing northwest under and to the west of the ridgeline toward Bells Canyon.

From the saddle at the head of Bells, the view is spectacular in every direction. Rugged peaks and ridgelines flank the saddle to the east and west, while the panorama of Box Elder Peak, Mount Timpanogos, and Utah Lake spreads to the south.

Dominated by an upper cirque, Bells Canyon descends to the north from a 10,400-foot saddle northwest of Lake Hardy. A nice side trip from here is to traverse northeast, climbing a few hundred feet under Thunder Mountain (11,154 feet). About 0.5 mile from the saddle above Bells, climb to the 11,000-foot saddle just north of Thunder. From here or from the clifftop perch on Thunder Mountain, the three cirques of Hogum Fork spread out to the east, while all of upper Little Cottonwood Canyon can be seen in the distance.

Pick your route carefully down to Upper Bells Canyon Reservoir. Use ridges and avoid the boulder accumulation in drainages when possible. Stay on the right (east) side of the canyon to find the upper reservoir, about 1.5 miles from the ridge.

As you descend Bells Canyon, observe the distinct vegetative changes. Keep an eye out for mountain goats, introduced from Washington by the Division of

Wildlife Resources. And note the cirques, basins, moraines, and polished tracks left by glaciers.

Just below Upper Bells Canyon Reservoir, a cairned route starts on the left (west) side of the creek. (Note: Older editions of the Dromedary Peak topo incorrectly show the trail on the other side.) Within 0.5 mile the stream cascades down a steep granite gorge and the trail veers farther left (west), continuing on the west side of a rocky ridge that divides the canyon. The trail passes amid dense spruce-fir forests, through a secluded willow and wildflower meadow, and, after another 0.5 mile, onto the center of a ridge dividing the upper forks of Bells Canyon Creek. From the ridge to this spot, you've descended about 2,000 feet.

Incredible avalanche debris obscures the trail. Stay out of the gullies and thread your way through the deadfall and sumac until you are above the ravine where the upper forks combine.

A small park is found half a mile down the canyon where the drainage from Thunder Mountain enters from the southeast. Reach it by hiking along the east side of the stream or climbing higher to the east and descending the ridge.

The trail is on the right (northeast) side of the stream here. Again, the USGS topo may be in error. Continue down the canyon on a good pathway to Lower Bells Canyon Reservoir, 2.5 miles below. Along the way, you'll hear many waterfalls; spur trails lead to scenic views.

Some of the lower sections of the trail are a bit tricky, since they are straight down the fall line and quite eroded—not pleasant hiking after a strenuous climb over the ridge.

When the canyon widens a mile before the lower reservoir, work your way through the confusion of trails to the right (north) side of the canyon, around the reservoir, and down the road to your car.

Remember that the final 0.75-mile stretch of the trail is on private property. Past complaints from landowners are the result of hikers straying off the trail here and using the lower reservoir. The Forest Service plans continuous improvement of the Bells Canyon Trail as finances permit, and access at the mouth of Bells is being negotiated.

The route from Dry Creek Canyon across the ridge and down Bells Canyon traverses a variety of land—private, watershed, Forest Service multiple use, and pristine wilderness. Treat each with equal respect.

Key Points

0.0 Start at the Schoolhouse Springs Trailhead.
4.5 Reach Lake Hardy.
6.0 Side trip to Thunder Mountain at 11,154 feet.
7.5 Arrive at Upper Bells Canyon Reservoir dam. Continue northwest.
11.0 Arrive at Lower Bells Canyon Reservoir.
12.0 Arrive at your vehicle at the dead end at the bottom of Bells Canyon.

Option: Better parking is available at the Dry Creek Trailhead, located east of Schoolhouse Springs. To reach this trailhead, continue eastward on Grove Drive to a T intersection and turn right. After crossing the bridge, turn left (you will still be on Grove Drive) and continue northeast for 0.25 mile. Grove Drive ends at the Dry Creek Trailhead. Take Dry Creek Trail 43 northeast, turn left (north) onto North Mountain Trail 42, and then turn right (north) onto Lake Hardy Trail 176 (also called "the Elevator" by some of the local folks) to access Lake Hardy. —*Originally contributed by Jim and Valerie Pissot*

8 Red Pine Lakes

A popular day hike or overnighter into the Lone Peak Wilderness, featuring beautiful views of Little Cottonwood Canyon, the Salt Lake Valley, and the Red Pine cirque, along with fishing for cutthroat trout. The hike is accessed via Little Cottonwood Canyon, 16 miles southeast of Salt Lake City.

Start: White Pine Trailhead.
Distance: 7 miles out and back.
Difficulty: Moderate.
Trail surface: Forest trail.
Seasons: Late spring through fall.
Land status: Wilderness area and national forest.
Nearest town: Salt Lake City.
Fees and permits: No fees or permits required.

Maps: USGS Dromedary Peak quad; Northern Utah Multipurpose Map; National Geographic Trails Illustrated Uinta National Forest Map.
Trail contacts: Public Lands Information Center, 3285 East 3300 S., Salt Lake City, UT 84109; (801) 466-6411. The land management agency is the Salt Lake Ranger District, Wasatch-Cache National Forest, 6944 South 3000 E., Salt Lake City, UT 84121; (801) 733-2660; www.fs.fed.us/r4/wcnf.

Finding the trailhead: Take Interstate 215 south from Salt Lake City and exit at 6200 South. Turn left under the highway overpass and continue 4 miles to the mouth of Little Cottonwood Canyon, passing the light at the mouth of Big Cottonwood Canyon along the way. Turn left and drive 6 miles up the canyon to the trailhead. Park at the White Pine parking area a mile beyond the Tanner Flat Campground. The lot is on the right (south) side of the road. A trail to both White Pine Lake and the Red Pine Lakes begins here. *DeLorme: Utah Atlas & Gazetteer: Page 53 C6.*

The Hike

This hike into Utah's first wilderness area is a popular one for Salt Lake Valley residents. The trailhead is forty minutes from downtown, and the trail ascends through some of the Wasatch's finest alpine terrain. Backcountry camping is permitted in Little Cottonwood Canyon. Remember that you are not permitted to camp within 200 feet of any water source or trail. Respect this regulation; Forest Service rangers

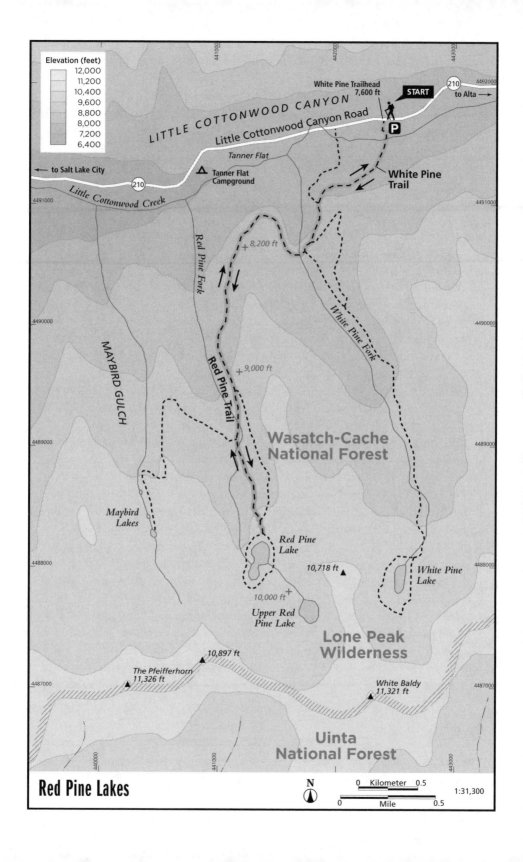

Red Pine Lakes

will be seeing that you do. Dogs are not allowed, and fines up to $299 are handed out regularly, so take note.

A well-constructed bridge crosses Little Cottonwood Creek 100 yards south of the parking lot amid a thick stand of aspen and spruce. The trail contours for a mile to the west and southwest amid several slide areas before reaching White Pine Fork. White Pine Trail cuts back sharply to the left (east) here. The Red Pine Trail branches off to the right and crosses a footbridge a few hundred feet upstream.

After crossing White Pine Fork, the trail contours for 0.5 mile north, west, and then south around a ridge into Red Pine Canyon, entering the Lone Peak Wilderness. Immediately after crossing into the wilderness, look to the right (northwest) and notice Little Cottonwood Canyon Road snaking its way west down the canyon toward the Salt Lake Valley. The view is beautiful, and it's not uncommon to come across a hiker snapping a few pictures here.

Many wildflower species show their colors along the trail in early summer, Uinta ground squirrels are common, and the remarkable forces of avalanches are evident on some of the steeper aspen and spruce-fir slopes. Notice the long ropelike strands of dirt in several areas along the trail. Pocket gophers have left these. They burrow through the snow during winter and push soft dirt into the tunnels. When the snow melts, the dirt settles to the ground in the many designs you see.

About a mile after you enter the wilderness, a trail crosses Red Pine Fork to the right (west) and continues into Maybird Gulch. Do not take this route; continue straight along the east side of the creek for almost a mile to Red Pine Lake.

The final stretch to the lake may have large patches of snow into midsummer, making the going sloppy and the trail difficult to locate in spots. If you run into this trouble, hike south into the basin above and you can't miss the lake.

Red Pine Lake—deep, clear, and with conifers around much of the perimeter—is one of the prettier of the Wasatch lakes. The granitic slopes of the Little Cottonwood–American Fork ridgeline loom to the south, and the knife-edge to the west above Maybird Gulch is spectacular. At the southeast end of the lake, a large boulder makes a perfect lunch spot. It is located where the stream from Upper Red Pine Lake enters. Sitting on the rock, look north down the lake and across Little Cottonwood Canyon to Twin, Dromedary, and Superior Peaks (all higher than 11,000 feet). Golden eagles often circle lazily on midday thermals above the ridgeline to the west.

Unfortunately this area shows signs of *Homo sapiens'* carelessness. Several old fire rings dot the area, and there is evidence of ax cuttings in standing trees. In a few locations trash has been burned carelessly and left for a more responsible person to pack out. A permanent fire closure is in effect for Red Pine and Maybird Lakes, and the regulations are strictly enforced.

Key Points

0.0   Start at the White Pine Trailhead.

1.0   The trail meets White Pine Fork. Turn right (southwest) onto the Red Pine Trail.

2.5 Junction with the trail to Maybird Gulch. Continue straight (south).

3.5 Arrive at Red Pine Lake.

7.0 Arrive back at the trailhead.

Options: For hikers interested in a lake with even more alpine qualities, Upper Red Pine Lake lies half a mile to the southeast over a steep knoll. There is no trail; you must scramble over large rocks near the lake. Talus slopes rise to the east and south, where you may hear the peculiar squeak of a pika. If you're observant, you might spot one of these small relatives of the rabbit and hare among the rocks above the lake. A yellow-bellied marmot may also waddle across your path. There are some nice cutthroat trout in the lake, but the fishing is usually slow until the water has warmed in midsummer. The lake can be icebound into late June.

If you're up for a final challenge before heading back down to Red Pine Lake and out to the trailhead, Thunder Mountain (10,718 feet), to the northeast, presents breathtaking views north across the canyon, east to White Pine Canyon and White Pine Lake, west to the Salt Lake Valley and the Pfeifferhorn (11,326 feet), and south along the Red Pine divide. Don't forget your camera. —*Originally contributed by Dave Hall*

9 The Pfeifferhorn

A very challenging day hike or overnighter to the crest of the Wasatch Mountains that offers spectacular views in rugged alpine country. The hike is accessed via Little Cottonwood Canyon, 16 miles southeast of Salt Lake City.

Start: White Pine Trailhead.
Distance: 10 miles out and back.
Difficulty: Strenuous.
Trail surface: Forest trail to Red Pine Lake, cross-country to the Pfeifferhorn.
Seasons: Summer through fall.
Land status: Wilderness area and national forest.
Nearest town: Salt Lake City.
Fees and permits: No fees or permits required.

Maps: USGS Dromedary Peak quad; Northern Utah Multipurpose Map; National Geographic Trails Illustrated Uinta National Forest Map.
Trail contacts: Public Lands Information Center, 3285 East 3300 S., Salt Lake City, UT 84109; (801) 466-6411. The land management agency is the Salt Lake Ranger District, Wasatch-Cache National Forest, 6944 South 3000 E., Salt Lake City, UT 84121; (801) 733-2660; www.fs.fed.us/r4/wcnf.

Finding the trailhead: Take Interstate 215 south from Salt Lake City and exit at 6200 South. Turn left under the highway overpass and continue 4 miles to the mouth of Little Cottonwood Canyon, passing the light at the mouth of Big Cottonwood Canyon along the way. Turn left and drive 6 miles up the canyon to the trailhead. Park at the White Pine parking area a mile beyond

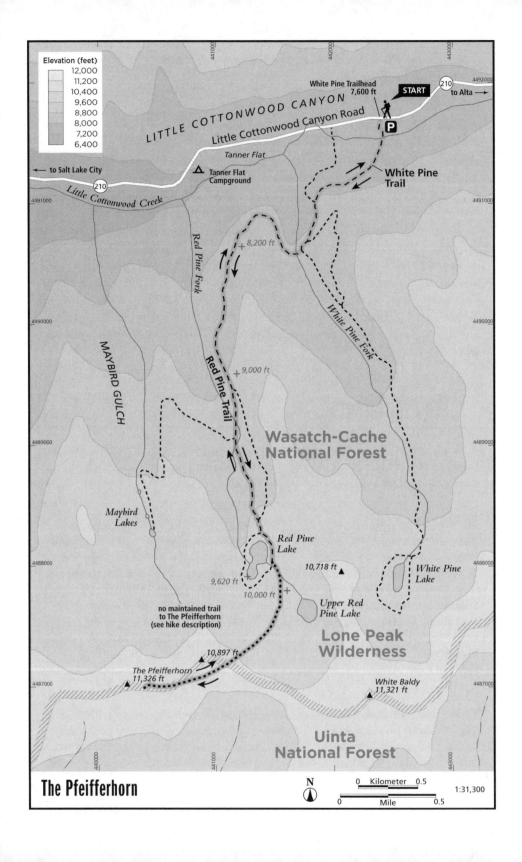

Elevation (feet)

	12,000
	11,200
	10,400
	9,600
	8,800
	8,000
	7,200
	6,400

White Pine Trailhead
7,600 ft

START

to Alta →

210

LITTLE COTTONWOOD CANYON

Little Cottonwood Canyon Road

Tanner Flat

White Pine
Trail

← to Salt Lake City

210

Tanner Flat
Campground

Little Cottonwood Creek

Red Pine Fork

+ 8,200 ft

White Pine Fork

MAYBIRD GULCH

Red Pine Trail

+ 9,000 ft

Wasatch-Cache
National Forest

Maybird
Lakes

Red Pine
Lake

White Pine
Lake

9,620 ft +

10,000 ft +

10,718 ft ▲

no maintained trail
to The Pfeifferhorn
(see hike description)

Upper Red
Pine Lake

Lone Peak
Wilderness

10,897 ft

The Pfeifferhorn
11,326 ft

White Baldy
11,321 ft ▲

Uinta
National Forest

The Pfeifferhorn

N

0	Kilometer	0.5
0	Mile	0.5

1:31,300

the Tanner Flat Campground. The lot is on the right (south) side of the road. A trail to both White Pine Lake and the Red Pine Lakes begins here. The hike to the Pfeifferhorn continues past Upper Red Pine Lake to the ridge. *DeLorme: Utah Atlas & Gazetteer:* Page 53 C6.

The Hike

Red Pine Lake offers access to many points along the rugged, winding ridge that divides Little Cottonwood Canyon from American Fork Canyon. Here the granite core of the range is exposed in a series of dramatic alpine peaks that provide spectacular views and immensely satisfying climbs. No technical equipment is required to ascend the Pfeifferhorn, at 11,326 feet the third highest summit on the ridge (after the Twin Peaks, at 11,489 and 11,443 feet).

Climbing the Pfeifferhorn from the White Pine Trailhead on Little Cottonwood Canyon Road is an all-day affair, involving about 10 miles for the round trip and 3,700 vertical feet. You should be in good condition and allow at least eight hours for the trip. Sunglasses and sunscreen are recommended, particularly early in the season. Backcountry camping is permitted in Little Cottonwood Canyon, so you may choose to camp at Red Pine Lake or at another suitable spot along the way. Remember that regulations specify that you make camp at least 200 feet from the nearest water source or trail.

From Red Pine Lake at 9,620 feet, follow the path along the intake stream from Upper Red Pine Lake. The path climbs steeply through conifers and soon bends away from the stream. As the ground becomes rockier, the path gets harder to follow, though a few cairns have been left by previous parties. Watch and listen for pikas in this rocky country. Climb across several small talus fields to a line of trees on the horizon marking the rim of Upper Red Pine Lake Basin—half a mile from Red Pine Lake.

You emerge on a low ridge about a quarter mile southwest of the upper lake. Climb along it southwest to the main ridge another 0.25 mile away. It's steep here, but the crest isn't far off. If you come in late July, you'll find the lovely magenta blossoms of Parry primrose nodding in shaded crevices, as well as fragrant pennyroyal with its delicate lavender pom-poms.

The crest of the ridge, about 1,000 feet above Red Pine Lake, is a good place to stop to catch your breath. Enjoy the exhilarating views of American Fork Canyon and Mount Timpanogos to the south, smoky blue in the midday light and marbled with snowfields. In midsummer large fields of lupine bloom in the meadows along this ridge, beautifully set off against the gray granite and pale green grass.

Contour westward, passing below peak 10,897 on your right, and rejoin the crest 0.25 mile later as it narrows to a knife-edged file of gigantic blocks. The easiest route keeps slightly below and to the left of the crest here, and requires both hands for safety and balance. The knife-edge is about 150 yards long.

You can see the pyramidal summit of the Pfeifferhorn straight ahead. The best route climbs alongside a steep, smooth granite chute. Keep to the left, where protruding rocks and grassy ledges make for easier going. It looks steep from a distance but turns out to be no worse than a staircase. Four hundred vertical feet bring you panting to the top.

The views from the Pfeifferhorn are among the most dramatic in the Wasatch. You can look northwest into the deep cirques of Hogum Fork and Bells Canyon as the ridge twists westward to Lone Peak. Beyond lie the Oquirrhs and the Stansbury Mountains; to the south, American Fork Canyon empties into Utah Lake; and far below, a matchstick city spreads toward the Great Salt Lake, a turquoise smear on the far horizon. Across the canyon to the north, the red summits of Twin, Dromedary, and Superior Peaks contrast handsomely with the younger, lighter granite exposed by the deep avalanche scars that corrugate their flanks. To the northeast, the main ridge pitches and zigzags toward Snowbird and Alta, with the dark, slablike Uinta Mountains just visible on the eastern horizon.

In early summer deep snow makes possible a variation on the descent. At the base of the summit cone, you can glissade down a snow-filled gully into Maybird Gulch, where within a mile the Maybird Gulch Trail rounds the dividing spur to meet Red Pine Fork and the Red Pine Trail less than a mile below Red Pine Lake. (In late summer this route is impractical, due to the extensive talus fields exposed on the floor of the gulch.) If you elect to descend by retracing your steps, simply cross the knife-edge (keeping below and to the right), contour to the right of peak 10,897, and meet the spur from Upper Red Pine Lake near a clump of wind-stunted evergreens. —*Originally contributed by John Tallmadge*

Key Points

0.0 Start at the White Pine Trailhead.

1.0 The trail meets White Pine Fork. Turn right (southwest) onto the Red Pine Trail.

3.5 Arrive at Red Pine Lake. The rest of the hike is cross-country.

5.0 Arrive at the summit of the Pfeifferhorn at 11,326 feet.

10.0 Arrive back at the trailhead.

10 Mount Timpanogos via Aspen Grove Trail

A spectacular—and popular—ascent to the summit of the second highest mountain in the Wasatch Range, this trek is suitable as a day hike or overnighter but most popular as a day hike. Timpanogos forms the eastern wall of Utah Valley and offers spectacular panoramas, one of the most beautiful glacial tarns in the state, and delightful approaches along sheltered cirques and exposed ridges.

Start: Aspen Grove Trailhead.
Distance: 12 miles out and back.
Difficulty: Moderate (more strenuous the last mile to the summit).
Trail surface: Forest trail.
Seasons: Late autumn, as the aspens turn brilliant gold. The terrain, however, is suitable for hiking from early summer to early winter.
Land status: Wilderness area.
Nearest town: Orem.

Fees and permits: A $3.00, three-day recreation pass is required and is available at the American Fork and Provo Canyons entrance stations.
Maps: USGS Aspen Grove and Timpanogos Cave quads; National Geographic Trails Illustrated Uinta National Forest Map.
Trail contacts: Pleasant Grove Ranger District, Uinta National Forest, Box 390 North 100 E., Pleasant Grove, UT 84062; (801) 785-3563; www.fs.fed.us/r4/uinta.

Finding the trailhead: Drive south from Salt Lake City on Interstate 15 and take exit 275, North Orem. Turn east onto 800 North Street (Highway 52) and drive to its junction with U.S. Highway 189. Turn left onto US 189, also known as the Provo Canyon Byway, which offers a graphic view of several noteworthy geologic formations. As you travel east on US 189, you pass through one of two tunnels and approach the junction of Highway 92 (aka the Sundance Turnoff). Turn left (northwest) onto Highway 92 past Sundance Resort, then continue past mile marker 23 and the Aspen Grove Family Camp. Just before you arrive at the Theater in the Pines picnic ground, you will pass the Aspen Grove entrance station where you can obtain the required $3.00 recreation user pass. Proceed west for half a block and turn left into the Aspen Grove (Theater in the Pines) parking lot and trailhead. The Aspen Grove Trail to the top of Mount Timpanogos begins in the northwest corner of the lot. *DeLorme: Utah Atlas & Gazetteer:* Page 53 D6.

The Hike

Mount Timpanogos, at 11,750 feet, is the most prominent mountain along the 200-mile length of the Wasatch Range. Its 7-mile crest, often said to resemble the profile of a reposing woman, rises abruptly 7,000 feet from the Utah Valley floor and provides a spectacular and—in winter—almost Himalayan backdrop to the communities of American Fork, Heber, Lehi, Midway, Pleasant Grove, and Orem. A wilderness area since 1984, the Mount Timpanogos Wilderness encompasses 10,750 acres of national forest system land.

Timpanogos is composed mostly of intermingled and horizontally bedded layers of limestone and quartzite and exhibits considerable evidence of glaciation along

Mount Timpanogos via Aspen Grove Trail

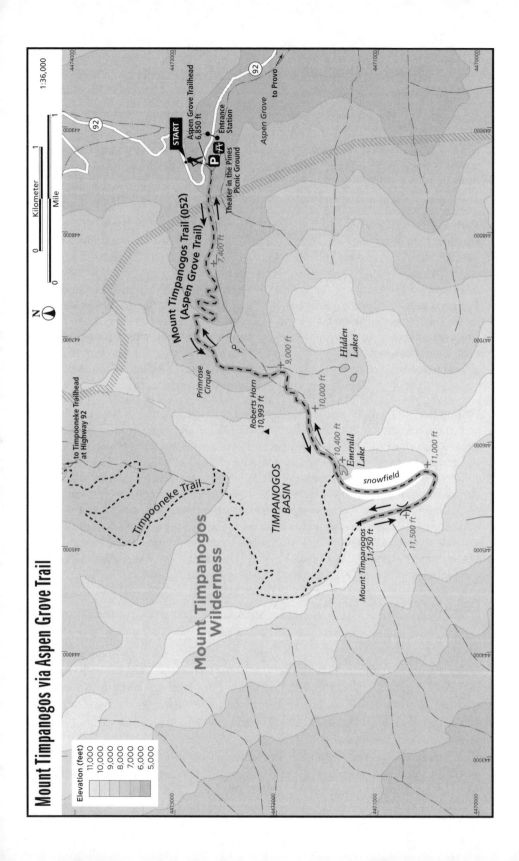

its eastern and northern flanks. Vegetation ranges from grasslands and mountain brush at lower elevations to lichens in the alpine regions. Mountain goats were introduced on Timpanogos in 1981 and are flourishing.

In the language of the Ute Indian tribe, *Timpanogos* originally meant "rocky stream" and referred specifically to the creek flowing down American Fork Canyon north of the mountain. During settlement of the area, the pioneers transferred the name to the river south of the mountain. Still later, the newly labeled Timpanogos River was renamed the Provo River for a fur trapper named Ernie Provost who explored the canyon. *Timpanogos* was then transferred again, this time to the only other nearby geologic feature of any prominence—the mountain itself.

According to legend (actually based on a story written in the twentieth century), the crest of Mount Timpanogos is a remnant of an Indian princess who slowly petrified as she languished for her warrior-husband-to-be while he was away on an "extended deer hunt."

Mount Timpanogos Trail 052 (aka the Aspen Grove Trail) begins at an elevation of 6,850 feet and proceeds almost directly westward through fir and aspen into the lower portion of Primrose Cirque. After a gentle 600-foot climb, the trail steepens as it begins to switchback up the headwall of the cirque. The switchbacks continue for about 2 miles as the trail ascends to an elevation of 10,000 feet and enters a hanging valley often covered with magnificent displays of mountain flowers. Another mile of very gentle hiking brings you to the traditional lunch knoll overlooking Emerald Lake and a nearby rock shelter. From here, the summit is visible another half mile to the southwest—1,300 feet straight up!

During lunch, area etiquette commands you to ponder the age-old question: Is it a glacier above Emerald Lake or a snowfield? For those who care to deliberate, it should be noted that at the time of the earliest-known "first winter ascent" of Timpanogos—February 19, 1916—a climber described a "large ice crevice" and a "number of deep beautiful crevices" along the upper area of what he called a "glacier."

The shelter near Emerald Lake was constructed in 1959 as an aid station/rest stop for use during annual community climbs of Mount Timpanogos, which would include thousands of participants attempting the summit on the same day. More than 8,000 hikers made the day hike one year. These one-day assaults were discontinued in 1970 due to resource damage. The Pleasant Grove Ranger District reports that the Aspen Grove side of the mountain may never recover from this overuse.

The route continues 0.75 mile up the gentle snowfield/glacier above the lake. The ascent is generally straightforward, though severe winter conditions can leave behind a very steep, sometimes overhanging, cornice at the top of the pass.

From the pass at 11,500 feet, the trail to the summit traverses in a northwesterly direction along the western slope of the ridge crest. The summit is three quarters of a mile beyond and 250 feet above the pass. A small, open, metal, hutlike structure, built as a triangulation station for the county, dominates the summit block, where dedicated hikers of the early 1920s danced at sunrise.

Key Points

0.0 Start at the Aspen Grove Trailhead.

4.5 Reach Emerald Lake.

6.0 Arrive at the summit of Mount Timpanogos at 11,750 feet.

7.5 Arrive back at Emerald Lake.

12.0 Arrive back at the trailhead.

Options: From the summit, three options are available for the descent to Aspen Grove. The first option retraces the ascent route. The second option follows a descending trail 0.8 mile northwest along the ridge to a pass, then swings back abruptly for a mile to Emerald Lake. From the lake, the descent to Aspen Grove retraces your ascent trail.

Many hikers prefer a third option, a route that does not return to Emerald Lake or to Aspen Grove. This route follows the ridge to the pass northwest of the summit but, instead of swinging back to Emerald Lake, continues about a mile into Timpanogos Basin and eventually terminates 5 miles farther at the Timpooneke Trailhead and ranger station 6 miles northwest of Aspen Grove. If two vehicles are available, a return shuttle can be organized in advance of the hike.

Incidentally, the Timpooneke Trail is also an excellent ascent route to Mount Timpanogos. It's a bit longer than the Aspen Grove route, but is a more gradual climb and is shaded during much of the morning. To reach the Timpooneke Trailhead, take exit 287, Alpine-Highland, off I–15 and turn east onto the Alpine Scenic Highway (Highway 92). Highway 92 is also known as the Alpine Loop Road and offers a scenic alpine route to Provo Canyon and US 189. As you enter American Fork Canyon, you will need to stop at the entrance station and obtain a $3.00 recreation user pass. Then proceed east until you almost reach mile marker 16, where Highway 92 forms a T intersection with the road into Timpooneke Campground. Turn right into Timpooneke and continue west 0.25 mile to the large asphalt-covered trailhead parking lot. Timpooneke Trail 053 begins on the west side of the double restroom located on the south side of the parking lot. —*Originally contributed by Alexis Kelner*

11 Santaquin Peak

A day hike or possible overnight trip to the top of 10,685-foot Santaquin Peak. A pleasing combination of alpine and pastoral scenery unfolds as the trail winds its way along several drainages. Along the way are views of Utah Lake and Mount Nebo.

Start: Loafer Mountain Trailhead on the Mount Nebo Scenic Byway (Nebo Loop Road).
Distance: 11 miles out and back.
Difficulty: Moderately strenuous.
Trail surface: Forest trail.
Seasons: Late spring and late summer through fall.
Land status: National forest.
Nearest town: Payson.

Fees and permits: No fees or permits required.
Maps: USGS Payson Lakes and Birdseye quads; National Geographic Trails Illustrated Uinta National Forest Map.
Trail contacts: Spanish Fork Ranger District, Uinta National Forest, 44 West 400 N., Spanish Fork, UT 84660; (801) 798-3571; www.fs.fed.us/r4/uinta.

Finding the trailhead: The hike begins from the Mount Nebo Scenic Byway, also called Nebo Loop Road or Forest Road 015. Take Interstate 15 to the Payson exit, 15 miles south of Provo. In Payson take 600 East heading south; this road leads into Payson Canyon. You will reach the Maple Dell Trailhead on the right after about 5.5 miles. There is a large metal bar gate here, used to close the road in winter and under other adverse conditions. Continue about 7 miles up the narrow, winding road to the Loafer Mountain Trailhead on the left, just north of Payson Lakes (about three-quarters of a mile before Payson Lakes Campground). *DeLorme: Utah Atlas & Gazetteer:* Page 45 B6.

The Hike

Santaquin Peak and Loafer Mountain provide a good change of pace from the more popular areas overlooking the Salt Lake Valley. From the trailhead at 7,700 feet, the trail climbs about 3,000 feet in a little more than 5.5 miles. It's a good day outing but certainly not overwhelming for hikers in good condition.

The route follows the well-marked Loafer Mountain Trail 098 about 4 miles to a saddle overlooking a cirque descending to the east. Bear left at the saddle on the obvious trail and hike in a northeasterly direction up the ridge, veering to the east within 0.25 mile toward the summit ridge. From Loafer Mountain (10,687 feet), Santaquin Peak is visible to the northwest, separated by a deep chasm.

Although the terrain is very steep in places, Santaquin Peak can be reached from the northern end of the Loafer Mountain ridge by descending through fir-covered slopes to the saddle connecting the two. From the low point, ascend the ridge to the summit of Santaquin Peak—about a mile and 450 vertical feet away.

Much of the area is open, providing a number of variations to adventuresome hikers armed with a topo map. Not all the contiguous land is national forest; be

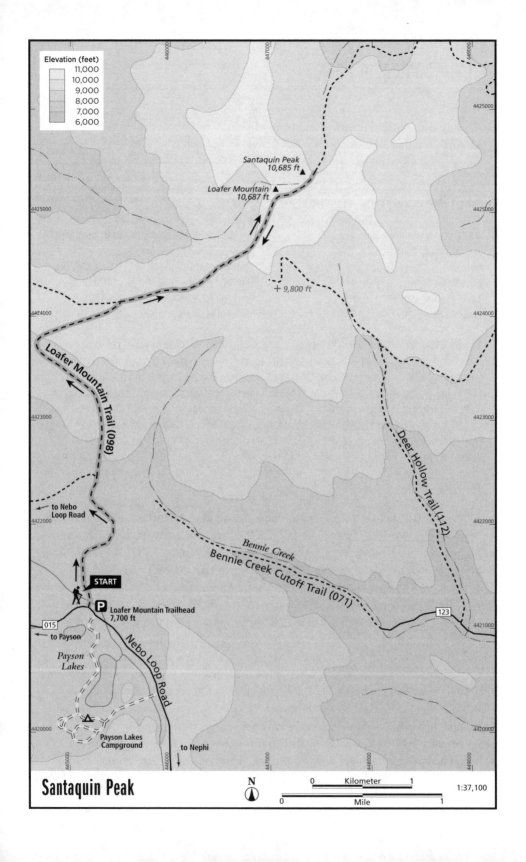

Elevation (feet)
11,000
10,000
9,000
8,000
7,000
6,000

Santaquin Peak
10,685 ft

Loafer Mountain
10,687 ft

+ 9,800 ft

Loafer Mountain Trail (098)

Deer Hollow Trail (112)

to Nebo
Loop Road

Bennie Creek
Bennie Creek Cutoff Trail (071)

123

START

P Loafer Mountain Trailhead
7,700 ft

015

to Payson

Payson
Lakes

Nebo Loop Road

Payson Lakes
Campground

to Nephi

Santaquin Peak

N

0   Kilometer   1

0   Mile   1

1:37,100

prepared to make local inquiries on the availability of private land for hiking. This is particularly true for the territory to the north overlooking Spanish Fork Canyon. Several hundred acres are involved, with access limited, if not forbidden.

Key Points

0.0 Start at the Loafer Mountain Trailhead on the Mount Nebo Scenic Byway (Nebo Loop Road).

4.0 Junction with Deer Hollow Trail 112 in a saddle overlooking a cirque. Hike northeast up the ridge.

4.5 Reach the summit ridge of Loafer Mountain.

5.5 Reach the summit of Santaquin Peak. Turnaround point.

7.0 Junction with Deer Hollow Trail 112. Stay right.

11.0 Arrive back at the trailhead.

Option: For a good overnight loop trip, backtrack to the saddle. The Loafer Mountain Trail connects with Deer Hollow Trail 112 at the saddle. The Deer Hollow Trail, although no longer maintained, winds its way 3 miles southeast to its end at Forest Road 123. Follow the road west about 0.5 mile to the Bennie Creek Cutoff Trailhead at the end of the road. Bennie Creek Cutoff intersects the Loafer Mountain Trail about 1 mile north of the trailhead and your vehicle. —*Originally contributed by Karin and Dennis Caldwell*

12 Mount Nebo

A strenuous 5,000-foot climb to the top of Mount Nebo's south summit in the Mount Nebo Wilderness. Spectacular views of northern and central Utah.

Start: Nebo Bench Trailhead.
Distance: 11 miles out and back.
Difficulty: Strenuous.
Trail surface: Forest trail.
Seasons: Late spring through fall.
Land status: Wilderness area.
Nearest town: Nephi.

Fees and permits: No fees or permits required.
Maps: USGS Mona and Nebo Basin quads; Northern Utah Multipurpose Map.
Trail contacts: Spanish Fork Ranger District, Uinta National Forest, 44 West 400 N., Spanish Fork, UT 84660; (801) 798-3571; www.fs.fed.us/r4/uinta.

Finding the trailhead: Take Interstate 15 to Nephi and turn east onto Highway 132 (at the light on 100 North). Continue east about 6 miles and turn left (north) onto the Mount Nebo Scenic Byway (Nebo Loop Road). Bear left in 3.3 miles onto Forest Road 48 and drive about 1.5 miles to the signed Nebo Bench Trailhead on the left, just past the Ponderosa Campground. *DeLorme: Utah Atlas & Gazetteer:* Page 45 C6.

The Hike

Mount Nebo is a demanding trip—not recommended for hikers looking for an easy day hike. The trek can be made in a day, but you may find a two-day backpack more enjoyable. You climb 5,000 feet in about 5.5 miles.

The Mount Nebo Bench Trail begins at 6,450 feet and climbs west for about 0.5 mile before swinging north on a long switchback. Several switchbacks in the next 0.5 mile ascend through sage and maple-oak thickets. It can be hot along this stretch, so bring plenty of water. Look back along the Andrews Creek drainage for a nice view.

After this first mile and a 1,400-foot elevation gain, the trail enters a relatively flat sagebrush-and-grass meadow. The views east to the Golden Ridge area, southeast to the Manti-LaSal National Forest, and north into the Salt Creek drainage are superb.

Follow the trail west 0.5 mile up another set of steep switchbacks to Andrews Ridge. Aspens and conifers become more common here. You will discover that the trail splits into two major routes and several side trails. From the junction, the left trail follows the south slope of Andrews Ridge, while the right trail (recommended) continues near the ridge. The trails rejoin after about half a mile.

At this junction an old trail heads south into Quaking Asp Canyon. Continue straight (northwest). The summit trail crosses two very small drainages and enters a third, larger one in the next 0.75 mile, climbing about 500 feet in the process. Even

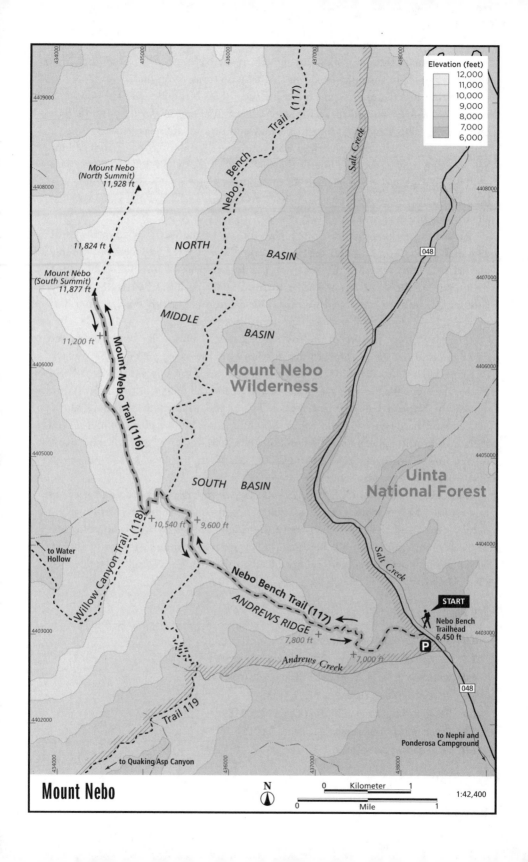

Mount Nebo
(North Summit)
11,928 ft

11,824 ft

Mount Nebo
(South Summit)
11,877 ft

11,200 ft

Trail (117)

Nebo

Bench

NORTH

BASIN

MIDDLE

BASIN

Mount Nebo
Wilderness

Mount Nebo Trail (116)

SOUTH   BASIN

Willow Canyon Trail (118)

10,540 ft   9,600 ft

to Water
Hollow

Nebo Bench Trail (117)

ANDREWS RIDGE

7,800 ft

Andrews Creek

7,000 ft

Salt Creek

Uinta
National Forest

Salt Creek

048

START

Nebo Bench
Trailhead
6,450 ft

P

048

to Nephi and
Ponderosa Campground

Trail 119

to Quaking Asp Canyon

Mount Nebo

N

0   Kilometer   1

0   Mile   1

1:42,400

late into summer, the snowfields that remain in the basins above the trail may provide some water in the gulches. Be sure to treat any water you find.

The trail forks after entering the third basin. The Nebo Bench Trail continues north. Turn left (west) and make the steep ascent (600 feet in 0.5 mile) to a saddle on the ridge. The views west into Juab Valley and beyond are spectacular.

Turn right (north) onto the ridge and continue 1.5 miles through stands of limber pine and then above tree line to the 11,877-foot south summit.

The final stretch is spectacular. At the southern end of the summit, there is a beautiful alpine meadow. A small snowbank to the east and below the ridge may last all year when the snowfall has been heavy.

An old flag-shaped sign sits on top, placed there by the Wasatch Mountain Club. The highest point on the ridge is actually two peaks north (11,928 feet), but the trail ends at the south summit. You can reach this higher peak by scrambling along the knife-edge to the north for 0.5 mile to the middle peak (11,824 feet) and then another 0.5 mile to the actual summit. Use caution along this precipitous ridge, however. If you have doubts about the climb, don't make it.

The views from the top of the south summit are fantastic. To the north are the other peaks of the Nebo ridge; to the northeast are the many peaks of the Wasatch that ring Utah Valley. Views to the east and south are of the Uinta and Manti-LaSal National Forests. To the west, you can see the basins and ranges of the Great Basin.

Mount Nebo has many plant species. The alpine zone has daisies, buckwheat, lichens, and hardy grasses. The subalpine zone hosts limber pine, lupine, several species of beardtongue, gentian, columbine, bluebells, Indian paintbrush, and many others. Lower down are aspen, Douglas fir, sagebrush, maple, oak, and numerous plants of the Compositae family.

This area is critical wildlife habitat. You may see rodents, grouse, and a variety of other birds. Hikers with keen eyes will see agile sharp-shinned hawks darting between trees and riding thermals above the ridges. The Nebo area is home to one of Utah's most important elk herds, and deer are also common. Recently, Rocky Mountain bighorn sheep were reintroduced to the area. —*Originally contributed by Gary McFarland*

Key Points

0.0 Start at the Nebo Bench Trailhead.

3.5 Junction with Willow Canyon Trail 118. Turn left (west).

4.0 Junction with Mount Nebo Trail 116. Turn right (north).

5.5 Arrive at the south summit at 11,877 feet.

7.0 Return to the junction with Willow Canyon Trail 118.

7.5 Return to the junction with Nebo Bench Trail 117.

11.0 Arrive back at the trailhead.

13 Daniels Canyon Nature Trails

Two interpretive trails in Daniels Canyon in the Uinta National Forest, Heber Ranger District. Both offer spectacular scenery and views, many interpretive signs, and diverse vegetation.

Start: The Whiskey Springs Nature Trail starts at the trailhead in the Whiskey Springs Picnic Area; the Foreman Hollow Trail begins at the trailhead in Lodgepole Campground.
Distance: The Whiskey Springs Nature Trail is a 500-foot loop; the Foreman Hollow Trail, a 4-mile loop.
Difficulty: Whiskey Springs, easy; Foreman Hollow, easy to moderate.
Trail surface: The Whiskey Springs Nature Trail is paved and gravel; the Foreman Hollow Trail is a well-maintained forest trail.
Seasons: June through October.

Land status: National forest.
Nearest town: Heber City.
Fees and permits: A $4.00 parking fee is charged at Whiskey Springs Picnic Area and at Lodgepole Campground.
Maps: USGS Center Creek and Twin Peaks quads; Northeastern Utah Multipurpose Map; Uinta National Forest Travel Plan Map.
Trail contacts: Heber Ranger District, Uinta National Forest, P.O. Box 190, Heber City, UT 84032; (435) 654-0470; www.fs.fed.us/r4/uinta.

Finding the trailhead: To reach the Whiskey Springs Trailhead, drive 8 miles southeast of Heber City on U.S. Highway 40 to the Uinta National Forest. The Whiskey Springs Picnic Area is located just inside the national forest boundary on the right (west) side of the road. Foreman Hollow Trail 090 is near the summit of Daniels Canyon, 16 miles from Heber City on US 40. A small section of paved campground road connects the loop. The trail can be accessed at either of the two gated, dirt maintenance roads that spur off the paved campground road. The trailheads for either end are found about half a mile past the gates, where the trail becomes easy-to-follow singletrack terrain. *DeLorme: Utah Atlas & Gazetteer:* Page 54 C1 and D2.

The Hike

The Whiskey Springs Nature Trai l and the Foreman Hollow Trail are two interpretive loop trails easily accessed from Heber City along US 40.

The 500-foot nature loop is an easy paved-and-gravel trail with interpretive plant signs along the way. It is a perfect complement to a leisurely afternoon picnic.

The Foreman Hollow Trail is a 4-mile loop that offers spectacular views of Strawberry Reservoir to the southeast, and Strawberry Peak (9,714 feet) and Twin Peaks (9,712 and 9,653 feet) to the southwest. Educational signs along the well-maintained trail note interesting facts about the native vegetation and wildlife. Campsites, water, and restrooms are available at Lodgepole Campground. *—Contributed by the Heber Ranger District*

(Note: Since two separate, short trails in the same vicinity are featured on this hike, no key points are provided.)

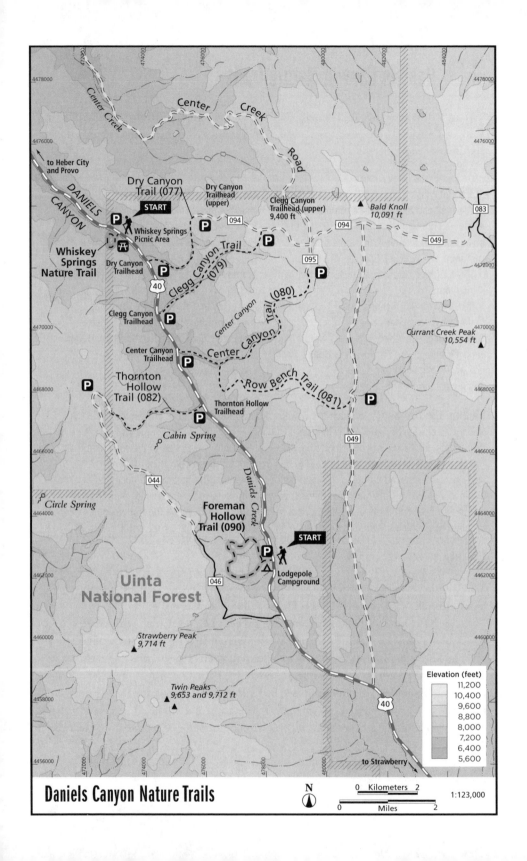

Daniels Canyon Nature Trails

14 Dry Canyon and Clegg Canyon

The Dry Canyon and Clegg Canyon Trails offer a number of day-hike opportunities in Daniels Canyon in the Uinta National Forest, Heber Ranger District. Both trails feature panoramic views, wildlife, and diverse vegetation.

Start: Dry Canyon and Clegg Canyon Trailheads off U.S. Highway 40.

Distance: The Dry Canyon Trail is 3 miles point to point; the Clegg Canyon Trail, 4 miles point to point.

Difficulty: Strenuous.

Trail surface: Forest trail.

Seasons: June through October.

Land status: National forest.

Nearest town: Heber City.

Fees and permits: No fees or permits required.

Maps: USGS Center Creek quad; Uinta National Forest Travel Plan Map; Northeastern Utah Multipurpose Map.

Trail contacts: Heber Ranger District, Uinta National Forest, P.O. Box 190, Heber City, UT 84032; (435) 654-0470; www.fs.fed.us/r4/uinta.

Finding the trailhead: To reach the lower end of Dry Canyon Trail 077, drive 9 miles southeast of Heber City on US 40. The trailhead is on the left (east) side of the highway, 1.5 miles past the Uinta National Forest boundary. To access the top of the Dry Canyon Trail for a vehicle shuttle, take Center Creek Road, which is just off US 40 in Heber City, and head east. After about 6 miles it becomes a dirt Forest Service road (039) that you will follow for another 6 miles (four-wheel drive is not required). Turn right (west) onto Forest Road 094, just past a small shack (the last turnoff before Center Creek Road ends). Follow this road west just over 0.5 mile past the sheep corrals at the Clegg Canyon Trailhead to a clearing with a 3-foot wire fence running north-south. The upper trailhead is just on the other side of this fence.

The lower end of Clegg Canyon Trail 079 is another mile along US 40, also on the left (east) of the highway. Access the upper end of this trail by taking the same route you used to the top of the Dry Canyon Trail. Watch for the upper trailhead at the sheep corrals about 1 mile after you've turned west onto FR 094. *DeLorme: Utah Atlas & Gazetteer:* Page 54 C1 and D1.

The Hike

These two point-to-point trails in Daniels Canyon are easily accessed off US 40 and connect via a Forest Service road, providing vehicle shuttle or loop hike opportunities. The area is used for grazing and has many sheep and cattle trails, which can cause some confusion. These two trails are maintained annually, but hiking with a map is strongly recommended. Water is not available along either route, so be sure to carry a sufficient supply, especially in the warm summer months. Be prepared, as well, for summer afternoon thunderstorms. Hiking information, maps, and supplies for your trip can be obtained at nearby Heber City.

The route that the Dry Canyon Trail follows from US 40 is quite steep and moderately difficult as it passes through a narrow canyon. The canyon forks halfway up;

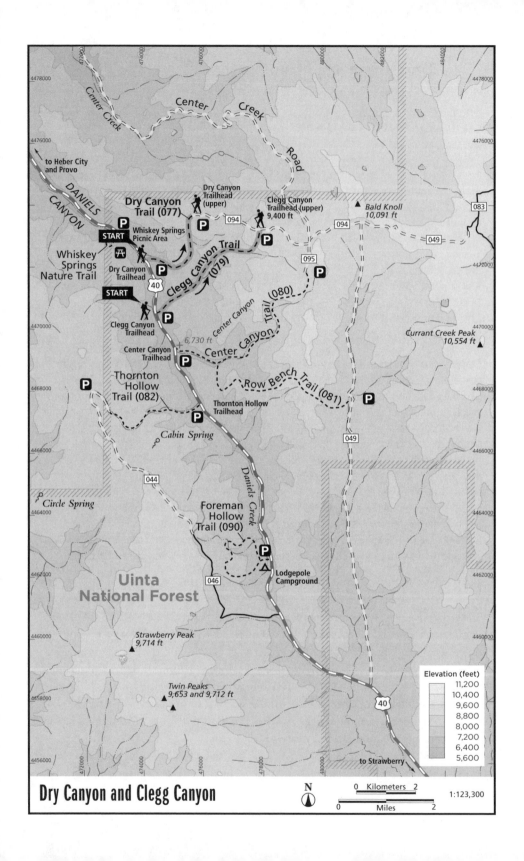

Dry Canyon and Clegg Canyon

stay right (south). At the top you cross an open meadow (stay northeast through the meadow), where you are treated to a breathtaking view of the surrounding mountains, including Bald Knoll (10,091 feet) to the east.

The Clegg Canyon Trail passes through canyon country, meadows, and evergreen and aspen stands. The trail is relatively flat at each end and steep in the middle, making it an easy to moderately difficult hike. Clegg Canyon is closed to all motorized traffic.

The Clegg Canyon and Dry Canyon Trails meet FR 094 within 1 mile of each other to create an 8.5- to 9.5-mile loop hike (depending on whether you left a second vehicle at either trailhead on the highway). —*Contributed by the Heber Ranger District*

(Note: Since two separate, short trails in the same vicinity are featured on this hike, no key points are provided.)

15 Center Canyon

A good day hike through imposing canyon walls, ending in a spectacular view of the Heber Valley. The trail, which offers panoramic views, wildlife, and diverse vegetation, is located in Daniels Canyon in the Uinta National Forest, Heber Ranger District.

Start: Center Canyon Trailhead off U.S. Highway 40.
Distance: 4.5 miles point to point.
Difficulty: Strenuous.
Trail surface: Forest trail.
Seasons: June through October.
Land status: National forest.
Nearest town: Heber City.

Fees and permits: No fees or permits required.
Maps: USGS Center Creek quad; Northeastern Utah Multipurpose Map; Uinta National Forest Travel Plan Map.
Trail contacts: Heber Ranger District, Uinta National Forest, P.O. Box 190, Heber City, UT 84032; (435) 654-0470; www.fs.fed.us/r4/uinta.

Finding the trailhead: Drive about 11 miles southeast of Heber City on US 40 and turn left (east) at the signed turnoff for Center Canyon. Park at the trailhead, located at a gate at the end of this turnoff, just off the highway. *DeLorme: Utah Atlas & Gazetteer:* Page 54 D1.

The Hike

Center Canyon Trail is open only to foot, horse, or mountain bike travel. Water is not available along the trail, so be sure to carry a sufficient supply, especially in the warm summer months. Be prepared for multiple stream crossings and afternoon thunderstorms during summer, too. Hiking information, maps, and supplies for your trip can be obtained at nearby Heber City.

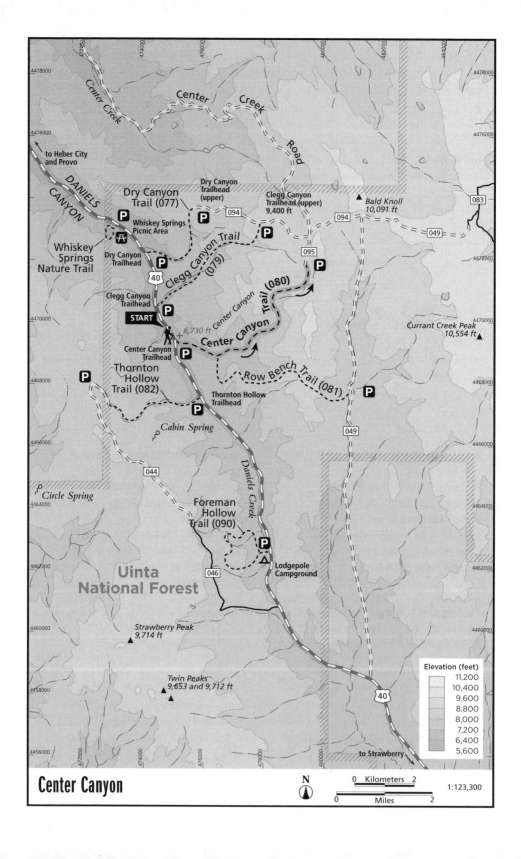

Center Canyon

The trail begins as an old Forest Service road, and after about 1.5 miles the road ends and the trail becomes singletrack. It's a relatively steep climb as the trail winds through Center Canyon to a ridge, following a small stream for most of its length. There are great views of the surrounding mountains, including Currant Creek Peak to the southeast at 10,554 feet and the east face of Mount Timpanogos to the west. Hiking through the canyon the entire way makes finding your sense of direction toward the top somewhat difficult, so bring a compass.

Center Canyon connects with Center Creek Road, which intersects Forest Road 094 about a half mile to the right (north). You could have a vehicle waiting here or hike west along FR 094 and pick up the Clegg Canyon or Dry Canyon Trails. —*Contributed by the Heber Ranger District*

Key Points

0.0   Start at the Center Canyon Trailhead off US 40.
1.5   The old dirt road turns to singletrack trail.
4.5   Junction with Center Creek Road.

16 Thornton Hollow

This short day hike in Daniels Canyon in the Uinta National Forest, Heber Ranger District, features rocky stream crossings, shady pine-needle-carpeted trail, aspen groves, and grassy meadows.

Start: Thornton Hollow Trailhead off U.S. Highway 40.
Distance: 4 miles out and back.
Difficulty: Moderate.
Trail surface: Forest trail.
Seasons: June through October.
Land status: National forest.
Nearest town: Heber City.

Fees and permits: No fees or permits required.
Maps: USGS Twin Peaks quad; Northeastern Utah Multipurpose Map; Uinta National Forest Travel Plan Map.
Trail contacts: Heber Ranger District, Uinta National Forest, P.O. Box 190, Heber City, UT 84032; (435) 654-0470; www.fs.fed.us/r4/uinta.

Finding the trailhead: Drive 12 miles southeast of Heber City on US 40. Thornton Hollow Trail 082 begins on the right (west) side of the highway. *DeLorme: Utah Atlas & Gazetteer:* Page 54 D1.

The Hike

The Thornton Hollow Trail is open only to foot, horse, or mountain bike travel. Water is not available along the trail, so be sure to carry a sufficient supply, especially

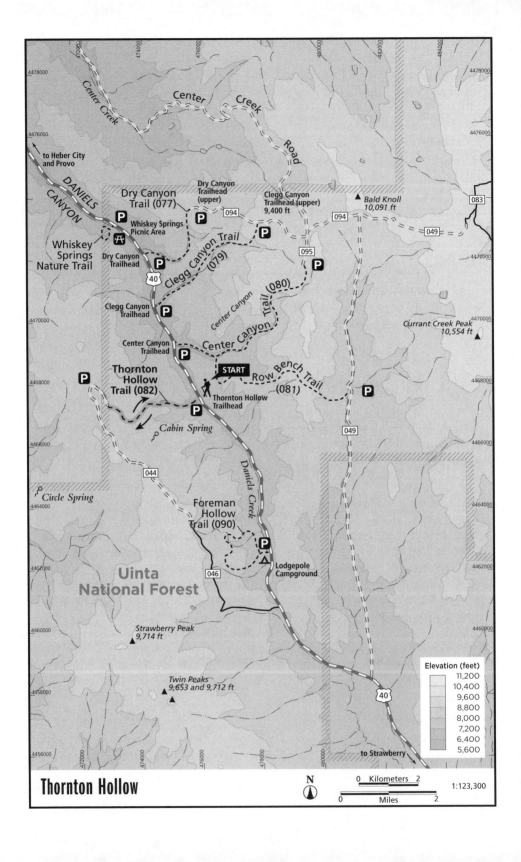

to Heber City
and Provo

DANIELS
CANYON

Dry Canyon
Trail (077)

Whiskey Springs
Picnic Area

Whiskey
Springs
Nature Trail

Dry Canyon
Trailhead

Clegg Canyon Trail
(079)

Clegg Canyon
Trailhead

Center Canyon
Trailhead

Thornton
Hollow
Trail (082)

Thornton Hollow
Trailhead

Cabin Spring

Circle Spring

Foreman
Hollow
Trail (090)

Uinta
National Forest

Strawberry Peak
9,714 ft

Twin Peaks
9,653 and 9,712 ft

Center Creek

Center
Creek
Road

Dry Canyon
Trailhead
(upper)

Clegg Canyon
Trailhead (upper)
9,400 ft

094

094

095

(080)

Center Canyon Trail

Center Canyon

START

Row Bench Trail
(081)

044

Daniels Creek

046

Lodgepole
Campground

Bald Knoll
10,091 ft

049

Currant Creek Peak
10,554 ft

049

083

to Strawberry

40

Thornton Hollow

N

Elevation (feet)
11,200
10,400
9,600
8,800
8,000
7,200
6,400
5,600

0   Kilometers   2

0   Miles   2

1:123,300

4478000
4476000
4474000
4472000
4470000
4468000
4466000
4464000
4462000
4460000
4458000
4456000

472000
474000
476000
478000
480000
482000
484000

in the warm summer months. Be prepared for summer afternoon thunderstorms. Hiking information, maps, and supplies for your trip can be obtained at nearby Heber City.

Thornton Hollow Trail 082 is a scenic shallow-canyon trail. It begins with a short, steep climb and then continues at a more gradual grade. The trail is shared by cattle, which have also made trails in the area. The cattle trails are usually narrow singletrack paths littered with fallen trees. The Thornton Hollow Trail is well maintained, with few fallen trees until the last quarter mile. At this point the fallen trees have been used to close the old road that you hike out on to vehicular traffic. Trail 082 connects with Forest Road 044 at the western boundary of the national forest.
—*Contributed by the Heber Ranger District*

Key Points

0.0 Start at Thornton Hollow Trail 082, just off US 40.

2.0 Reach FR 044. Turnaround point.

4.0 Arrive back at the trailhead.

17 Log Hollow

An enjoyable day trip on a loop trail, with another trailhead for an optional side trip nearby. The trail is in the Uinta National Forest near the western boundary of the High Uintas Wilderness and features spectacular views, wildlife, and diverse vegetation.

Start: Nobletts parking area on Highway 35.
Distance: 7-mile loop.
Difficulty: Moderate.
Trail surface: Forest trail.
Seasons: June through October.
Land status: National forest.
Nearest town: Francis.
Fees and permits: No fees or permits required.

Maps: USGS Soapstone Basin quad; Northeastern Utah Multipurpose Map; Uinta National Forest Travel Plan Map.
Trail contacts: Heber Ranger District, Uinta National Forest, P.O. Box 190, Heber City, UT 84032; (435) 654-0470; www.fs.fed.us/r4/uinta.

Finding the trailhead: Drive 8 miles north from Heber City on U.S. Highway 40, turn right (east) onto Highway 32, and drive 7 miles to Francis. Take Highway 35 southeast along the South Fork Provo River for about 10 miles. The eastern trailhead is located about 2 miles from the Uinta National Forest boundary on the left (north) side of the highway and can be accessed from the large Nobletts parking lot at this location. You passed the Log Hollow parking area and western trailhead 1 mile earlier. *DeLorme: Utah Atlas & Gazetteer:* Page 54 C2.

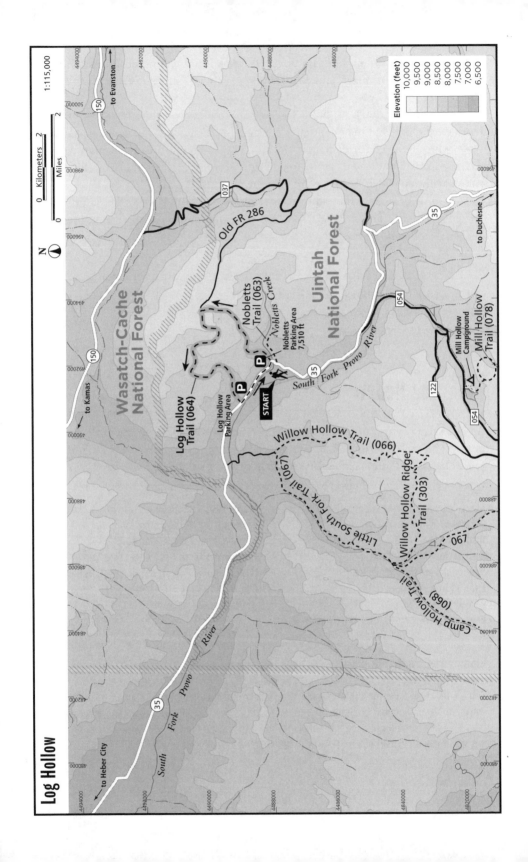

Log Hollow

1:115,000

to Evanston

Wasatch-Cache National Forest

Uintah National Forest

Old FR 286

Nobletts Trail (063)

Nobletts Creek

Nobletts Parking Area 7,510 ft

Log Hollow Trail (064)

Log Hollow Parking Area

P

P

START

South Fork Provo River

Willow Hollow Trail (066)

Little South Fork Trail (067)

Willow Hollow Ridge Trail (303)

Camp Hollow Trail (068)

Mill Hollow Campground

Mill Hollow Trail (078)

to Duchesne

to Kamas

to Heber City

South Fork Provo River

N

0   Kilometers   2
0   Miles   2

Elevation (feet)
10,000
9,500
9,000
8,500
8,000
7,500
7,000
6,500

The Hike

This hike follows a trail that makes a pleasant loop lined with conifer and aspen stands and scrub oak. Log Hollow Trail 064 is initially rather steep as it follows the left fork of Nobletts Creek. At the top of the canyon, the trail meets an old road (Forest Road 286), which you want to follow for about 0.25 mile. Look for where the road continues right (east) and is closed to the left (west); head left. The trail soon meanders along the ridge and winds through a grassy meadow. You can enjoy spectacular views of the surrounding valleys and peaks, including Iron Mine Mountain to the east and Soapstone Mountain to the southeast. As the ridge ends, the trail turns south down Log Hollow Canyon, where again there is evidence of an old road. Shortly you will arrive at a fork as you are making the descent from the ridge. Stay to the right. All is not lost, by the way, if you accidentally veer left: Both routes take you to the bottom of the mountain, but the trail to the left is not maintained and is very hard to follow. Descend from the ridge to the Log Hollow parking area, which is just about 1 mile west of where you started on Highway 35. The hike is 6 miles if you left a shuttle car at this parking area.

Key Points

0.0 Start at the Nobletts parking area off Highway 35.

6.0 Reach the Log Hollow parking area off Highway 35.

7.0 Arrive back at the Nobletts parking area.

Options: For a slightly easier route, you can hike the trail backward starting at the western access point (Log Hollow parking area).

If you have plenty of time, you might begin the day by hiking the short, generally easy Nobletts Creek Trail 063, located a quarter mile south of the Nobletts parking area off Highway 35. This 1.5-mile point-to-point, well-maintained trail passes through some interesting geologic formations and unique stream patterns. The key feature is Nobletts Creek, an underground stream that surfaces as a large spring and waterfall near the end of the trail. It makes for a quick, easy, and beautiful hike. —*Contributed by the Heber Ranger District*

18 Round, Sand, and Fish Lakes

A rigorous overnighter to three lakes in the upper Weber River drainage in the western Uinta Mountains. Good fly fishing for grayling and brook trout.

Start: Dry Fork Trailhead.
Distance: 9 miles out and back (to Fish Lake).
Difficulty: Strenuous.
Trail surface: Forest trail.
Seasons: Late June through September.
Land status: National forest.
Nearest town: Oakley.

Fees and permits: No fees or permits required.
Maps: USGS Whitney Reservoir quad; Northeastern Utah Multipurpose Map.
Trail contacts: Kamas Ranger District, Wasatch-Cache National Forest, P.O. Box 68, Kamas, UT 84036; (435) 783-4338; www.fs.fed.us/r4/wcnf.

Finding the trailhead: Take Interstate 80 east from Salt Lake City and exit at Wanship. Drive about 10 miles to Oakley on Highway 32. Turn left onto Weber Canyon Road (a quarter of a mile north of the Oakley General Store—your last stop for trail munchies), a county road that provides access to a number of Forest Service trails. The intersection is clearly marked with a sign indicating WEBER CANYON, SMITH AND MOREHOUSE. The trailhead is 19 miles from this intersection. After 12 miles the pavement ends and you begin traveling on an improved dirt road. The road to Smith and Morehouse Reservoir turns right at this point. Continue straight and pass the Thousand Peaks Ranch sign. After 4 miles on the dirt road, bear right at a minor intersection. Before long you cross the Weber River. About 0.25 mile beyond, pass the entrance to Holiday Park. Do not enter the park; rather, bear left and continue 0.5 mile to the trailhead, which is on the left just after you cross Dry Fork Creek. The trailhead is on private land, so respect the landowner's rights. There is a small dirt parking area. Camping and campfires are not permitted at the trailhead. *DeLorme: Utah Atlas & Gazetteer:* Page 54 B3.

The Hike

These lakes are for well-conditioned trekkers seeking good high-country fishing, particularly for the beautiful Arctic grayling. The trailhead is less than two hours from Salt Lake City, including several miles over improved dirt road suitable for passenger cars.

The Dry Fork Trail begins at 8,000 feet and climbs through a rocky fir forest, ending below timberline in a broad, U-shaped basin boasting many small ponds and lakes. Round Lake sits just below 10,000 feet; Sand and Fish Lakes are about 200 feet higher. Fish Lake is about 4.5 miles from the trailhead. This trail attracts heavy horse traffic, so expect to see a few ruts and mud holes on the steeper sections of the route.

From the trailhead, the route heads northeast through an aspen grove for 0.25 mile to the first crossing of Dry Fork Creek. Watch this crossing very carefully, especially with small children in tow. Normally low and easily waded, Dry Fork Creek

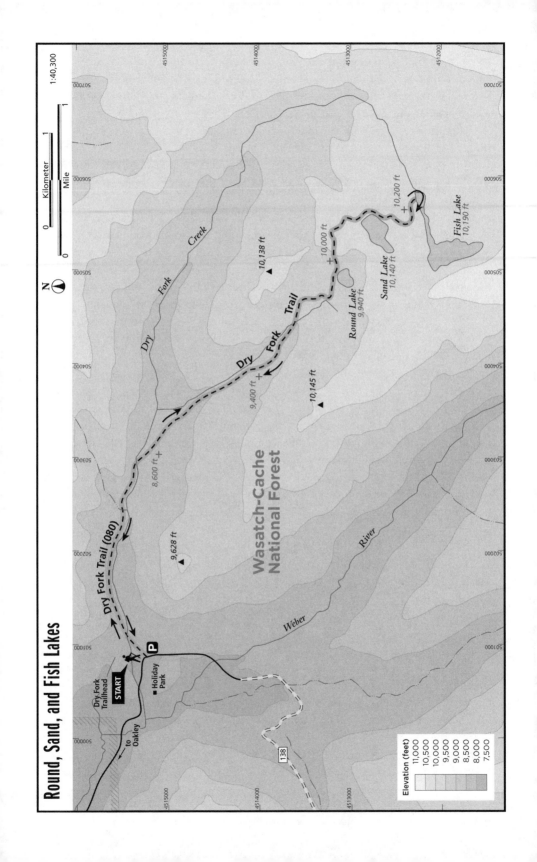

Round, Sand, and Fish Lakes

1:40,300

N

0 Kilometer 1

0 Mile 1

Dry Fork Trailhead

START

to Oakley

Dry Fork Trail (080)

P

Holiday Park

138

Weber

River

9,628 ft ▲

8,600 ft +

9,400 ft +

10,145 ft ▲

Dry Fork Trail

Dry

Fork

Creek

10,138 ft ▲

10,000 ft +

Round Lake
9,940 ft

Sand Lake
10,140 ft

Fish Lake
10,190 ft

10,200 ft +

Wasatch-Cache
National Forest

Elevation (feet)

11,000
10,500
10,000
9,500
9,000
8,500
8,000
7,500

can quickly rise to hazardous levels in midsummer due to upstream releases for irrigation. With care, older children and adults can cross safely at any time. Incidentally, you follow the stream for nearly 1.5 miles, so don't overload your water bottles yet. There's plenty ahead (be sure to treat all water).

After the stream crossing, the trail proceeds east along Dry Fork's left (north) side through lodgepole pines and firs. The trail becomes rocky, climbing slowly. While you still have your wind and energy, relax and enjoy the abundant wildflowers. You should see yarrow, cinquefoil, assorted sunflowers and daisies, Indian paintbrush, geranium, and monkshood.

After climbing about 600 feet in almost 1.5 miles, cross Dry Fork Creek again in a large clearing near the downstream end of an old washed-out beaver pond. Watch carefully for this spot, where the trail heads south for about 100 feet after the crossing. (Note: On the USGS map, the crossing is mistakenly shown as being past the upstream end of the clearing; other than this error, that map's trail description is accurate.) While at the clearing, look upward to the southeast at a knobby peak (10,138 feet). You ascend the slope to the right and pass the peak on the south side. Check your water now. While there are creeks in the next stretch of trail, none is reliable, and they may all be dry when you hike.

From Dry Fork Creek, head south on a smooth, gentle trail for about 100 feet, then bear left (east). In about 0.25 mile, at 8,600 feet, begin climbing a rocky trail, still tracking southeast. The trail again levels out, but you'll soon hit a steep stretch looking much like a streambed. Keep your eyes and wildflower guide open, because you'll spot white columbine, parrot's-beak, monkshood, false hellebore, cow parsnip, purple penstemon, red and yellow monkey flowers, bluebells, wild strawberry, and others. This damp area is ideal habitat for many of the showier wildflowers.

From here on, continue to the southeast until you reach Round Lake about 2 miles from the crossing. It seems like 5 miles, especially just before Round Lake where the trail is steepest. Cross the outlet stream from Round Lake, which actually is the trail for about 50 feet. Be careful—the alga-coated rocks are slippery.

Round Lake is small and sits at 9,940 feet in elevation. The one good campsite is on the northwest corner where the trail meets the lake and will accommodate three small tents. Don't pitch tents close to the water's edge, because the area is fragile and the water typically creeps up overnight following irrigation releases upstream. Do other hikers a favor and pack out some of the extra garbage in the area.

Round Lake has been stocked with Arctic grayling and brook and cutthroat trout. All readily take small flies, especially dries. The north and northeast shores are best for fly casting, but the largest fish may be on the other side, where many trees have fallen into the water. While fishing, note all of the elephant-head plants in the wet meadows around the lake.

Sand Lake is just southeast of Round Lake, 0.5 mile on the trail. At about the halfway mark, you skirt a large meadow on the north side. Look to your right (south) and notice a beautiful waterfall against the heavily timbered hillside. This cascade is the stream outlet from Sand Lake.

Sand Lake has only a few poor to fair campsites on its north and northwest corners, plus one just below the dam (not shown on the USGS map). The largest site could accommodate one party with up to three small tents. The inlet meadow on the southwest corner of the lake is wet and muddy.

Sand Lake contains small grayling and has poor fly fishing due to the steep, timbered, debris-ridden shoreline. Round Lake certainly is more productive and attractive for anglers.

Fish Lake is due south of Sand Lake, another 0.5 mile on an easy trail. The trail meets Fish Lake at a long, narrow arm extending northeast from the main lake body. Although not shown on the USGS map, Fish Lake has a rock dam at the extreme northeast end of the arm.

The plant community around Fish Lake is similar to that around Round and Sand Lakes, and you are still below timberline. The lake has many good shoreline campsites, particularly on its long arm. It contains mostly brook trout and grayling and often has good fly fishing. The outlet stream looks as if it could hold some nice trout as well.

The Round/Sand/Fish Lakes area has received no official Forest Service wilderness designation. However, the area is part of the Lakes Roadless Area, recommended for wilderness by Utah conservationists.

Hikers can enhance the wilderness qualities of this area by packing out some of the accumulated trash, which the Forest Service says has become a particular problem here in recent years. —*Originally contributed by Bill Geer*

Key Points

0.0 Start at the Dry Fork Trailhead.

0.25 Cross Dry Fork Creek. Hike east on the north side of the creek.

1.5 Cross Dry Fork Creek again. Head south, then bear left (east).

3.5 Reach Round Lake. Continue southeast.

4.0 Reach Sand Lake. Continue south.

4.5 Arrive at Fish Lake.

9.0 Arrive back at the trailhead.

19 Three Divide Lakes

A day hike or overnighter to beautiful terrain in the Uinta Mountains. There are numerous lakes along the entire hike, with alpine scenery and good fishing.

Start: Crystal Lake Trailhead.
Distance: 6-mile loop.
Difficulty: Easy.
Trail surface: Forest trail.
Seasons: Late spring through fall.
Land status: National forest.
Nearest town: Kamas.

Fees and permits: A $3.00-per-day per vehicle recreation pass is required. Weekly and annual passes are available.
Maps: USGS Mirror Lake quad; Northeastern Utah Multipurpose Map.
Trail contacts: Kamas Ranger District, Wasatch-Cache National Forest, P.O. Box 68, Kamas, UT 84036; (435) 783-4338; www.fs.fed.us/r4/wcnf.

Finding the trailhead: Drive about 26 miles east of Kamas on Highway 150 (Mirror Lake Highway). Turn left toward Trial Lake at a long, 180-degree turn to the right. Drive on pavement for a few hundred yards, continuing on a gravel road for 0.75 mile. Turn right toward Crystal Lake (signs mark the spot). The trailhead is half a mile ahead at the end of the road, just north of a horse ramp at the west end of the parking area. This trailhead leads to many areas of the upper Provo and Weber drainages, so don't be discouraged if you see several cars in the trailhead parking area. *DeLorme: Utah Atlas & Gazetteer:* Page 54 B3.

The Hike

The western Uinta Mountains, from Kamas east to Bald Mountain, offer spectacular high lake country and a family of peaks at more than 10,000 feet. This is the Lakes Roadless Area, headwater country of the Provo and Weber Rivers.

The Three Divide Lakes are about 3 miles from the trailhead and only about 400 feet higher in elevation, so the hike is relatively easy. These beautiful alpine lakes sit among a cluster of lakes at just over 10,400 feet. The area is bordered by the Notch Mountain peaks to the north (11,263 feet is the tallest) and by boulder-strewn Mount Watson (11,521 feet) to the southwest.

Beginning at about 10,000 feet, the trail passes Lily Lakes in a few hundred yards, then contours north for a mile before reaching the Notch Mountain Trail just south of Wall Lake. This section of trail, incidentally, is not shown on the 1972 Mirror Lake topographic map.

At Wall Lake the trail angles to the east through a lovely series of ponds and small meadows and then ascends several switchbacks for 0.75 mile to the broad meadows near Twin Lakes.

The Notch, a 10,000-foot pass leading to Lovenia and Ibantik Lakes and the upper Weber drainage, is a quarter mile to the north. Leave the trail here, proceeding

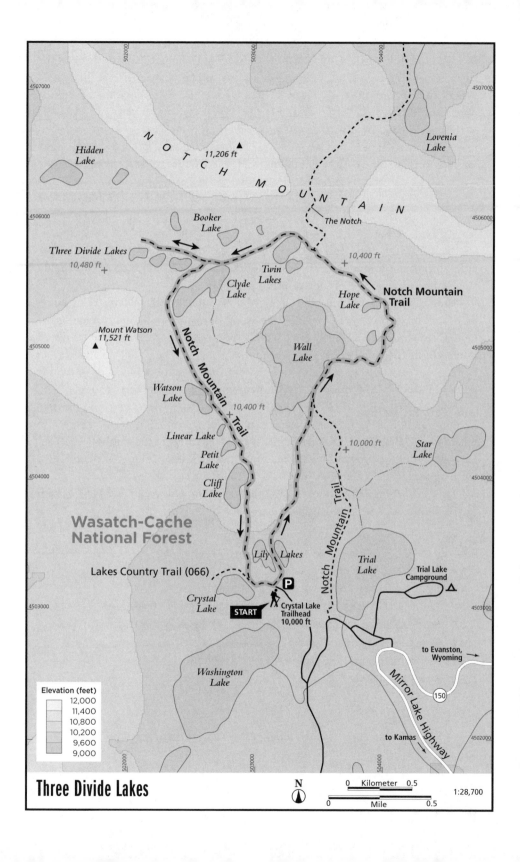

Hidden
Lake

N O T C H
11,206 ft

M O U N T A I N

The Notch

Lovenia
Lake

Booker
Lake

Three Divide Lakes

10,480 ft +

Twin
Lakes

10,400 ft
+

Clyde
Lake

Hope
Lake

**Notch Mountain
Trail**

Mount Watson
11,521 ft

Notch Mountain Trail

Wall
Lake

Watson
Lake

Linear Lake

10,400 ft
+

Petit
Lake

Star
Lake

Cliff
Lake

10,000 ft
+

**Wasatch-Cache
National Forest**

Lily Lakes

Notch Mountain Trail

Trial
Lake

Trial Lake
Campground

Lakes Country Trail (066)

Crystal
Lake

P

START

Crystal Lake
Trailhead
10,000 ft

to Evanston,
Wyoming

Washington
Lake

Mirror Lake Highway

150

to Kamas

Elevation (feet)

| 12,000 |
| 11,400 |
| 10,800 |
| 10,200 |
| 9,600 |
| 9,000 |

Three Divide Lakes

N

0   Kilometer   0.5

0   Mile   0.5

1:28,700

due west 0.8 mile to Twin Lakes. A path runs 0.5 mile along the north shore of the larger upper lake, up a series of boulders, and on to large Clyde Lake at the base of Mount Watson. From Clyde Lake, the Three Divide Lakes are all within 0.5 mile to the north.

Fishing is good here, particularly for small brook trout. There are also cutthroats in some of the nearby lakes. Campsites are plentiful in the many stands of spruce and fir, with springwater available throughout the year. Be sure to treat all water.

From a base camp near any of the Three Divide Lakes, you can take side trips through the Notch to Lovenia Lake. You can make the 1,100-foot climb up Mount Watson or explore the Hidden Lake area to the northwest on the shoulder of the Middle Fork Weber River. This is a lovely area in the shadow of Mount Watson.

Because of this area's proximity to Mirror Lake Highway, it gets heavy use, especially during the midsummer months. But it's wide-open country, and you should be able to find a quiet niche for your campsite.

Mule deer, some moose, and elk inhabit the area. Small mammals, including weasels, voles, and muskrats, provide interesting diversions from your hiking in the high lakes country. Extensive pine marten research was done on the northern reaches of the Middle Fork Weber River.

You can retrace your steps to your car, but the loop route offers an intriguing cross-country hike and more of a wilderness experience in the lakes region.

After backtracking to Clyde Lake, hike around its west end and find the trail heading south. Follow a series of terraces and lakes (Watson, Linear, and Petit) 0.75 mile down to Cliff Lake. Foot traffic has created a path from the south end of Cliff Lake along the west edge of Lily Lake, connecting to Lakes Country Trail 066. Turn left here for less than a quarter mile back to the trailhead.

There are numerous options in this splendid alpine wilderness, but we'll leave it to you to discover them. —*Originally contributed by Margaret Pettis*

Key Points

0.0   Start at the Crystal Lake Trailhead.

1.0   Junction with the Notch Mountain Trail. Continue north.

3.2   Reach Clyde Lake. Turn right (northwest) to the first of the Three Divide Lakes.

3.6   Reach the third and westernmost of the Three Divide Lakes. Turnaround point.

4.0   Arrive back at Clyde Lake. Turn right (southwest).

5.75 Junction with Lakes Country Trail 066. Turn left (southeast).

6.0   Arrive back at the trailhead.

20 Four Lakes Basin

A popular backpack to alpine lakes in the western Uinta Mountains. There are beautiful views of the western Uintas, including the upper Duchesne River and Rock Creek country.

Start: Highline Trail Trailhead.
Distance: 16 miles out and back.
Difficulty: Moderate.
Trail surface: Rocky forest trail.
Seasons: Summer through early fall.
Land status: Wilderness area.
Nearest town: Kamas.
Fees and permits: A Mirror Lake Area Recreation Pass is required for trailhead parking: $3.00 per day, $6.00 per week, $25.00 per year. Golden Eagle/Age/Access Passports are accepted. Passes are available at Forest Service offices in Kamas and Evanston, Wyoming, the Bear River Station and Beaver Creek Station, several self-issue stations in the national forest, and several local vendors in Kamas and Evanston. Voluntary trailhead registration is strongly encouraged.
Maps: USGS Hayden Peak quad; Northeastern Utah Multipurpose Map; National Geographic Trails Illustrated High Uintas Wilderness Map; Ashley National Forest Map.
Trail contacts: Duchesne Ranger District, Ashley National Forest, P.O. Box 981, Duchesne, UT 84021; (435) 738-2482; www.fs.fed.us/r4/ashley. Also, Kamas Ranger District, Wasatch-Cache National Forest, P.O. Box 68, Kamas, UT 84036; (435) 783-4338; www.fs.fed.us/r4/wcnf.

Finding the trailhead: Take Highway 150 (Mirror Lake Highway) east from Kamas into the Uinta Mountains. About 2.5 miles past Mirror Lake and just after passing from Duchesne County into Summit County, turn right (east) into the Highline Trail parking lot. Expect to find the large lot filled, especially at the height of the hiking season. *DeLorme: Utah Atlas & Gazetteer:* Page 54 B3.

The Hike

Although not as remote and quiet as some other Uinta Mountains hikes, this trip is considered a basic west-side approach to the interior High Uintas Wilderness. You get there quickly, too—just off Highway 150 north of Mirror Lake. Once on the trail, you're soon in roadless country.

This route is also the most popular access to the Highline Trail, which courses across the great backbone of the east–west Uinta Mountains. At first you will see many hikers, some out for a stroll to Scudder Lake. Then there are the more serious hiker-anglers who find solitude and fast fishing off the main trail at Wilder, Wyman, and Packard Lakes, about 3.5 miles in. Most of the traffic, however, is to the many lakes in Naturalist Basin, located to the north of the Highline Trail in the shadow of Mount Agassiz (12,428 feet) and Spread Eagle Peak (12,540 feet). Farther east along the Highline Trail is grayling-filled Carolyn Lake, then the invitingly cold water of

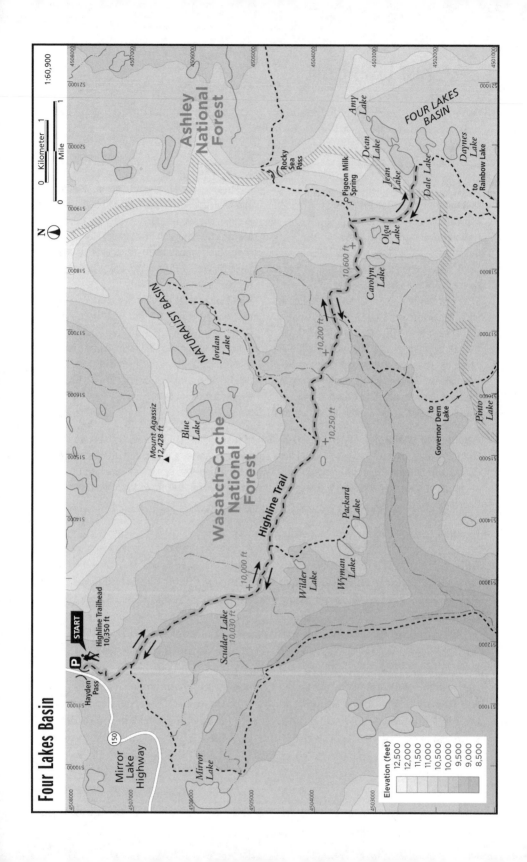

Four Lakes Basin

1:60,900

Elevation (feet)
12,500
12,000
11,500
11,000
10,500
10,000
9,500
9,000
8,500

Pigeon Milk Spring, followed by Rocky Sea Pass and access to the upper Rock Creek drainage to the north, but you will head south past Olga Lake to Four Lakes Basin.

From the trailhead just east of Hayden Pass (10,347 feet), the trail descends 2 miles to a point just east of Scudder Lake, a popular destination for day hikers. A mile beyond, a trail heads right (south) to Wilder, Wyman, and Packard Lakes. Continue straight (east) here, mostly contouring on the gently undulating trail below Mount Agassiz.

The steep trail to Naturalist Basin heads left (north) as you pass around the rocky spur south of Agassiz. The basin and its lakes make a nice side excursion, but be prepared to see many other hikers.

In 1.5 miles the trail heading south to Pinto and Governor Dern Lakes and Grandaddy Basin exits to the right (south). The Highline Trail continues eastward, beginning to climb after this junction. The trail ascends about 600 feet in slightly more than a mile—the only real climb you have into Four Lakes Basin.

About a quarter mile before the rocky ridge to the east, the trail south to Four Lakes Basin exits to the right. However, you should hike an additional few hundred yards east toward Rocky Sea Pass to Pigeon Milk Spring. The water is cold and delicious here, and many hikers go a bit out of their way to fill their water bottles. Pigeon Milk was named for the sometimes slightly discolored glacial "milk" flowing here. As with any natural source, water quality is highly changeable, and the water at Pigeon Milk may not always be safe to drink.

Heading south and then east for 1.2 miles, you wind around the rockslides protecting Four Lakes Basin. Your first glimpse of the basin is of Jean and Dean Lakes, visible from the 10,900-foot ridge to the west. Dale and Daynes Lakes are a bit lower to the southeast.

Swampy meadows, almost the type you would expect to see dinosaurs rise from, grace the scenery throughout this region. These meadows are found so consistently that they seem almost deliberately spaced for variety. Some of the lakes, including those back toward the trailhead, are often eerily forged with cold morning mist.

Nearly all the lakes offer fine fly fishing due to open meadow shorelines and cooperative, while not large, trout. The west end of Dean Lake along the open cliffs is an especially productive site for catching hungry cutthroats.

You may want to make this hike before branching out into the remainder of the Uintas. It is the doorstep to almost all the trails on the west side of these unique and scenic mountains. —*Originally contributed by Hartt Wixom*

Key Points

0.0 Start at the Highline Trail Trailhead.

2.0 Reach Scudder Lake.

3.0 Junction with the trail to Wilder, Wyman, and Packard Lakes. Continue straight (east).

4.0   Junction with the trail to Naturalist Basin. Continue straight (east).

5.5   Junction with the trail to Pinto and Governor Dern Lakes and Grandaddy Basin. Continue straight (east).

6.8   Junction with the trail to Four Lakes Basin. Turn right (south).

8.0   Arrive in Four Lakes Basin.

16.0   Retrace your steps to arrive back at the trailhead.

THE HIGH UINTAS Northeastern Utah's High Uinta Mountains are a range of superlatives.

They embrace the state's highest peak—13,528-foot Kings Peak—and the headwaters of major rivers that produce 90 percent of Utah's in-state water. They are important habitat for large big-game herds as well as for more secretive and rare species. Three-quarters of the state's bird species are found in the Uintas. There are hundreds of alpine lakes sprinkled through the many drainages.

The Uintas are an isolated and biologically intact alpine sanctuary. From the high, rugged peaks along the range's 11,000-foot, 70-mile backbone to the willow-covered and richly forested river basins, the High Uintas are more like the northern Rockies than are other inter-mountain ranges.

On the North Slope long meadows are flanked by virgin lodgepole pine and spruce forests, harboring rare species such as the pine marten, goshawk, black bear, and cougar. Research is being conducted to verify the possible presence of the Canadian lynx, wolverine, and timber wolf. Utah's largest elk and moose herds are found here, and mule deer are common. In addition, there are bald and golden eagles, ospreys, owls, hawks, weasels, mink, and the ever-present beavers.

The Uinta's largest rivers begin on the South Slope, high in the alpine basins, 15 to 20 miles from any trailheads. The lower Yellowstone River tumbles through steep, heavily timbered country, and the Uinta River slices an 80-foot vertical gorge through the range's largest glacial canyon.

Historically the Uintas are a lively chapter in the discovery of the American West. First recorded by Father Escalante in 1776 and then by John Wesley Powell in 1869, the Uintas have been hunted by the Utes, trapped by the pioneer Rocky Mountain Fur Company (notably Jim Bridger, William Ashley, and Andrew Henry), surveyed by great American explorer-geologists Hayden, Agassiz, Gilbert, Cleveland, and others, tie-hacked for construction of the Union Pacific Railroad across Wyoming, and grazed by Uinta Basin and southern Wyoming sheepherders.

Today the Uintas offer spectacular opportunities for family camping, rugged hiking and climbing, riding, fishing, and hunting for thousands of visitors yearly.

Established in 1931 as a Forest Service primitive area, 247,000 acres of the Uintas were granted protection from commercial timber harvesting, road construction, summer housing expansion, off-road vehicles, and mining (after 1983). In 1984 the High Uintas Wilderness was established, encompassing 456,704 acres of the Uinta Mountains.

While considerable North Slope acreage was added to the High Uintas Wilderness, some of the most pristine middle-elevation North Slope lands were ignored along with the alpine eastern Bollies. Conservationists continue to push for wilderness designation of this primeval landscape. Critical issues surrounding oil and gas leasing on the East Fork of the Blacks Fork and Stillwater drainages, and timber-harvesting proposals by the Ashley National Forest on the South Slope and eastern reaches of the range, still threaten the integrity of the area.

Since the High Uintas Wilderness was designated, two herds of native bighorn sheep have been reintroduced in the area. For a decade the Utah Wilderness Association (now the High Uintas Preservation Council) pushed for reintroduction of this extirpated species into its native habitat. When considerable acreage on the eastern North Slope was closed to sheep grazing, the dream became reality. This has renewed interest in seeking ways to further reduce domestic sheep grazing in key areas in the Uintas to allow the existence of the native bighorn.

In 1991 a High Uintas Wilderness Limits of Acceptable Change (LAC) Task Force was created to properly manage the wilderness to ensure that the wild values would not get trampled by growing numbers of wilderness users, horse packers, sheep grazers, and a host of other management concerns. Following the LAC effort, the High Uintas Wilderness Management Plan was completed in 1997, amending the Ashley and Wasatch-Cache National Forest plans. Current management direction for the High Uintas Wilderness is provided by this plan. —*Originally contributed by Margaret Pettis and Dick Carter*

(Note: For more information on the Uintas, contact the High Uintas Preservation Council, P.O. Box 72, Hyrum, UT 84319; 435-245-6747; www.hupc.org.)

21 Stillwater Drainage

Several short two-day hikes or a longer five-day trip in the High Uintas. Cirques and massive peaks ring the upper basins, and there is good fishing on Stillwater Fork.

Start: Christmas Meadows Trailhead.
Distance: Various.
Difficulty: Moderate.
Trail surface: Forest trail.
Seasons: Late spring through fall (snow may restrict upper basin travel into July).
Land status: Wilderness area.
Nearest town: Kamas.
Fees and permits: A Mirror Lake Area Recreation Pass is required for trailhead parking: $3.00 per day, $6.00 per week, $25.00 per year. Golden Eagle/Age/Access Passports are accepted. Passes are available at Forest

Service offices in Kamas and Evanston, Wyoming, the Bear River Station and Beaver Creek Station, several self-issue stations in the national forest, and several local vendors in Kamas and Evanston.
Maps: USGS Hayden Peak and Christmas Meadows quads; Northeastern Utah Multipurpose Map; High Uintas Wilderness Map.
Trail contacts: Evanston Ranger District, Wasatch-Cache National Forest, P.O. Box 1880, Evanston, WY 82930; (307) 789-3194 or (801) 642-6662 (June through October); www.fs.fed.us/r4/wcnf.

Finding the trailhead: From Kamas on the west end of the Uinta Mountains, take Highway 150 (Mirror Lake Highway) over Bald Mountain Pass, past Mirror Lake and the Highline Trailhead (which serves the western end of the High Uintas Wilderness), toward Evanston, Wyoming. About 15 miles north of Mirror Lake and shortly after crossing a bridge over the Bear River, turn right onto the dirt road to Christmas Meadows Campground. Follow this road 4.5 miles to the end, where you will find the trailhead. (From Evanston, this road is about 33 miles south on Highway 150.) *DeLorme: Utah Atlas & Gazetteer:* Page 55 A4.

The Hike

The Stillwater drainage of the Bear River offers three destinations: West Basin, with Kermsuh Lake; Middle Basin, with McPheters and Ryder Lakes; and Amethyst Basin, containing Amethyst and Ostler Lakes. Each has incredibly beautiful alpine scenery of high rock walls, pockets of spruce, scattered ponds, and wet meadows. Good fishing exists throughout the three basins, and water is abundant.

You could easily spend a week in this beautiful drainage, visiting each of the three basins. For a weekend outing, choose one of the three.

The trail to the three basins begins at 8,800 feet at the south end of the Christmas Meadows Campground. If you choose to follow Stillwater Fork itself for the first 1.5 miles, rather than the trail, you'll find good trout fishing in its deep, clear pools. The trail stays on the east flank of the drainage, passing beaver ponds, springs, and aspen and talus slopes.

After 2.5 miles the Amethyst Basin Trail heads to the left (east). It climbs a steep, rocky slope for 1,000 feet before leveling out on the north shoulder of Ostler Fork,

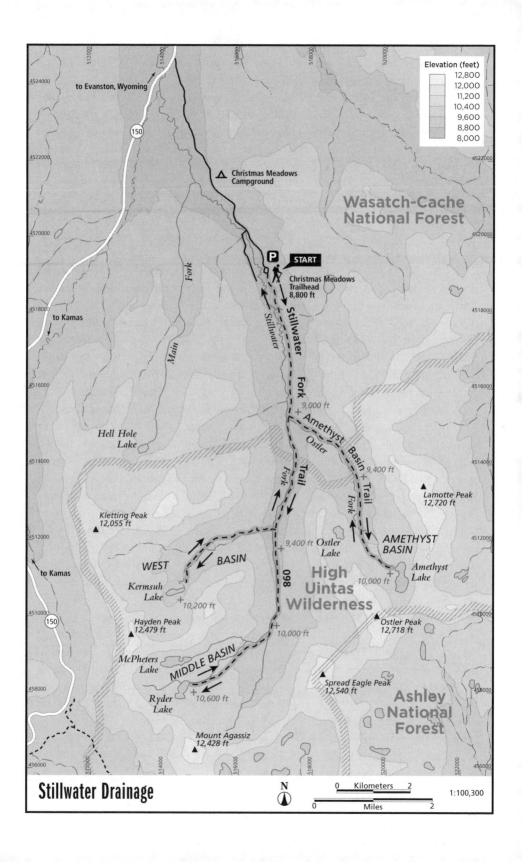

Elevation (feet)
12,800
12,000
11,200
10,400
9,600
8,800
8,000

to Evanston, Wyoming

150

△ Christmas Meadows
Campground

Wasatch-Cache
National Forest

P START

Christmas Meadows
Trailhead
8,800 ft

to Kamas

Main Fork

Stillwater

Stillwater

Stillwater Fork

9,000 ft

Amethyst Basin + Trail

Hell Hole
Lake

Ostler

Ostler Trail

9,400 ft

Fork

Lamotte Peak
12,720 ft

Kletting Peak
12,055 ft

Fork

Amethyst Basin + Trail

9,400 ft   Ostler
Lake

AMETHYST
BASIN

WEST   BASIN

Kermsuh
Lake

10,200 ft

High
Uintas
Wilderness

10,000 ft   Amethyst
Lake

Hayden Peak
12,479 ft

860

10,000 ft

Ostler Peak
12,718 ft

McPheters
Lake

MIDDLE BASIN

Ryder
Lake

10,600 ft

Spread Eagle Peak
12,540 ft

Ashley
National
Forest

150

Mount Agassiz
12,428 ft

Stillwater Drainage

N

0   Kilometers   2

0   Miles   2

1:100,300

north of Salamander Lake. Hidden in the lodgepole pines across Ostler Fork, the route to this little lake is a real test of orienteering.

Hike south through several meadows, spruce parklands, and finally a spectacular broad meadow from which the first unobstructed view of magnificent LaMotte and Ostler Peaks can be enjoyed. The trail to Amethyst Basin splits at the base of this large meadow. A faint, unreliable trail heads half a mile southwest to Ostler Lake; continue straight (south) for another mile to Amethyst Lake, nestled in the farthest crook of the basin.

This large, picturesque lake sits at the base of centuries of talus from the Ostler-LaMotte ridge. Wind-scoured spruce dot its rocky shore and fingerling meadows. If you camp here, Ostler, Toomset, and two small unnamed lakes are within an hour to the northwest.

If you choose to stay on the main Stillwater Fork trail, continue 2 miles past the Amethyst Basin Trail and find the trail on the right (west) to West Basin and Kermsuh Lake. Cross Stillwater Fork and immediately climb a series of switchbacks and several steep pitches. The trail sits high above West Basin Creek, making water along this stretch unreachable. Older editions of the topographic map are in error at this point: The trail does not cross the creek flowing out of West Basin but remains high on the north side of the deep creekbed and enters a sizable open meadow. It then crosses the creek and offers a stunning view of the walled head basins.

The trail winds about 2 miles through a diverse forest to kidney-shaped Kermsuh Lake. The large meadow mentioned earlier and several others along the northern shore of Kermsuh offer excellent campsites and abundant water. There are hidden ledges and potholes with much evidence of wildlife, exquisite ancient pockets of spruce, and a lovely lake that drains into Kermsuh from the south. Rugged, vertical Hayden Peak (12,479 feet) looms above this small lake to the southwest, and Kletting Peak (12,055 feet) to the northwest provides a wall of stone above the tiny basin.

To reach Ryder, McPheters, and the other lakes of the Middle Basin, follow the main Stillwater trail past the West Basin turnoff. After 2 miles the trail crosses the Stillwater Fork and climbs 500 feet up a steep shoulder on the south bank of Middle Basin Creek. The trail leads westerly another mile to Ryder Lake, which, with McPheters and more than two dozen tiny lakes and potholes, offers an incredible view of the bowl, nestled close to 11,000 feet. Surrounding the bowl are Mount Agassiz (12,428 feet) on the south, Hayden Peak on the northwest, and, across the Stillwater Fork, magnificent Spread Eagle Peak (12,540 feet) and Ostler Peak (12,718 feet). These splendid peaks form a narrow ring encircling the lakes of the Middle Basin.

Just over the Agassiz–Spread Eagle ridge are the lakes of Naturalist Basin; beyond the Spread Eagle–Ostler ridge lies Rock Creek. This is high-alpine country at its finest—spectacular scenery and outstanding opportunities for exploration. —*Originally contributed by Margaret Pettis*

(Note: Since this hike covers an area with three different route options of various lengths, no key points are provided.)

22 West Fork Blacks Fork

An overnighter to the headwaters of the Blacks Fork River. There are lush alpine meadows, good fishing, and excellent opportunities to view wildlife. Golden eagles are a common sight.

Start: The major ford of the West Fork Blacks Fork River, south of Lyman Lake.

Distance: 22 miles out and back.

Difficulty: Easy.

Trail surface: Jeep trail, forest trail.

Seasons: Late spring through fall (be prepared for snow in early spring).

Land status: National forest, wilderness area.

Nearest town: Kamas.

Fees and permits: A Mirror Lake Area Recreation Pass is required for trailhead parking: $3.00 per day, $6.00 per week, $25.00 per year. Golden Eagle/Age/Access Passports are accepted. Passes are available at Forest Service offices in Kamas and Evanston, Wyoming,

the Bear River Station and Beaver Creek Station, several self-issue stations in the national forest, and several local vendors in Kamas and Evanston.

Maps: USGS Lyman Lake, Elizabeth Mountain, Explorer Peak, and Red Knob quads; Northeastern Utah Multipurpose Map; National Geographic Trails Illustrated High Uintas Wilderness Map.

Trail contacts: Evanston Ranger District, Wasatch-Cache National Forest, P.O. Box 1880, Evanston, WY 82930; (307) 789-3194 or (801) 642-6662 (June through October); www.fs.fed.us/r4/wcnf.

Finding the trailhead: Take Highway 150 (Mirror Lake Highway) east from Kamas. Pass the Bear River Ranger Station on the right after about 45 miles. Two miles beyond, turn right onto North Slope Road. This graded, well-traveled route across the Uinta North Slope provides access to many of the drainages. Drive about 13 miles to Elizabeth Pass (10,235 feet), which divides the Bear River drainage of the Great Basin from the Blacks Fork drainage of the Green River. Cross Elizabeth Pass and drive another 5 miles, passing Fish Lake, to the Lyman Lake junction. Turn right here (south, then west) back along the river. Follow this rocky road (eroded in spots but usually passable for two-wheel-drive vehicles) about 4.5 miles to a major river crossing. Park here to begin the hike.

The more adventurous with four-wheel drive can ford the river again and continue for another 1.5 to 2 miles. The Forest Service has plans to eventually route the traffic that uses this ford across a bridge farther downstream and then up the eastern side of the river to the trailhead located where the Bear River/Smiths Fork Trail crosses the West Fork Blacks Fork Trail. *DeLorme: Utah Atlas & Gazetteer:* Page 55 A4.

The Hike

The West Fork Blacks Fork River is a superb journey into the northwestern portion of the High Uintas Wilderness. This drainage is replete with moose, mule deer, elk, small mammals, and raptors. The hike offers level traversing of lush meadowlands, a

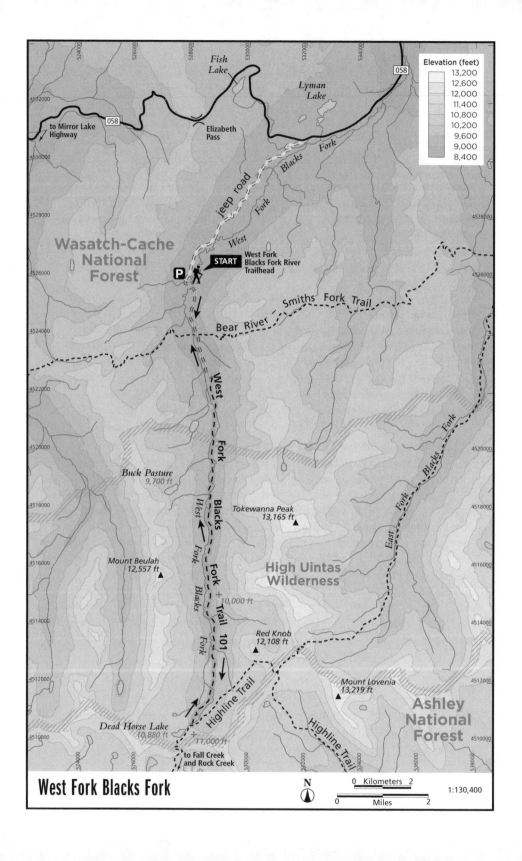

Elevation (feet)

	13,200
	12,600
	12,000
	11,400
	10,800
	10,200
	9,600
	9,000
	8,400

Fish Lake

Lyman Lake

058

to Mirror Lake Highway

058

Elizabeth Pass

Blacks Fork

West Fork

jeep road

Wasatch-Cache National Forest

P START

West Fork Blacks Fork River Trailhead

Bear River — Smiths Fork Trail

West Fork Blacks Fork + Trail 101

West Fork Blacks Fork

Buck Pasture 9,700 ft

Tokewanna Peak 13,165 ▲ ft

Mount Beulah 12,557 ft ▲

High Uintas Wilderness

East Fork *Blacks Fork*

+ 10,000 ft

Red Knob 12,108 ft ▲

Mount Lovenia 13,219 ft ▲

Ashley National Forest

Dead Horse Lake 10,880 ft

Highline Trail

+ 11,000 ft

Highline Trail

to Fall Creek and Rock Creek

West Fork Blacks Fork

N

0	Kilometers	2
0	Miles	2

1:130,400

survey of rich wildlife habitat, and an ascent into the alpine lakes and ponds for which the Uintas are famous. This is the High Uintas at its finest.

The hike is gentle, about 11 miles (and about 1,600 feet of elevation gain) from the trailhead to Dead Horse Lake—a popular destination below the Uinta backbone. Plan to spend two to four days in the upper drainage in order to explore it fully. The upper meadows, the alpine potholes on the high western ledge and below Dead Horse Lake, and the lake itself offer the finest Uintas scenery.

The hike begins at about 9,300 feet and climbs slowly along a jeep trail for 4.5 miles to Buck Pasture at 9,700 feet. The trail begins on the east side of the river and then makes several crossings before passing the wilderness boundary and reaching the long meadow. Several pothole lakes lie to the west of Buck Pasture.

There is some off-road vehicle damage in a few of the lower meadows resulting from ORV use during wet spring conditions. This activity has posed a real management problem for the Forest Service. However, a new travel plan was implemented in 2003, which prohibits motorized vehicle use away from designated routes.

The trail follows the river's course through a series of rich meadows and offers superb scenery of the high ridgelines paralleling the river. The ridgeline exceeds 11,000 feet to the east and west, with 12,557-foot Mount Beulah to the southwest of Buck Pasture and 12,108-foot Red Knob and 13,165-foot Tokewanna Peak to the southeast. Forests of lodgepole pine, subalpine fir, and eventually spruce harbor deer, elk, pine martens, goshawks, and other interesting wildlife species. Moose are common and can be seen leaving the willows for the forest each evening.

This drainage is also grazed by domestic sheep under an approved grazing permit. These sheep bands follow a regulated schedule, so hikers can find out where they are on a particular weekend and plan their visit accordingly. Grazing in the wilderness by domestic livestock is an allowed activity under the Wilderness Act.

Once you reach Buck Pasture, Dead Horse Lake is another 6.5 miles. Here the rugged Uinta spine looms to the south more than 1,000 feet above. Water abounds in the West Fork drainage, and campsites are readily available. Use of a stove when camping not only makes your presence less noticeable to future hikers, but also increases your chances of seeing moose near the river.

Key Points

0.0 Start at the major ford of the West Fork Blacks Fork River, south of Lyman Lake.

4.5 Reach Buck Pasture.

11.0 Arrive at Dead Horse Lake.

22.0 Retrace your steps to arrive at the trailhead.

Options: From Dead Horse Pass at just under 11,600 feet, high above its namesake lake, you can drop to the south into the head of Fall Creek (by way of Ledge and Phinney Lakes) and Rock Creek (by way of Lightning, Helen, Triangle, and

Reconnaissance Lakes), thus exploring the very head of the South Slope drainage. Allow several more days to see this spectacular alpine country.

Another side trip is the route along the Highline Trail, out of the east side of the head basin, over to the East Fork Blacks Fork. This spectacular route passes between Red Knob and 13,219-foot Mount Lovenia. Allow an additional day for this trip. —*Originally contributed by Margaret Pettis*

23 Kings Peak

A multiday backpack to Utah's highest peak—13,528-foot Kings Peak. Along the way you'll enjoy emerald green Henrys Fork Basin and a dozen lakes below 13,000-foot peaks.

Start: Henrys Fork Trailhead.
Distance: 32 miles out and back.
Difficulty: Strenuous.
Trail surface: Forest trail, cross-country.
Seasons: Mid-July to mid-August.
Land status: Wilderness area.
Nearest town: Mountain View, Wyoming.
Fees and permits: No fees or permits required.
Maps: USGS Gilbert Peak NE, Bridger Lake,

Mount Powell, and Kings Peak quads; Northeastern Utah Multipurpose Map; National Geographic Trails Illustrated High Uintas Wilderness Map.
Trail contacts: Mountain View Ranger District, Wasatch-Cache National Forest, 321 Highway 414 E., P.O. Box 129, Mountain View, WY 82939; (307) 782-6555; www.fs.fed.us/r4/wcnf.

Finding the trailhead: To reach the trailhead, take Interstate 80 east from Evanston, Wyoming, and turn right onto the I-80 business route to Fort Bridger. Drive about 3 miles and turn right onto Wyoming Highway 414 toward Mountain View. In Mountain View pick up Wyoming Highway 410 toward Robertson. About 7 miles south of Mountain View, WY 410 makes a ninety-degree turn to the west. Continue south here into the Uintas and drive toward the Bridger Lake Guard Station. After about 13 miles turn left toward the Henrys Fork. In another 11 miles, just before the road crosses the river, turn right toward the Henrys Fork Campground—about 0.75 mile along the west side of the river. *DeLorme: Utah Atlas & Gazetteer:* Page 55 A6.

The Hike

Many hikers just *have* to scale the highest peak around. In Utah that means 13,528-foot Kings Peak, a rocky spire in the eastern half of the High Uintas Wilderness. What makes Kings Peak such a fine backpack is not only the exciting scramble to the summit, but also the beautiful alpine terrain and trout fishing along the way.

Choose the time of your hike carefully. Snow remains in the high country into summer, and the mountains are crowded on the July 4 and later July weekends. Any

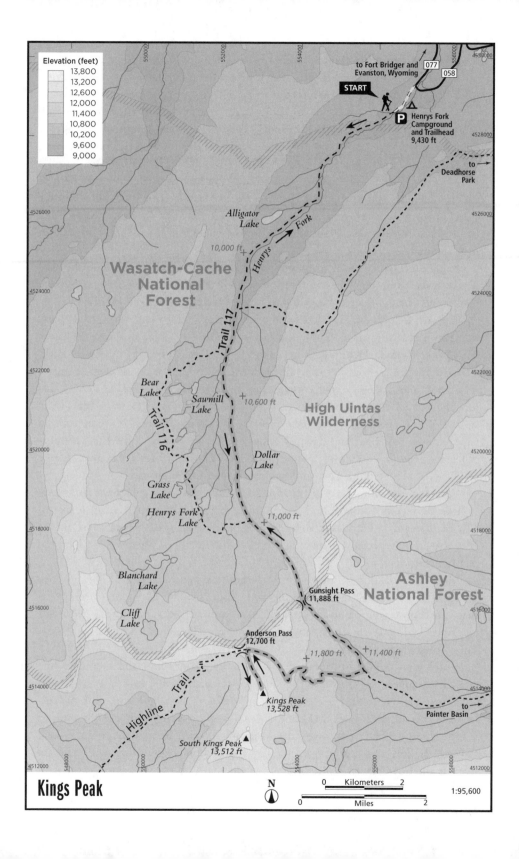

Kings Peak

hike above timberline in the Uintas should be planned with weather in mind. After-noon thunderstorms are the norm, which means lightning. Don't be caught trying to climb Kings Peak in a thunderstorm.

There are several approaches to Kings Peak, from both north and south. Many hikers consider the route along the Henrys Fork the best because the distance from the trailhead to Kings Peak, about 16 miles, is shorter than two alternate routes along the Yellowstone and Uinta Rivers on the Uintas' South Slope. However, because the Henrys Fork route is the shortest, it is also the most heavily used. If your wilderness experience tastes run to the more pristine end of the spectrum, this trail is not for you. Lots of Boy Scout groups and folks more interested in "bagging" Kings Peak use this trail. In addition, several permitted sheep bands graze the Henrys Fork Basin each summer.

From the Henrys Fork Campground Trailhead at about 9,430 feet, the trail climbs more than 4,100 feet to the top. At the trailhead a wooden Forest Service map points out the many lakes and peaks located in the area you'll be hiking.

The trail follows the Henrys Fork for 5.5 miles, gaining about 700 feet of eleva-tion before reaching a junction in a meadow northeast of Bear and Sawmill Lakes. The quickest route to Kings Peak heads past Dollar Lake to the east of Henrys Fork. Cross the stream on your left over the primitive footbridge or by fording the stream if conditions are safe. The trail continues up the east side of the stream. (Don't fol-low the old trail, which in the past continued straight, on the west side of the stream.) Many hikers choose to take an extra day on the "scenic" route by turning right (west)—past Bear and Sawmill Lakes and on to Henrys Fork Lake, about 4 miles from the junction. This loop rejoins Trail 117 past Dollar Lake about a mile southeast of Henrys Fork Lake and before reaching Gunsight Pass.

Camping and fishing along this route are excellent. Above Henrys Fork Lake (follow the creek), you will find good fishing at Lake Blanchard, the small lake to Blanchard's east, and at Castle and Cliff Lakes. These lakes offer fast fly fishing for cutthroat trout, especially at inlets and outlets; the stream just below Blanchard has plenty of big ones.

Most of the lakes here are above timberline, leaving the area near Henrys Fork Lake—at about 10,800 feet—with the best campsites. The Forest Service suggests that you choose your campsite carefully. Areas around lakes and streams get heavy use. Water is abundant in the basin, but treatment is recommended to avoid the pos-sibility of contracting giardiasis.

Watch for wildlife in this region and also notice Kings Peak to the south. On a clear day it appears as an inverted V-notch just above the large rockslide.

Where the trails rejoin at 11,000 feet, east of the Henrys Fork and south of Dol-lar Lake, it is about 2 miles to 11,888-foot Gunsight Pass. The entrance to the pass is, indeed, shaped like a rifle's sight, and you can't miss it. The trail does not continue through the low notch as easily as it may appear from below, however. There are thickets and boulders here, and the trail switches back up the west slope to the pass.

If you're lucky enough to find clear weather at the pass, you'll have beautiful views down into Painter Basin on the Uintas' South Slope, as well as back down the Henrys Fork.

Since the trail to Kings Peak drops toward Painter Basin and then climbs westward to Anderson Pass, there is a strong temptation to avoid loss of altitude by crossing onto the steep, rubble-strewn rockslides to the south. This is a mistake, as anyone who's tried it has quickly discovered. The rocks are loose and dangerous, and you eventually have to drop down to the meadow below.

So follow the trail down from Gunsight Pass. The trail descends about 400 feet quickly, then heads through the flats 1.5 miles to the Highline Trail. Turn right (west) here and begin climbing toward Anderson Pass.

The trail climbs 1,400 feet over the next 3 miles, including an 800-foot climb in just over a mile. The east slope of Kings Peak looms to the west, then south, as you climb, and the views down along the upper Uinta River are spectacular.

At Anderson Pass you get your first glimpses of the spacious Yellowstone drainage to the southwest. In fact, the Highline Trail now contours to the west and then drops down into the basin. But you head southwest here, up the ridge to the top of Kings Peak.

It's less than a mile to the top, but you've got more than 900 vertical feet, and there is no trail. You have to hop the boulders. Near the top, watch your step carefully, because there is considerable exposure to the west. You know you're at the top—even in a blowing mist—by the plaque commemorating mountain explorer and scientist Clarence King. A mailbox offers a diary in which you can record your experience.

With any luck in the weather, you can enjoy a remarkable view from the top of Kings. The Yellowstone drainage to the southwest looks like moonscape photos— tundra without timber. In the Uinta River Basin to the east, you see forested slopes near Lake Atwood bordered by rocky ridges. Several small lakes lie below you in cliff country. And one of the most beautiful views is right down the Henrys Fork Basin to the north, where you can admire many lakes and emerald meadows. —*Originally contributed by Hartt Wixom*

Key Points

0.0 Start at the Henrys Fork Trailhead.

5.5 Junction with Trail 116 to Bear Lake. Continue straight (south).

8.3 Arrive at a second junction with Trail 116. Continue straight.

10.4 Reach Gunsight Pass.

11.9 Turn right (west) at the Anderson Pass cutoff.

15.0 Reach Anderson Pass. Head southwest, up the ridge.

16.0 Summit of Kings Peak at 13,528 feet.

32.0 Retrace your steps to arrive back at the trailhead.

24 Rock Creek

A three- to five-day backpack in the Rock Creek drainage on the south slope of the Uinta Mountains. Rock Creek is a vast wilderness drainage with many lakes, abundant wildflowers and wildlife, good fishing, solitude, and views, plus easy access to other areas of the High Uintas.

Start: Rock Creek Trailhead.
Distance: 28-mile lollipop loop.
Difficulty: Moderately difficult.
Trail surface: Rocky forest trail.
Seasons: Summer and early fall.
Land status: National forest, wilderness area.
Nearest town: Duchesne.
Fees and permits: No fees or permits required. Voluntary trailhead registration is strongly encouraged, however.

Maps: USGS Tworoose Pass and Explorer Peak quads; Northeastern Utah Multipurpose Map; National Geographic Trails Illustrated High Uintas Wilderness Map; Ashley National Forest Map.
Trail contacts: Duchesne Ranger District, Ashley National Forest, P.O. Box 981, Duchesne, UT 84021; (435) 738-2482; www.fs.fed.us/r4/ashley.

Finding the trailhead: To reach the trailhead at the Upper Stillwater Reservoir, take Highway 87 (Moon Lake Highway) north from Duchesne about 16 miles and turn left onto Forest Road 134. Drive about 3 miles into Mountain Home, turning left again. Follow the signs to Rock Creek. You cross Mountain Sheep Pass about 9 miles west of Mountain Home, then enter the spectacular Rock Creek Canyon, which rapidly deepens as you head upstream (northwest) into the mountains. The road is paved to the trailhead, which is about 25 miles from Mountain Home at a parking lot with restrooms and a horse ramp. (Note: The Rock Creek Trail, along Stillwater Reservoir—about 2 miles—is closed from November 1 through June 30 every year due to safety hazards associated with heavy rockfall.) *DeLorme: Utah Atlas & Gazetteer:* Page 55 C4.

The Hike

Rock Creek drains a large region on the South Slope of the Uinta Mountains. Its deep, forested canyon offers leisurely woodland walking and good trout fishing, while its upper basins provide alpine camping and climbing, with easy access to other parts of the range via major passes and trails. Many routes can be planned from the trailhead near the Upper Stillwater Reservoir, and loop trips of three to seven days are particularly convenient.

The extended backpack follows Rock Creek for about 10 miles, then angles northeast another 4 miles to Phinney and Anderson Lakes in the heart of the High Uintas Wilderness. The return trip parallels a long ridge extending south from Explorer Peak, drops into beautiful Squaw Basin, then follows the East Fork to Rock Creek and the trailhead.

The 14-mile trip up Rock and Fall Creeks gains 2,400 feet through some of the Uintas' finest country. If you don't have the time for this loop, however, you can take

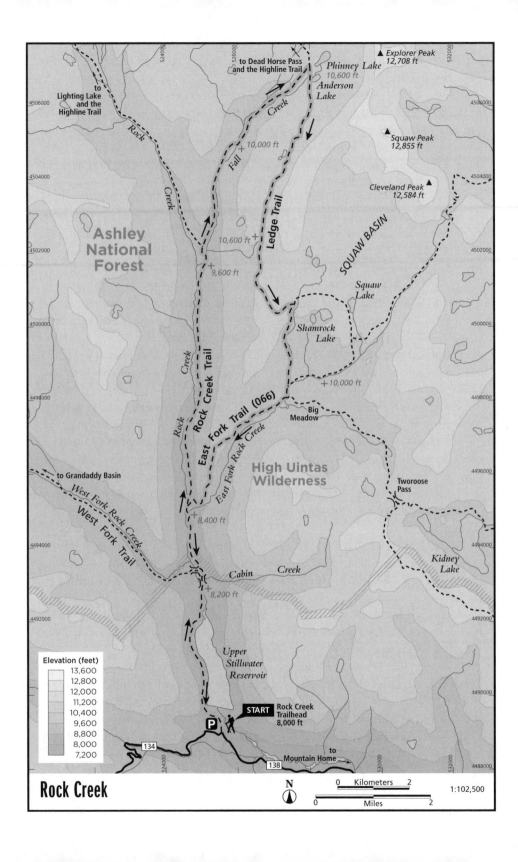

▲ Explorer Peak
12,708 ft

to Dead Horse Pass
and the Highline Trail

Phinney Lake
10,600 ft

Anderson
Lake

to
Lighting Lake
and the
Highline Trail

Fall Creek

+ 10,000 ft

▲ Squaw Peak
12,855 ft

Ledge Trail

Cleveland Peak
12,584 ft ▲

Rock Creek

Ashley
National
Forest

+ 10,600 ft

SQUAW BASIN

+ 9,600 ft

Squaw
Lake

Rock Creek Trail

Shamrock
Lake

Squaw
Lake

+ 10,000 ft

East Fork Trail (066)

East Fork Rock Creek

Big
Meadow

High Uintas
Wilderness

Twooroose
Pass

to Grandaddy Basin

West Fork Rock Creek

East Fork Rock Creek

West Fork Trail

+ 8,400 ft

Kidney
Lake

Cabin Creek

+ 8,200 ft

Upper
Stillwater
Reservoir

Elevation (feet)

13,600
12,800
12,000
11,200
10,400
9,600
8,800
8,000
7,200

START Rock Creek
Trailhead
8,000 ft

P

134

138

Mountain Home

to

Rock Creek

N

0   Kilometers   2

0   Miles   2

1:102,500

a shorter trip by hiking up the East Fork on the way in and spending a day or two in Squaw Basin.

Because of the reservoir, older editions of the Tworoose Pass topographic map do not correctly show the first few miles of the trail. Rather than climbing along the east side of Rock Creek, the trail now heads north along the left (west) side of the reservoir. You can see the spectacular peaks at the head of Rock Creek from here, but the trail soon enters the forest, and the peaks disappear from view until you get to the meadows below Phinney Lake.

About 2.5 miles from the trailhead, Cabin Creek enters from the right (east), and the West Fork comes in from the left (west) a few hundred yards farther on. The West Fork Trail heads to Grandaddy Basin, Naturalist Basin, and Four Lakes Basin. The Rock Creek Trail drops down to cross the creek here, continuing north along the east side as shown on the Tworoose topo map.

About 1.25 miles past the West Fork junction, you cross the East Fork and meet the trail to Squaw Basin. If you choose to make the shorter trip and climb to Squaw Basin from here, you'll gain 1,300 feet in 1.5 miles, with no water and very little shade. In 1974 a great forest fire burned 2,900 acres in Rock Creek Canyon, and this steep, exposed trail still shows evidence of its effects. However, the area is healing well and is now thick with lodgepole pine. In early summer you're also likely to find lupine, fireweed, and other pioneer flowers in bloom.

Still, the main trail offers a more pleasant, if lengthier approach to Squaw Basin, particularly in the heat of summer. Continue up Rock Creek Canyon, through the burned-over forest where, curiously, occasional clusters of pines appear to have escaped the fire. There are numerous camping spots along the rocky floor of the canyon, if you are inclined to spend the first night in the forest.

If you come in June or July, you can find water trickling in small rivulets from melting snow far above. This water and water from the creek should be treated to prevent giardiasis.

About 1.75 miles above the East Fork junction, the trail bends away from the creek and continues along the base of the steep mountain slope that bounds the Rock Creek floodplain. You can hear the stream along here, although it is hidden in the trees.

Four and a half miles above the junction, the trail crosses Fall Creek and forks, the left branch ascending Rock Creek to Lightning Lake and the Highline Trail, the right fork climbing along Fall Creek for 4 miles to Phinney Lake.

Take the right (more northerly) fork. Immediately past the junction, the Fall Creek Trail begins to climb steeply, but after about a mile it levels off in a meadow at about 9,600 feet. In another mile the trail crosses the creek, and 0.75 mile beyond, you come to one of the world's greatest (but extremely cold) swimming holes.

As Fall Creek crosses the 10,000-foot contour, it cuts into a thin formation of red and blue shale. This very soft rock weathers easily; in fact, you could crumble it in your hand. The creek slices through it in a narrow chute, with several cold, deep plunge pools.

Just above the falls, two streams meet to form the main creek, and the shale between them is so neatly beveled it looks engineered, like the prow of a ship or a concrete bridge pylon. Below these cliffs you can find perfect skipping rocks, flat flakes of shale whose edges have been scoured and rounded by the stream. This is a wonderful spot for lunch, photography, or a cold swim after a hot day of hiking.

Beyond the falls, the trail ascends a ridge dividing the two tributaries, and the forest opens into broad alpine meadows in about 0.75 mile. Suddenly you are surrounded by the huge peaks of the High Uintas, gigantic crumbling piles of buff, gray, and rust-colored metamorphic rocks. Explorer Peak (12,708 feet) and Squaw Peak (12,855 feet) rise on your right, with Yard Peak (12,706 feet) and Dead Horse Pass on your left. Phinney Lake lies half a mile farther, just past the junction with the Ledge Trail. There are eight lakes in this basin, with plenty of camping and fishing. Phinney and Continent Lakes are particularly good for brook and cutthroat trout.

At the junction with the Ledge Trail, a quarter of a mile before Phinney Lake, you can turn left (northwest) to meet the Highline Trail in a mile and ascend Dead Horse Pass (11,600 feet) to the West Fork Blacks Fork on the Uintas' North Slope.

To complete the trip to Squaw Basin, turn right (south) onto the Ledge Trail and contour along the base of the huge talus slopes below Explorer Peak. Here the red quartzite that forms the bulk of the High Uintas has been quarried by frost into great rectangular blocks, forming labyrinths for small mammals. The rocks look bare from a distance, but up close they reveal gaudy mats of lichen—slate gray, black, clay blue, and bright chartreuse.

The trail winds to the south among numerous small unnamed lakes fed by snowmelt. This is forested country broken by numerous meadows and immense fields of wildflowers. Often you will see trails of flowers snaking up toward the talus along hidden drainages. At times the trail climbs up rocky spurs, offering splendid views of the gray peaks across the headwaters of Rock Creek. If you take the Ledge Trail late in the day, you are likely to see moose and deer, not to mention a spectacular sunset over the far peaks.

Four miles from the junction at Phinney Lake, the trail turns left (east) and climbs 450 vertical feet in 0.75 mile. From the ridge, you can see the densely forested floor of Squaw Basin. Squaw Peak (12,855 feet) and Cleveland Peak (12,584 feet) border the basin to the north, with Cleveland Pass and the immense, mesalike Brown Duck Mountain to the east.

Descend a steep 0.5 mile to the junction with the East Fork Trail on the floor of the basin. Take Trail 066 for 1.5 miles to Big Meadow. You can also bushwhack 0.5 mile east to Shamrock Lake.

At Big Meadow the trail to Tworoose Pass and Brown Duck Basin enters from the east. Fly fishers enjoy casting for small, feisty brook and cutthroat trout in the East Fork's deep meanders.

The trail climbs out of the meadow gradually, entering the burned-over area and reaching 9,744 feet in 1.5 miles before descending toward Rock Creek.

It's a steep, hot, dusty descent, but you'll be glad you're not climbing it. Take a moment on top to view the immense area of the burn (recovery has progressed considerably; you may not notice the fire damage).

In 1.25 miles you arrive at Rock Creek. From there, it's about 4 gentle miles back to the trailhead. —*Originally contributed by John Tallmadge*

Key Points

0.0 Start at the Rock Creek Trailhead.

2.5 Cabin Creek comes in from the right (east).

4.0 Junction with the East Fork Trail. Continue straight (north).

10.0 Junction with the Fall Creek Trail. Bear right (north).

14.0 Arrive at Phinney Lake. Turn right (south) onto the Ledge Trail.

18.5 Junction with the East Fork Trail. Bear right (southwest).

24.0 Junction with the Rock Creek Trail. Bear left (south).

28.0 Arrive back at the trailhead.

25 Yellowstone Drainage

An extended trip to the many lakes and high basins of the upper Yellowstone drainage in the High Uintas Wilderness. This is one of the Uintas' longest, most primitive, and most scenic basins.

Start: Center Park Trailhead.
Distance: Various.
Difficulty: Moderate.
Trail surface: Forest trail.
Seasons: Mid-July to late August.
Land status: Wilderness area, national forest.
Nearest town: Mountain Home.
Fees and permits: No fees or permits required.

Maps: USGS Burnt Mill Spring, Lake Fork Mountain, Garfield Basin, and Mount Powell quads; Northeastern Utah Multipurpose Map; National Geographic Trails Illustrated High Uintas Wilderness Map.
Trail contacts: Roosevelt Ranger District, Ashley National Forest, 650 West Highway 40, P.O. Box 127, Roosevelt, UT 84066; (435) 722-5018; www.fs.fed.us/r4/ashley.

Finding the trailhead: Drive about 20 miles north on Highway 87 from U.S. Highway 40 in Duchesne through Mountain Home until you enter the Uinta and Ouray Indian Reservation. Continue another 4 miles, then turn right at the Yellowstone Creek turnoff. Cross the Lake Fork River, turn left within 0.25 mile, and head north again. About 0.25 mile after entering the Ashley National Forest, the Hells Canyon Road forks to the left. This is a rough road and may not be suitable for some two-wheel-drive vehicles, especially in inclement weather. Forest Service side roads exist along the way, so follow your topo maps carefully for about 10 miles to the trailhead

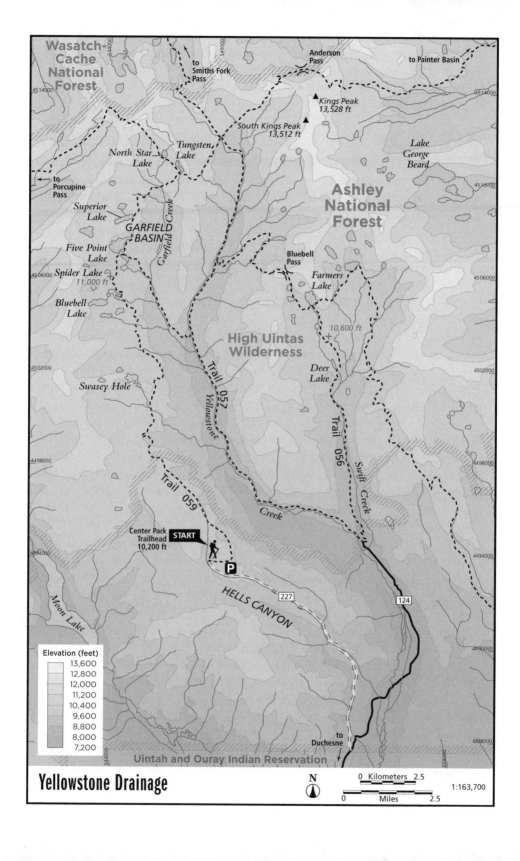

Yellowstone Drainage

at Center Park. Look for the trailhead sign to Swasey Hole. (If you encounter trouble on this road, an alternate trailhead is at the end of the maintained road to the east. Forest Road 119 parallels the Yellowstone River, which shortly becomes Yellowstone Creek.) *DeLorme: Utah Atlas & Gazetteer:* Page 55 B5.

The Hike

The more than 20-mile length of the Yellowstone drainage has just about everything typical of the entire 100-mile-long Uinta Mountains. From the 10,200-foot trailhead near the end of the Hells Canyon Road (or alternate but longer trail at road's end on Yellowstone Creek), you climb on Trail 059 through vast forests of Engelmann spruce and lodgepole pine, then into the treeless tundra in the Garfield Basin. No drainage in the Uinta Mountains has more trout-filled lakes and streams than this one, and in a variety of meadow, cliff-edge, and arcticlike waters.

After 4.5 miles the trail skirts to the east of Swasey Hole. Several peaks of more than 11,300 feet protect this pothole-filled area on the west and north. You might see deer and elk anywhere from Swasey Hole on. Moose are less numerous in the southern Uintas than they are to the north, but seeing one of these beautiful animals is possible, as the big mammals have moved over the summit in some regions. Bird life of all kinds is especially abundant before you get beyond timberline. You may see blue grouse, hawks, eagles, and Clark's nutcrackers. Various sparrows and finches are also common.

Four miles beyond Swasey Hole, you reach Bluebell and Spider Lakes. Five Point and Superior Lakes are another 1 and 2 miles, respectively.

Around the sprawling Spider Lake, meadows stretch everywhere, with excellent fly fishing in clear, cold feeder ponds. Wherever trees form a windbreak, there are luxuriant campsites. And you are never without scenic mountain backdrops, including the highest point in the Uintas, 13,528-foot Kings Peak (and slightly lower South Kings) in the northeast corner of Garfield Basin.

Around all these 11,000-foot lakes, you find lush meadows and plenty of firewood. But a backpacker stove with ample fuel is recommended, especially in the treeless terrain north of Superior Lake.

There is a fair amount of hiking traffic in midsummer near trailside lakes such as Five Point. But there are nevertheless some oversize fish in all of these lakes. Five Point, Superior, and Little Superior have produced trout to six pounds. The best part, however, is that you never know when a little pond nearby may yield a surprise catch.

One thing you are certain to see is the result of glacial action, including cirques at most of the stream canyon heads, smoothed-over ridges, and gouged-out lake basins.

The ridgetops, incidentally, provide some scenic routes if you prefer to travel that way rather than on the forested trails. But be sure to pick out a prominent landmark (such as the Wilson Peak ridge, north of Five Point Lake on the north side of Garfield Basin) to keep track of your location. You can find most of the lakes in this basin, too, by merely following streams into the high meadows below the baldies.

Two lakes in the uppermost Yellowstone drainage, North Star and Tungsten—about 3 miles beyond Superior Lake—have a reputation for growing giant cutthroat trout. In this alpine country that means two- to four-pounders, with an occasional shorter, but possibly heavier, brook trout.

And no matter how far you look in this basin, you won't see air or water pollution, telephone lines, pavement, or likely anything artificial. The terrain is as harsh as it is wildly scenic; a snowstorm in July is not uncommon at this elevation of around 11,500 feet.

In such country, particularly considering the long distances back to civilization, make certain you have sufficient supplies of food, matches, and warm clothing and are wearing top-notch hiking boots. If you don't like one lake or meadow, you can find another nearby. Truly, the Yellowstone has everything, including 12,700-foot Anderson Pass into Painter Basin just north of Kings Peak.

You are unlikely to find other campers or hikers north of Superior Lake in this upper terrain. The Yellowstone backcountry offers plenty of room for exploration, and you can't always be certain what you'll find next. —*Originally contributed by Hartt Wixon*

(Note: Since a variety of hiking options in the same area are featured on this hike, no key points are provided.)

26 Eastern Uintas Highline Trail

A multiday backpack along the summit of the Uinta Mountains to the eastern edge of the High Uintas Wilderness. The Highline Trail offers high-altitude views of the eastern Uinta Mountains as well as good fishing and camping.

Start: Leidy Peak Trailhead.
Distance: 21 miles point to point.
Difficulty: Moderate.
Trail surface: Forest trail, cross-country.
Seasons: July 15 through September 15.
Land status: National forest.
Nearest town: Vernal.
Fees and permits: No fees or permits required.

Maps: USGS Leidy Peak, Whiterocks Lake, and Chepeta Lake quads; National Geographic Trails Illustrated Flaming Gorge/East Uintas Map; Ashley National Forest Map.
Trail contacts: Vernal Ranger District, Ashley National Forest, 355 North Vernal Avenue, Vernal, UT 84078; (435) 789-1181; www.fs.fed.us/r4/ashley.

Finding the trailhead: There are two main vehicle access routes to the Highline Trail. To begin the hike on the eastern end, drive 20 miles north from Vernal on U.S. Highway 191 to the Red Cloud Loop junction (Forest Road 018). Turn left onto this paved road for about 2.5 miles, then make another left onto a gravel road (still FR 018) for about 11 miles to the Leidy Peak–Hacking Lake junction (Forest Road 043). Follow this road about 10 miles to its end at the trailhead. *DeLorme: Utah Atlas & Gazetteer:* Page 56 B2.

Eastern Uintas Highline Trail

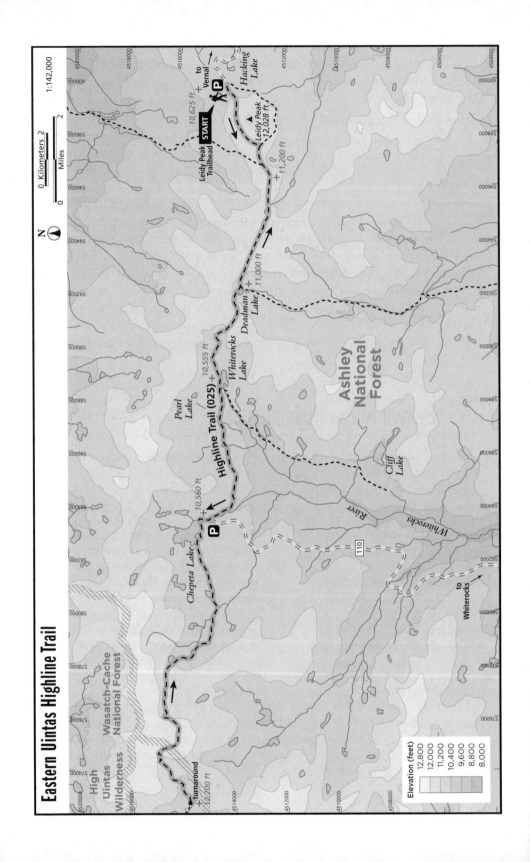

1:142,000

N

0 Kilometers 2

0 Miles 2

Leidy Peak Trailhead

to Vernal

10,625 ft

START

Hacking Lake

Leidy Peak
12,028 ft

+11,200 ft

+11,000 ft

Deadman Lake

Whiterocks Lake

Highline Trail (025) +10,555 ft

Pearl Lake

Chepeta Lake

+10,560 ft

Cliff Lake

Whiterocks River

110

to Whiterocks

Ashley National Forest

Wasatch-Cache National Forest

High Uintas Wilderness

+12,200 ft turnaround

Elevation (feet)

12,800
12,000
11,200
10,400
9,600
8,800
8,000

The other route is accessed by traveling west from Vernal on Highway 121 through Lapoint, then north to Whiterocks. Pick up Forest Road 117 by the Elkhorn Guard Station, just north of Whiterocks, and drive about 12 miles to the junction of Forest Road 110 to Chepeta Lake, about 9 miles farther. *DeLorme: Utah Atlas & Gazetteer:* Page 56 B1.

The Hike

Those who enjoy leaving the bustle of everyday life behind, and who wish to avoid the crowds in some backcountry areas, will enjoy the remoteness of this trail. The Highline Trail is so named because it follows the high summits of the entire Uinta Mountains. This section of trail winds through the Uinta Mountains to the eastern edge of the High Uintas Wilderness. The trail continues west through the wilderness area to its end at the Mirror Lake Highway.

Although the Highline Trail is marked and maintained by the Forest Service, some portions of trail above timberline do not have an established path but are clearly marked with rock cairns. Areas below timberline are marked with blazes on trees. Count on at least a day to hike from the beginning of the trail on the eastern end to Chepeta Lake, and another two days to hike to the wilderness boundary and back.

The trail is used by both backpackers and horsepackers. All drinking water obtained along the trail should be treated before use to ensure its purity.

Hikers should be in good physical condition for this trip. You are hiking primarily above timberline, where the terrain is mostly open and rocky. The altitude climbs from 10,625 feet at Hacking Lake to an elevation of 11,500 feet near Leidy Peak, descending to 10,560 feet at Chepeta Lake and climbing again to a high point of 12,200 feet at the wilderness area boundary.

There are several trails that tie in with the Highline Trail. Numerous backcountry lakes with trout-fishing opportunities dot these side trails as well as the main trail. Hiking, fishing, and exploring possibilities are endless. —*Originally contributed by Michael Bergfeld*

(Note: Since this hike covers an area with two possible access points and route options of various lengths, no key points are provided.)

27 Jones Hole Creek

A moderate day hike or overnighter in Dinosaur National Monument. The Jones Hole Trail follows the clear, spring-fed waters of its namesake creek in a deep, scenic canyon. Special attractions include trout fishing and prehistoric Indian rock art.

Start: Jones Hole National Fish Hatchery.
Distance: 8 miles out and back.
Difficulty: Moderate.
Trail surface: Dirt trail.
Seasons: Spring through fall.
Land status: National monument.
Nearest town: Vernal.
Fees and permits: A $10.00-per-vehicle entrance fee ($5.00 on foot or bicycle), valid for seven days, is charged to enter the

national monument. A free backcountry use permit is required for overnight trips; call (435) 781-7700.
Maps: USGS Jones Hole quad; National Geographic Trails Illustrated Dinosaur National Monument Map.
Trail contacts: Dinosaur National Monument, Quarry Visitor Center, P.O. Box 127, Jensen, UT 84035; (435) 781-7700; www.nps.gov/dino.

Finding the trailhead: From U.S. Highway 40 (Main Street) in Vernal, take U.S. Highway 191 north for 5 blocks, turn right onto 500 North Street, and, after about 2 miles, bear left past the county dump. The hatchery is 35 miles farther on a well-signed, paved road. Park in the visitor parking area at the fish hatchery.

From the Dinosaur Quarry Visitor Center, the route is more difficult, but a free map and directions are available at the visitor center information desk. To reach Dinosaur Quarry, drive 13 miles southeast of Vernal on US 40. Turn left in Jensen onto Highway 149 and continue another 7 miles to Dinosaur National Monument and the Quarry Visitor Center. With directions in hand, drive about one hour along Brush Creek Road and Diamond Mountain Road to the fish hatchery. *DeLorme: Utah Atlas & Gazetteer:* Page 57 C5.

The Hike

You won't see any dinosaur bones in Jones Hole, but you will see country typical of the rest of Dinosaur National Monument—deep, sheer-walled canyons etched into the high plateaus at the eastern end of the Uinta Mountains. Jones Hole Creek, rushing from limestone springs to join the Green River, has carved a gorge more than half a mile deep. An easy trail follows the creek for 4 miles, descending more than 500 feet to its confluence with the Green River in Whirlpool Canyon.

The trail begins at a signed trailhead on the east bank of Jones Hole Creek and follows the creek closely for most of its length. Surrounded by semiarid sagebrush and piñon-juniper uplands, Jones Hole is an oasis. The stream issues from several springs in the limestone canyon walls just above the hatchery and tumbles through a boulder-strewn channel lined with box elder, watercress, horsetail, and, in early summer, an explosion of yellow monkey flower. Drawn by the water and the lush

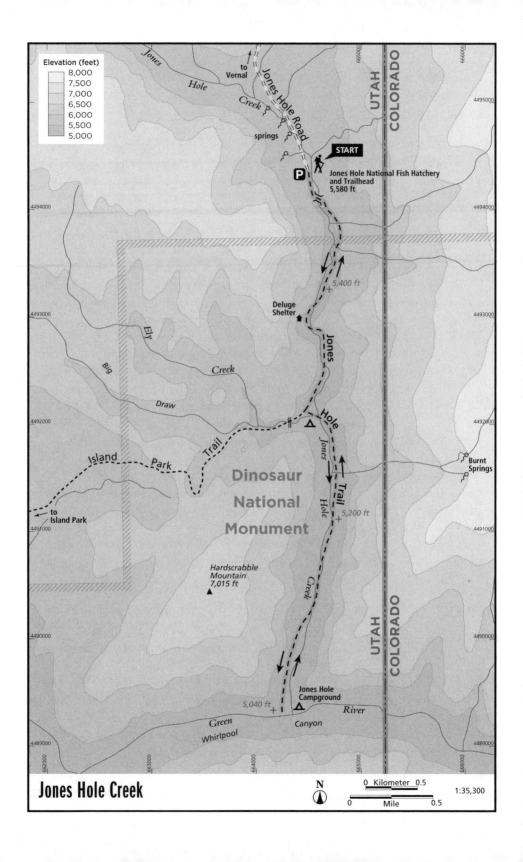

Elevation (feet)

8,000
7,500
7,000
6,500
6,000
5,500
5,000

to
Vernal

Jones

Hole

Creek

springs

Jones Hole Road

UTAH

COLORADO

START

P

Jones Hole National Fish Hatchery
and Trailhead
5,580 ft

5,400 ft

Deluge
Shelter

Jones

Ely

Creek

Big

Draw

Island   Park   Trail

Hole

△

Jones

Burnt
Springs

to
Island Park

Dinosaur

National

Monument

Hole

Trail

5,200 ft

Hardscrabble
Mountain
7,015 ft
▲

Creek

UTAH

COLORADO

Jones Hole
Campground
△

5,040 ft

River

Green

Whirlpool

Canyon

Jones Hole Creek

N

0   Kilometer   0.5

0   Mile   0.5

1:35,300

growth, wildlife concentrates in the canyon. You might see a mule deer ducking through the underbrush or hear a yellow-bellied marmot whistling from its hideout on a talus slope. Canyon wrens and other songbirds add their tunes to the constant background music of the creek.

About 1.5 miles down the trail, a plank bridge crosses the creek. A short side trail just beyond this bridge leads to a group of 1,000-year-old pictographs from the Fremont culture, known as the Deluge Shelter. If you visit the pictographs, please don't touch them—the iron-oxide paint used by the Fremonts has withstood centuries of weather, but the pressure of many fingers, as well as the acids and oils in your skin, can quickly wear away this prehistoric art.

At about 1.8 miles is a junction with the Island Park Trail at Ely Creek, a tributary stream entering from the right (west). It's only a quarter mile up this trail to a small waterfall on Ely Creek, a scenic spot shaded by Douglas fir and birch trees.

Buff-colored Weber sandstone dominates the upper part of Jones Hole and forms monolithic walls reminiscent of Zion Canyon. When you cross Ely Creek, however, you also cross the Island Park Fault and step back about 200 million years in time. Older rocks have been uplifted into view on the downstream side of the fault, forming stepped walls as hard limestone and sandstone layers alternate with softer shale beds. A close look at trailside boulders and ledges may reveal fossils of corals, crinoids, and brachiopods, which lived in the ancient seas that left these strata.

About 2 miles beyond Ely Creek, the trail ends at the Jones Hole Campground, a popular stop for raft parties floating the Green River. Overnight use of the campsites is reserved for river groups only, but hikers may picnic.

There is an established campsite at the mouth of Ely Creek (the only designated backcountry campsite in the monument); camping elsewhere along Jones Hole Creek is not permitted. If you plan an overnight hike in the Jones Hole area, you must reserve one of the two sites there and obtain a free backcountry use permit and zero-impact camping handout at the Dinosaur Quarry Visitor Center. Water from both Jones Hole Creek and Ely Creek must be boiled or chemically purified before drinking. Bring your backpacker stove; campfires are prohibited since wood is not plentiful and fires, however small, create ash and debris that mar the site and are difficult to erase.

There is some good fishing for brown and rainbow trout in Jones Hole Creek. Remember that a Utah fishing license is required even though you are in a national monument. Special catch limits apply, and you are responsible for knowing the regulations.

Pets are not allowed on the trail. And, as in all backcountry areas, carry out what you carry in. Be particularly careful with garbage—scavenging skunks have become a problem at the river camp. As in any national park or monument, do not disturb any natural, historic, or archaeological resource. Let those who come after you enjoy all that you have enjoyed. —*Originally contributed by Linda West*

Key Points

0.0   Start at the Jones Hole Trailhead at the Jones Hole Fish Hatchery.

1.8   Junction with the Island Park Trail. Continue south.

2.0   Cross Ely Creek.

4.0   Arrive at the Green River.

8.0   Return to the trailhead at the fish hatchery.

Honorable Mentions

Northern Utah

A Smithfield Dry Canyon Trail

Dry Canyon is the easily accessible starting point for a number of day hike and overnight backpack options in the rugged 44,964-acre Mount Naomi Wilderness, north of Logan, which was designated under the Utah Wilderness Act of 1984. Trail 060 winds through the rather narrow canyon, which opens up into subalpine bowls covered by lupine, columbine, buttercup, and penstemon as you work your way toward Bear River Ridge at 9,200 feet. The trail skirts 8,848-foot Mount Jardine and, 7.5 miles from the trailhead, intersects Trail 005, which continues on to Mount Elmer, Tony Grove Lake, Mount Naomi, and High Creek Lake.

In Smithfield turn right off U.S. Highway 91 onto 300 South and drive 10 miles to a rock barrier. The Forest Service trailhead is 1 mile farther up the gravel road. This section is on private property—please be courteous and stay on the road. For more information contact Logan Ranger District, Wasatch-Cache National Forest, 1500 East Highway 89, Logan, UT 84321; (435) 755–3620; ww.fs.fed.us/r4/wcnf. *DeLorme: Utah Atlas & Gazetteer:* Page 62 B3. —*Contributed by the Logan Ranger District*

B Alexander Basin

Alexander Basin has several features to attract the travel-weary hiker tired of long drives to the Uintas or southern Utah. This beautiful basin, with its trailhead just a few minutes from Salt Lake City in Mill Creek Canyon, offers solitude and plenty of opportunity for exploration. Moreover, overnight camping is permitted in Mill Creek, and if you have a dog who enjoys hiking as much as you do, don't leave him behind. Dogs are permitted in the canyon as well. (Dogs are not allowed in most of the other nearby canyons.) This 3-mile round-trip hike offers an ideal day excursion or a pleasant overnighter. Alexander Basin also presents the opportunity to scale 10,246-foot Gobblers Knob or to head west into Bowman Fork and south past 10,241-foot Mount Raymond and into Big Cottonwood Canyon. Side hikes into other drainages are possible from Alexander Basin. Climbing Gobblers Knob brings you to the Mill Creek Canyon–Big Cottonwood Canyon crest, and several hikes are possible into this canyon to the south. The trail west from Alexander Basin into Bowman Fork and Porter Fork leads to Baker Spring and to Big Cottonwood Canyon. All offer fine alpine hiking, but if you choose to stay put, spending all your time in Alexander Basin, you'll discover why this area is one of the Wasatch's special attractions.

Take Interstate 215 south in Salt Lake City and exit onto the 39th South off-ramp. Turn left under the interstate and turn left again at the light onto Wasatch Boulevard. Drive north for 1 block and turn right onto Mill Creek Canyon Road. Continue about 8.5 miles to the Alexander Basin Trailhead on the right side of the road, about a mile beyond the Fircrest and Clover Springs Picnic Grounds. For more information contact the Public Lands Information Center, 3285 East 3300 S., Salt Lake City, UT 84109; (801) 466–6411. The land management agency is the Salt Lake Ranger District, Wasatch-Cache National Forest, 6944 South 3000 E., Salt Lake City, UT 84121; (801) 733–2660; www.fs.fed.us/r4/wcnf. *DeLorme: Utah Atlas & Gazetteer:* Page 53 B6. —*Originally contributed by Dave Hall*

Ⓒ Lone Peak via Draper Ridge

Should a monument be erected at the base of Lone Peak, its bronze plaque might read: "Lone Peak stands as a memorial to the dedication and perseverance of many conscientious Utahans who, over a period of nearly fifteen years and against almost insurmountable political and bureaucratic odds, succeeded in securing for the enjoyment of present and future generations a nearly pristine piece of Utah's rapidly vanishing wilderness." In addition to its unique position as part of Utah's first congressionally designated wilderness in 1977, Lone Peak, the pièce de résistance of the Lone Peak Wilderness, is among the most delightful mountain experiences in the Wasatch Range. There is irony in the proximity of the Lone Peak Wilderness to Utah's capital city, but the area's convenience is unparalleled, and to optimistic wilderness advocates Lone Peak is a reminder that hard-fought battles can mean environmental victories.

The relatively long (6 miles) and steep ascent to Lone Peak cirque and the summit at 11,253 feet via the Draper Ridge route is on public and private lands of diverse ownership. Because no public agency has assumed responsibility for its maintenance, the Draper Ridge "trail" consists of linearly connected—and sometimes interconnected—segments of firebreaks, jeep trails, horse, game, and foot trails. There's a good chance you will see deer, mountain goats, and pikas (rock rabbits) during your climb to the top.

Take Interstate 15 south of Salt Lake City to exit 291 (Bluffdale) and turn east onto Highland Drive. Follow Highland Drive, continuing under the railroad overpass, in an easterly direction for approximately 3.5 miles, to the Ballard Equestrian Center. In the southeast corner of the large asphalt parking lot is the trailhead sign for equestrian user access to Corner Canyon (equestrian users may park their trailers in this trailhead location). Directly south of the equestrian parking area, on the other side of Highland Drive, is the access road to the Corner Canyon Trailhead for non-equestrian users. There also is a sign at this point indicating public access to Corner Canyon. The road is open to two-wheel-drive vehicles; it is a bit rough, however, so travel is recommended via high-clearance vehicles. The Corner Canyon–Draper

Ridge Trailhead is located approximately 2 miles southeast of the Highland Drive entrance. Draper City maintains a trailhead sign at this location, and parking is available. For more information contact Pleasant Grove Ranger District, Uinta National Forest, 390 North 100 E., Pleasant Grove, UT 84062; (801) 785–3563; www.fs.fed.us/r4/uinta. Also, Salt Lake Ranger District, Wasatch-Cache National Forest, 6944 South 3000 E., Salt Lake City, UT 84121; (801) 733–2660; www.fs.fed.us/r4/wcnf. *DeLorme: Utah Atlas & Gazetteer:* Page 53 C5. *—Originally contributed by Alexis Kelner*

D Great Western Trail–Uinta National Forest

The Great Western Trail, planned as a continuous route from Mexico to Canada, traverses some of the most spectacular scenery in the West. As a way to represent the pioneer spirit, the trail is marked with the symbol of a covered wagon inside the silhouette of Utah and is open to hikers, horses, and mountain bikers. All-terrain vehicles are allowed in designated locations. Hiking possibilities incorporating the Great Western Trail in the Uinta National Forest are endless. Numerous trails and roads intersect the route, providing various access opportunities. Study a map and choose a portion that piques your interest.

The trail enters the Uinta National Forest at its northern edge, northeast of Lone Peak Wilderness. Take Highways 209 and 210 east of Sandy past the Snowbird and Alta ski resorts. Half a mile past Alta, the road continues as Forest Road 028. Just before Albion Campground, you'll find the trailhead to Lake Mary on the left side of the road. The portion through the Uinta National Forest stretches for 65 miles and skirts the Lone Peak and Timpanogos Wilderness Areas, then travels the spine of the Uinta National Forest—Strawberry Ridge—to Spanish Fork Canyon. The Uinta portion of the Great Western Trail finishes at the Big Sky Cafe on U.S. Highway 50/6 in Spanish Fork Canyon. For more information contact Uinta National Forest, 88 West 100 N., P.O. Box 1428, Provo, UT 84603; (801) 342–5100; www.fs.fed.us/r4/uinta. *DeLorme: Utah Atlas & Gazetteer:* Page 53 C6. *—Originally contributed by the Heber Ranger District*

E Row Bench

Row Bench is a moderate day hike with a wide range of wilderness scenery and route options, located in Daniels Canyon in the Uinta National Forest, Heber Ranger District. Initially the trail is steep, but it then levels out and meanders along the ridgeline through stands of aspen and Gambel oak with brief patches of grassy meadow. Water is not available along the trail, so be sure to carry a sufficient supply, especially in the warm summer months. Be prepared for summer afternoon thunderstorms. Hiking information, maps, and supplies for your trip can be obtained at nearby Heber City.

To reach Row Bench Trail 081, drive about 11 miles south from Heber City on U.S. Highway 40, then turn left (east) at the Center Canyon turnoff. Park at the trailhead, located at a gate at the end of this turnoff, just off the highway. Hike along the old dirt road for about 1 mile. You will reach an inconspicuous fork where the road continues east as Center Canyon Trail. To the right (south), Row Bench Trail begins. For more information contact Heber Ranger District, Uinta National Forest, P.O. Box 190, Heber City, UT 84032; (435) 654–0470; www.fs.fed.us/r4/uinta. *DeLorme: Utah Atlas & Gazetteer:* Page 54 D1. —*Contributed by the Heber Ranger District*

F Hidden Lake

This Hidden Lake truly is hidden—some experienced backcountry hikers have gotten lost along the way. So follow your topo maps carefully and keep your compass handy. The hike is not difficult—about 4 miles to the lake with a net loss in elevation of about 300 feet. Whatever difficulty you may encounter will be in orienteering on the second half of the trip in. The intermittent, unsigned trail has few distinct landmarks. Along the way you pass numerous lakes, including Long Lake, Weir Lake, Pot Lake, and Duck Lake. Hidden Lake has a few good campsites, mostly on its southeast side. There are a few deep holes in the lake, offering a good opportunity for a midday dip. Some large cutthroat and brook trout lurk in the depths and occasionally dimple the surface in the shallows. They're not easy to catch, but when you do hook into one, it will give you a fine fight.

Drive about 26 miles east of Kamas on Highway 150 (Mirror Lake Highway). Turn left toward Trial Lake at a long, 180-degree turn to the right. Drive on pavement for a few hundred yards, continuing on a gravel road for 0.75 mile. Turn right toward Crystal Lake (signs mark the spot). The trailhead is half a mile ahead at the end of the road, just north of a horse ramp at the west end of the parking area. This trailhead leads to many areas of the upper Provo and Weber drainages, so don't be discouraged if you see several cars in the trailhead parking area. For more information contact Kamas Ranger District, Wasatch-Cache National Forest, P.O. Box 68, Kamas, UT 84036; (435) 783–4338; www.fs.fed.us/r4/wcnf. *DeLorme: Utah Atlas & Gazetteer:* Page 54 B3. —*Originally contributed by Dave Hall*

G Burnt Fork

Hiking opportunities in the eastern Uinta Mountains are often ignored, but the area has spectacular terrain, abundant wildlife, fast fishing, and only moderate (although increasing) hiking pressure. Beginning at the Spirit Lake Campground at 10,200 feet, this hike traverses the upper reaches of the middle and north forks of Sheep Creek and then enters the Burnt Fork drainage. The Burnt Fork Lakes sit at around 10,700 feet, so elevation gains from the trailhead amount to less than 600 feet. The 11-mile hike to Island Lake passes other beautiful alpine lakes that offer excellent campsites. And the upper Burnt Fork region along the way boasts several small but fish-filled lakes requiring off-trail exploring.

To reach the trailhead, take Interstate 80 east of Evanston, Wyoming, and turn right onto the I–80 Business Route to Fort Bridger. Drive about 3 miles and turn right onto Wyoming Highway 414. Follow WY 414 through Mountain View, Lonetree, and Burntfork. Turn right about 2.5 miles past Burntfork and drive on the graded road for about 13.5 miles. Turn right toward Spirit Lake and continue another 6 miles on rough road to the trailhead. You will find the trailhead 0.25 mile past the Spirit Lake Campground on the left. Parking is not available at the trailhead, but the Spirit Lake Lodge will watch your car for a fee. For more information contact Mountain View Ranger District, Wasatch-Cache National Forest, 321 Highway 414 E., P.O. Box 129, Mountain View, WY 82939; (307) 782–6555; www.fs.fed.us/r4/wcnf. *DeLorme: Utah Atlas & Gazetteer:* Page 56 A1. *—Originally contributed by Hartt Wixom*

H Dinosaur National Monument

Dinosaur National Monument is a land that has changed little over the past hundred years. While the park has few trails developed and marked in the traditional sense, there is unequaled opportunity to travel undeveloped "routes" through narrow slickrock canyons or along benches with vast, sweeping views. You can stop at any visitor center or ranger station to discuss the hiking potential of a particular area and obtain a free backcountry use permit, which is required for overnight trips. Dinosaur National Monument can provide the backcountry traveler with an isolated wilderness experience in rugged terrain amid dramatic scenery, almost total silence (actually measured at less than twelve decibels of ambient sound!), and surprises only the desert can provide.

Drive 13 miles southeast of Vernal on U.S. Highway 40. Turn left in Jensen onto Highway 149 and continue another 7 miles to Dinosaur National Monument and the Quarry Visitor Center. For more information contact Dinosaur National Monument, Quarry Visitor Center, P.O. Box 128, Jensen, UT 84035; (435) 781–7700; www.nps.gov/dino. For information on the Colorado portion of the park, contact Dinosaur National Monument, 4545 East Highway 40, Dinosaur, CO 81610; (970) 374–3000; www.nps.gov/dino. *DeLorme: Utah Atlas & Gazetteer:* Page 57 C4. *—Originally contributed by Herm Hoops*

Central Utah:
The Great Basin, Fishlake National Forest, Wasatch Plateau, San Rafael River, and Book Cliffs

28 Tule Valley

A little-known hike in a greasewood desert and wetlands ecosystem, located west of the House Range, 50 miles west of Delta. You'll find solitude at its best in this undeveloped valley with wetlands and warmwater springs.

Start: The corral at Tule Spring.
Distance: About 13 miles out and back.
Difficulty: Easy, depending upon weather conditions.
Trail surface: Dirt road.
Seasons: Fall, winter, spring.
Land status: Bureau of Land Management (BLM).
Nearest town: Delta.

Fees and permits: No fees or permits required.
Maps: USGS Chalk Knolls, Coyote Knolls, and Swasey Peak NW quads; Northcentral Utah Multipurpose Map.
Trail contacts: Fillmore Resource Area, Bureau of Land Management, P.O. Box 778, Fillmore, UT 84631; (435) 743-3100; www.ut.blm.gov.

Finding the trailhead: Take U.S. Highway 6/50 southwest from Delta for about 12 miles to the dirt Antelope Spring Road. Turn right and continue about 24 miles. Turn right again toward Antelope Spring. Proceed another 22 miles through the House Range via Dome Canyon Pass to Tule Spring. A dirt road turns to the right and continues a few hundred yards to a corral at Tule Spring. *DeLorme: Utah Atlas & Gazetteer:* Page 35 A4.

The Hike

Most wilderness hikes in Utah are in the high country or the canyons. Tule Valley is a change of pace. Located in the Great Basin, west of the House Range, Tule is an undeveloped desert valley sprinkled with wetlands. The hike is on an old road with virtually no elevation change.

At Tule Spring (4,422 feet), where the hike begins, a rough road heads north 6.5 miles to Coyote Spring. Interestingly, although you gain and lose some elevation along the way, Coyote Spring is at 4,424 feet—a net gain of 2 feet over more than 6 miles. The water at Tule Spring and Coyote Spring, as well as other springs nearby, has not been tested and may be of questionable quality. The BLM recommends that you treat water from the springs or bring your own.

There is a sizable wetland 2.5 miles north of the trailhead on the left (west). Another 0.5 mile beyond, a rise of a few hundred feet offers a break in the scenery. If you plan an overnighter, this is an interesting camping area. From the top of the hillock, you can look south and see your car at the trailhead.

Views from Tule Valley include the steep side of the House Range to the east, the Deep Creek Mountains to the northwest, and the low-lying Confusion Range to the west. Nevada's Mount Moriah and Wheeler Peak are also on the western horizon. Twisters and storms are often seen kicking up salt in the adjacent salt flats.

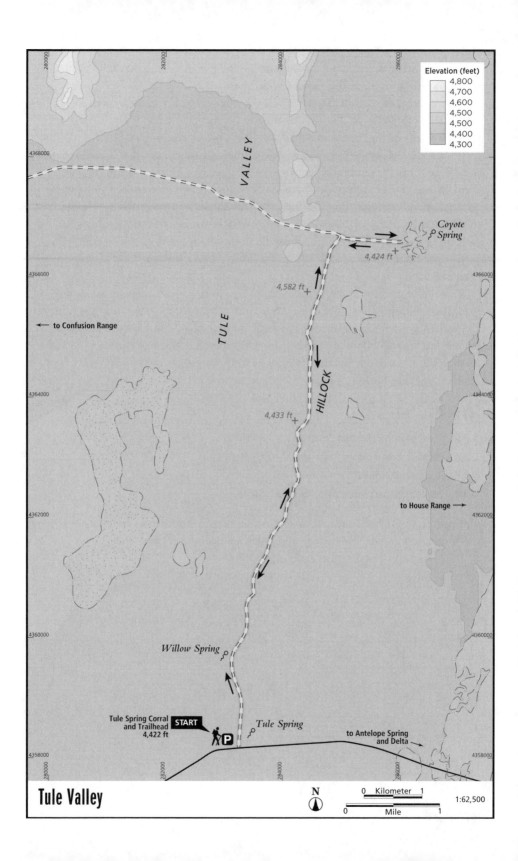

Elevation (feet)

	4,800
	4,700
	4,600
	4,500
	4,500
	4,400
	4,300

Coyote Spring

4,424 ft

VALLEY

4,582 ft

← to Confusion Range

TULE

HILLOCK

4,433 ft

to House Range →

Willow Spring

Tule Spring Corral
and Trailhead
4,422 ft

START

Tule Spring

to Antelope Spring
and Delta →

Tule Valley

N

0   Kilometer   1

0   Mile   1

1:62,500

Hiking in stormy weather is an experience, watching clouds swirl around the peaks of the House Range and the Deep Creek Mountains.

Tule Valley was once an extension of Lake Bonneville. If you look carefully, you'll see ancient shorelines on the mountains around the valley. Tule Valley has approximately twenty springs, most of which originate below the surface (1,500 to 3,000 feet), causing warm water temperatures. Cattle and sheep use the water, and the marshes and water provide habitat for waterfowl, marsh hawks, blackbirds, rails, and marsh wrens, as well as for relic populations of the western spotted frog and a species of leech and giant water bug. You may find obsidian chips around and between the springs, left by prehistoric Native Americans. (Remember that archaeological artifacts are protected by federal law; please do not take any artifacts as souvenirs.) Most certainly, the springs were stop-off points during travel and provided an important source of food.

After hiking north about 6 miles from Tule Spring, you intersect an east–west road. Turn right (east) and continue 0.5 mile to Coyote Spring. You may spot ducks and even a goose or two on the open water here. Most waterfowl in the general vicinity are found 30 miles to the north at the Fish Springs National Wildlife Refuge, but Coyote Spring attracts birds as well.

From Coyote Spring, you can backtrack to your car.

Key Points

0.0   Start at the corral at Tule Spring.

6.0   Intersect a road running east-west. Turn right (east).

6.5   Reach Coyote Spring.

13.0 Retrace your steps to arrive back at Tule Spring.

Option: From Coyote Spring, using your topo map, you can take an overland route southwest back to the trailhead. —*Originally contributed by Peter Hovingh*

29 Swasey Peak

A day hike or backpack in the Great Basin region of the House Range with spectacular views of the Great Basin in Utah and Nevada. The area also features a small population of bristlecone pine.

Start: The parking area off Sinbad Spring Road.
Distance: 4.5-mile loop.
Difficulty: Moderate, depending upon weather.
Trail surface: Cross-country, dirt road.
Seasons: Late spring through fall.
Land status: Bureau of Land Management (BLM).

Nearest town: Delta.
Fees and permits: No fees or permits required.
Maps: USGS Swasey Peak and Marjum Pass quads.
Trail contacts: Fillmore Resource Area, Bureau of Land Management, P.O. Box 778, Fillmore, UT 84631; (435) 743-3100; www.ut.blm.gov.

Finding the trailhead: Take U.S. Highway 6/50 southwest from Delta for about 12 miles and turn right onto Antelope Spring Road. After another 24 miles, turn right (northwest) toward Antelope Spring. Travel 9 more miles into the House Range. As the road swings west and then south toward Dome Canyon Pass, Sinbad Spring Road exits to the right. Turn right (north) and drive to Antelope Spring, just off the road to the north. (Incidentally, there are extensive trilobite beds here. You may want to stop briefly to hunt for some of these fossils.) Continue 3.2 miles beyond this junction to a large open area. Park here. *DeLorme: Utah Atlas & Gazetteer:* Page 35 A5.

The Hike

At 9,669 feet, Swasey Peak is the highest point in the House Range. From the top, after an off-trail, 1,700-foot climb, you'll have a panoramic view northwest to the Deep Creeks, northeast to Whirlwind Valley and Mount Nebo, southeast to the Tushar Mountains and 12,169-foot Delano Peak, south to the dry Sevier Lake, and west across Tule Valley to the Confusion Range. In addition, Wheeler and Pilot Peaks and Mount Moriah are visible in Nevada.

You begin by bushwhacking up the slope on the right (northeast) side of the road. There is no water on the mountain, so plan on toting a supply with you. The first section of the hike may not appear difficult when you consult the appropriate topo maps. You climb about 600 feet in less than a mile and overlook a steep drop-off to the west. But the thick mountain mahogany can be a nuisance until you reach the ridge.

A small population of bristlecone pine exists along the ridge. Continue northeast 0.5 mile to the first of two lower summits. The top is another 0.5 mile along the ridge.

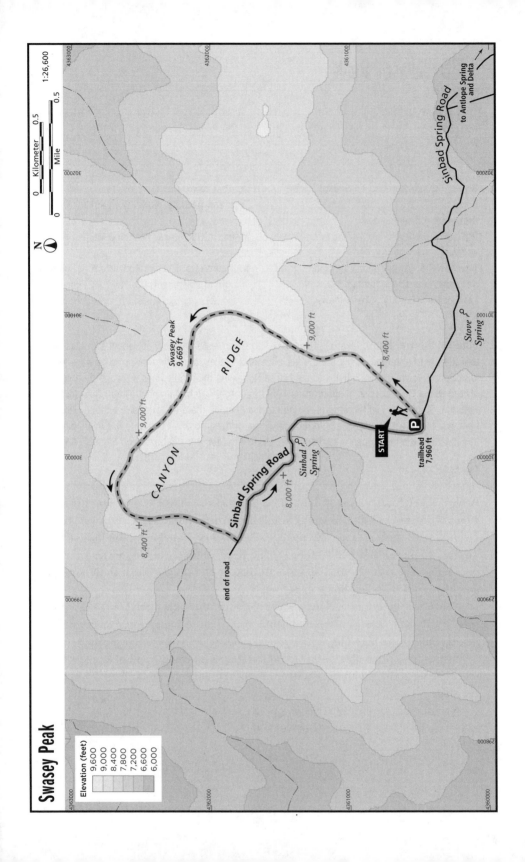

Swasey Peak

1:26,600

N

Elevation (feet)
9,600
9,000
8,400
7,800
7,200
6,600
6,000

Kilometer
Mile

CANYON

RIDGE

Swasey Peak
9,669 ft

+ 9,000 ft

+ 9,000 ft

+ 8,400 ft

+ 9,000 ft

+ 8,400 ft

+ 8,000 ft

Sinbad Spring Road

end of road

Sinbad
Spring

Sinbad Spring Road

to Antlope Spring
and Delta

Stove
Spring

START

trailhead
7,960 ft

P

To return to your car, hike down the ridge to the northwest. After 0.75 mile swing to the west and then south, staying above the steep terrain to the west. You meet Sinbad Spring Road in a flat, southwest of Swasey Peak. Follow the road to the left (southeast) about a mile to your car. —*Originally contributed by Peter Hovingh*

Key Points

0.0   Start at the open parking area off Sinbad Spring Road.

1.9   Reach Swasey Peak at 9,669 feet.

3.5   Arrive at Sinbad Spring Road.

4.5   Arrive back at the parking area.

30 Notch Peak

A day hike to the top of 9,655-foot Notch Peak in the House Range, 44 miles southwest of Delta. The area offers solitude, bristlecone pines, and spectacular views of the Great Basin in Utah and Nevada.

Start: The trailhead at the end of Miller Canyon Road.
Distance: 9 miles out and back.
Difficulty: Moderate.
Trail surface: Gravel road, dry wash, cross-country.
Seasons: Spring and fall.
Land status: Bureau of Land Management (BLM) wilderness study area.

Nearest town: Delta.
Fees and permits: No fees or permits required.
Maps: USGS Notch Peak and Miller Cove quads.
Trail contacts: Fillmore Field Office, Bureau of Land Management, P.O. Box 778, Fillmore, UT 84631; (435) 743-3100; www.ut.blm.gov.

Finding the trailhead: Drive southwest from Delta on U.S. Highway 6/50 for about 38 miles. Turn right onto a dirt road. This road is not signed, and you may miss it unless you watch carefully. After 4.7 miles turn left; continue another 1.3 miles and then turn right onto Miller Canyon Road. A sign marks the spot. In 5.5 miles bear left into Miller Cove. About 3 miles farther along, there is an old stone cabin on the right. At one time an active mining claim, the cabin now is a historical structure owned by the BLM. Please respect this property. Continue past the cabin to the trailhead, which is marked by wilderness study area signs. Park where the road is closed. *DeLorme: Utah Atlas & Gazetteer:* Page 35 B4.

The Hike

The 9-mile round trip to the top of Notch Peak (9,655 feet)—part of an 80,000-acre Bureau of Land Management wilderness study area—offers an opportunity to get away from throngs of hikers in more popular backcountry areas. The hike is not

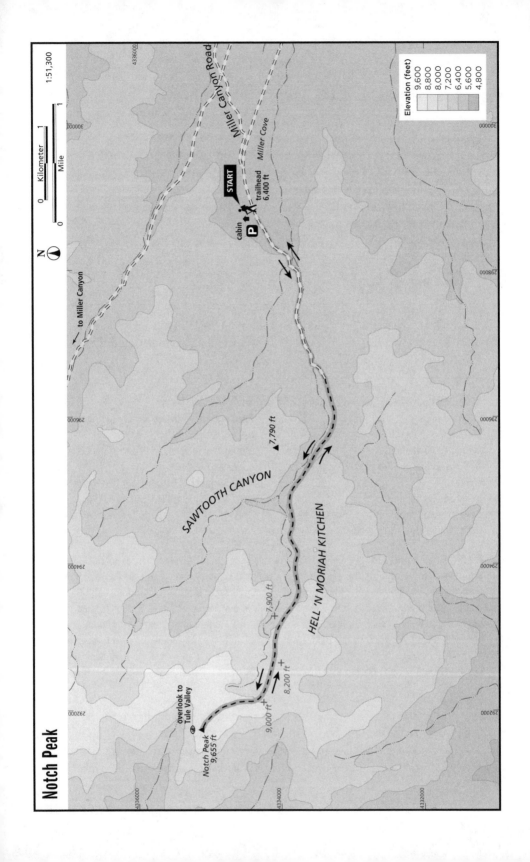

Notch Peak

N

1:51,300

Elevation (feet)
9,600
8,800
8,000
7,200
6,400
5,600
4,800

Miller Canyon Road

to Miller Canyon

START

trailhead
6,400 ft

cabin

P

Miller Cove

▲ 7,790 ft

SAWTOOTH CANYON

HELL 'N MORIAH KITCHEN

7,900 ft

8,200 ft

9,000 ft

overlook to
Tule Valley

Notch Peak
9,655 ft

difficult, despite a 3,000-foot climb. Most of the trip is along a dry wash. Only the final 0.25 mile to the top is relatively steep. No water exists along the route, so be certain to fill water bottles in Delta before driving to the trailhead. Flash flooding can be a problem in late summer and early fall.

Start by hiking along the gravel road to the west, passing through a deeply cut canyon. The walls on the left (south) side rise several hundred feet. The hiking is easy here—along the rough gravel road on relatively flat terrain.

After 0.5 mile the canyon opens and the drainage splits. Hike to the left (southwest) of a large, rounded knob that you can see straight ahead. There is no conspicuous trail here, but the open wash makes the going easy.

Occasionally the walls of the meandering wash narrow, and the hiking is similar to canyon hiking in southeastern Utah. Normally, however, dry slopes rise from the wash. Piñon and juniper dot the sage-covered hillsides at the lower elevations. Fir and mountain mahogany become more common as you climb.

About 3.5 miles from the trailhead, the wash becomes steeper, and you climb over a few tricky ledges. A good lunch spot is just above a massive tree that has fallen across the canyon. Slightly above the trunk is a bristlecone pine—one of the first you'll see along the trail.

In another 0.5 mile the wash becomes indistinct. Begin climbing on the sage–mountain mahogany hillsides, heading northwest 0.5 mile to an obvious saddle east of Notch Peak. At the saddle look at the spectacular chasm on the mountain's west side, dropping 4,500 feet to Tule Valley.

Notch Peak is a steep quarter of a mile to the west. The views from the top are rewarding, including the Deep Creek Mountains to the northwest, the Confusion Range to the west, the Wah Wahs to the south, and Sevier Lake and the mountains of the Fishlake National Forest to the east.

The Wasatch Mountain Club has left a small mailbox in a rock cairn at the top. Among those who have signed the log are a few hang-glider pilots who packed their gear to the peak for an aerial descent to Tule Valley. The message in the log indicated that they were scared, but there was pride and a $500 bet on the line.

On the trip down you may want to take a brief side trip to a small bristlecone pine grove on the southeast side of the knob east of Notch Peak. A 0.25-mile hike from the saddle and around the knob brings you there. —*Originally contributed by Dave Hall*

Key Points

0.0 Start at the trailhead on Miller Canyon Road.

4.5 Reach Notch Peak at 9,655 feet. Turnaround point.

9.0 Arrive back at the trailhead.

31 Wah Wah Mountains

An interesting day hike into a remote Great Basin range. You'll hike cross-country from one high point to another along the ridgeline of the Wah Wah Mountains, enjoying wildlife, views, and solitude.

Start: The high point in the road on the spine of the Wah Wah Mountains.
Distance: 5 to 7 miles out and back.
Difficulty: Moderate.
Trail surface: Cross-country, game trails.
Seasons: Late spring through fall.
Land status: Bureau of Land Management (BLM).
Nearest town: Milford.

Fees and permits: No fees or permits required.
Maps: USGS Lamerdorf Peak quad; Southwestern Utah Multipurpose Map.
Trail contacts: Cedar City Field Office, Bureau of Land Management, 176 East D. L. Sargent Drive, Cedar City, UT 84720; (435) 586-2401; www.ut.blm.gov.

Finding the trailhead: Take Highway 21 west from Milford for about 24 miles, passing through the San Francisco Mountains, and turn left onto a gravel road near mile marker 54. Bear right in about 2.5 miles and continue southwest another 13 miles to the backbone of the Wah Wahs. Park at the high point (about 8,000 feet). If you continue on to the west side of the Wah Wahs, you descend into Pine Grove, where the remains of several small mines are visible. *DeLorme: Utah Atlas & Gazetteer:* Page 24 B3.

The Hike

This excursion into the Wah Wah Mountains makes an easy day hike. Most hikers eat lunch at one of the summits 1 or 2 miles in and make the round trip in four to five hours. Overnight hikes heading farther into the range are possible but not popular due to the scarcity of water.

Part of the attraction of the Wah Wahs, like other Great Basin ranges, is their remote nature and the stark contrast they present with the desert below. Just getting to the mountains is an interesting trip. You won't see many people on the way to the trailhead, and the chance of seeing someone on the hike is even slimmer.

There is no formal trailhead by the road, and travel in the backcountry is mostly cross-country. A few game trails exist, but consider the ridgeline your guide. Springs just a few miles to the west in Pine Grove provide the only water.

Beginning at the high point in the road, climb northeast through the forest for 0.5 mile to a knoll. A fence here runs north–south. Follow it north another 0.5 mile to the next high point, at around 8,600 feet.

About 0.75 mile from the trailhead, look for signs of revegetation following a burn approximately fifty years ago. Mule deer and even antelope have been spotted here, as well as a long list of birds.

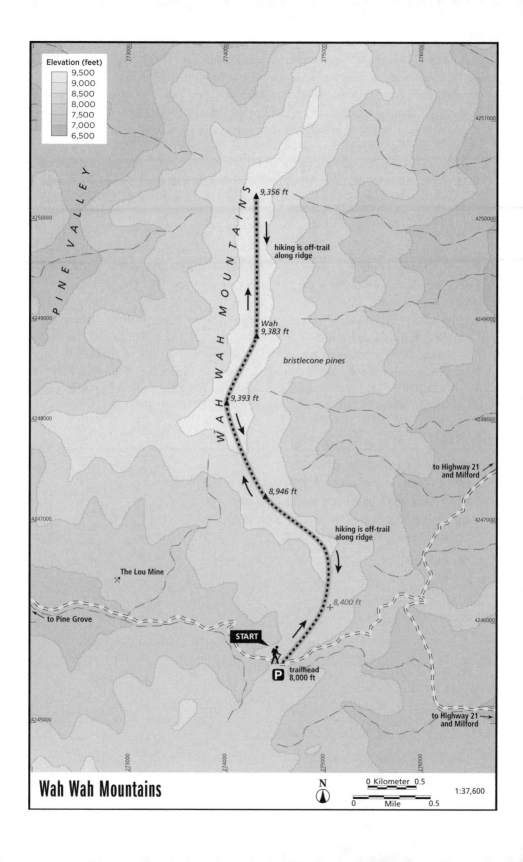

Wah Wah Mountains

Elevation (feet)
9,500
9,000
8,500
8,000
7,500
7,000
6,500

9,356 ft

hiking is off-trail
along ridge

Wah
9,383 ft

bristlecone pines

9,393 ft

to Highway 21
and Milford

8,946 ft

hiking is off-trail
along ridge

8,400 ft

The Lou Mine

to Pine Grove

START

P trailhead
8,000 ft

to Highway 21
and Milford

P I N E   V A L L E Y

W A H   W A H   M O U N T A I N S

N

0 Kilometer 0.5

0 Mile 0.5

1:37,600

Continue the gentle ridge walk through conifers to an unnamed peak (9,393 feet) a mile to the northwest, passing over one high point (8,946 feet) along the way. Heading northeast, you leave the forest and enter more open country that falls off to the west. There are splendid views of Pine Valley, more than 4,000 feet below.

Wah Peak (9,383 feet) is half a mile to the north. Bristlecone pines (some several thousand years old) can be found on the ridge to the east of Wah.

Hike another mile along the ridge, soaking in the views and the solitude, before making the return to your car. An option is to take an extended trip to the north. The Wah Wah Mountains continue north for about 15 miles to Highway 21 and beyond, about 15 miles more. Little water is available, however, so most hikers do the short day hike.

When you make the Wah Wah trip, plan to spend some time exploring the Great Basin in your car at the end of the hike. Some fascinating abandoned towns and old mining operations are in the area, and each dirt road you take will almost always offer new attractions.

The old mining town of Frisco—now a ghost town—is particularly interesting. It's in the San Francisco Mountains just off Highway 21 and makes an easy side trip after leaving the Wah Wahs. Following the discovery of silver here in the late 1800s, there were 4,000 residents. Today, although a few of the claims have been reactivated, there is little left other than the remains of some old buildings. —*Originally contributed by Bill Viavant*

Key Points

0.0 Start at the high point in the road.

2.0 Reach an unnamed peak at 9,393 feet. Continue northeast.

2.5 Arrive at Wah Peak at 9,383 feet. Continue north.

3.5 Turnaround point along the ridgeline at 9,356 feet.

7.0 Arrive back at the trailhead.

32 Skyline National Recreation Trail

A day hike along the "skyline" of the Tushar Mountains with spectacular views of several ranges and the east and west side of the Tushar Mountains.

Start: Various trailheads.
Distance: Big Flat to Lake Stream Trailhead is 7.7 miles; Lake Stream to Big John Flat Trailhead, 5.8 miles; Big John Flat Trailhead to Mud Lake, 4 miles.
Difficulty: Moderate.
Trail surface: Forest trail.
Seasons: July through October.
Land status: National forest.
Nearest town: Beaver.

Fees and permits: No fees or permits required.
Maps: USGS Delano Peak and Shelly Baldy Peak quads; National Geographic Trails IIllustrated Fishlake National Forest Map; Fishlake National Forest Travel/Visitor Map.
Trail contacts: Beaver Ranger District, Fishlake National Forest, P.O. Box E, Beaver, UT 84713; (435) 438-2436; www.fs.fed.us/r4/fishlake.

Finding the trailhead: There are three different trailheads on this hike. A good beginning is at the Big Flat Trailhead. Take Highway 153 about 20 miles east from Beaver past Elk Meadows Ski and Summer Resort to Puffer Lake. The highway is paved up to Puffer Lake, then turns to gravel. Big Flat is another 3 miles south. The trailhead is located about a quarter mile south of the Big Flat Guard Station where the road leaves the timber and enters the Big Flat meadow. There is a sign with directions to the trailhead at this junction. The actual trailhead lies 200 yards east of Highway 153 where there is an unloading ramp for horses.

The Lake Stream Trailhead is accessed by Forest Roads 129 and 642 northeast of Puffer Lake. To access Big John Flat, drive 16 miles east of Beaver on Highway 153 to Forest Road 123. Turn left (north) and drive about 5 miles to the trailhead at the north end of Big John Flat. High-clearance vehicles are recommended for most forest roads. *DeLorme: Utah Atlas & Gazetteer:* Page 26 B3.

The Hike

The Skyline Trail was placed on the National Recreation Trail system in 1979. Craggy peaks around the trail give the impression of being on top of the mountains near the "skyline."

Closed to all motorized travel, this trail is an excellent one for those people looking for solitude on foot, mountain bike, or horseback. As a whole the Skyline Trail is rated easy to moderate in difficulty, with only a few short, strenuous sections. All trailheads and junctions along the way are well signed. Since there are different trailheads along this trail, you can plan a short half-day hike or a point-to-point trek with a vehicle shuttle. Several trails interconnect with the Skyline for those who want to spend more than just one day.

The trail crosses elevations ranging from 10,100 feet to 11,100 feet. Mountain peaks seen from the trail range from City Creek Peak (11,161 feet) to Delano Peak

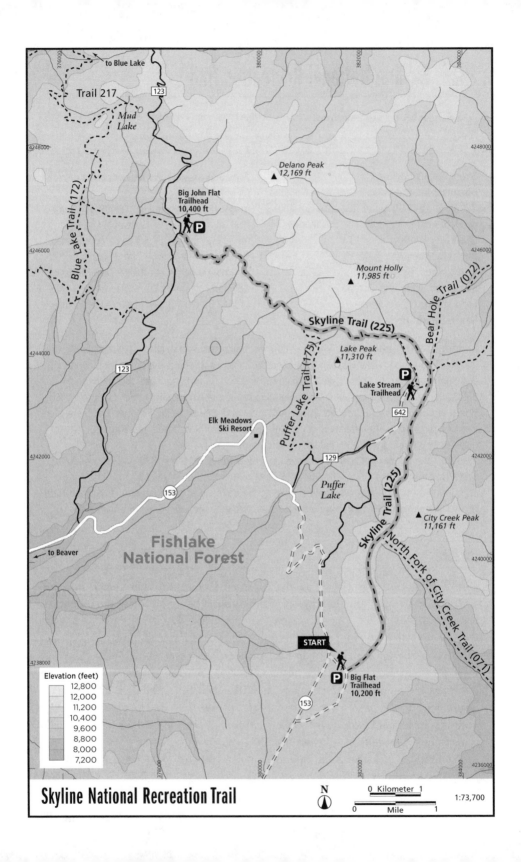

to Blue Lake

Trail 217

123

Mud
Lake

Blue Lake Trail (172)

123

Delano Peak
12,169 ft

Big John Flat
Trailhead
10,400 ft

P

Mount Holly
11,985 ft

Skyline Trail (225)

Bear Hole Trail (072)

Lake Peak
11,310 ft

P

Puffer Lake Trail (175)

Lake Stream
Trailhead

642

Elk Meadows
Ski Resort

129

Skyline Trail (225)

153

Puffer
Lake

City Creek Peak
11,161 ft

to Beaver

Fishlake
National Forest

North Fork of City Creek Trail (071)

START

P

Big Flat
Trailhead
10,200 ft

153

Elevation (feet)

| 12,800 |
| 12,000 |
| 11,200 |
| 10,400 |
| 9,600 |
| 8,800 |
| 8,000 |
| 7,200 |

Skyline National Recreation Trail

N

0   Kilometer   1

0   Mile   1

1:73,700

(12,173 feet). The Piute Reservoir area and the lowlands to the east of the trail in the Circleville Valley lie at 6,000 feet in elevation.

From the Big Flat Trailhead, Skyline Trail 225 heads north past City Creek Peak and the auxiliary trails North Fork of City Creek (071) and Bear Hole (072). After the Bear Hole Trail intersection, Skyline turns left (west) up a short, steep section to the Lake Stream Trailhead. Another steep section takes you past Lake Peak (11,310 feet). Puffer Lake Trail 175 intersects Skyline from the south another 0.5 mile farther and is another good choice for a point-to-point trip. After passing Mount Holly (11,985 feet) and Delano Peak (12,169 feet) on your right (north), the trail ends at the Big John Flat Trailhead.

In 1994 the Skyline National Recreation Trail was extended from the Big John Flat Trailhead northwest to Blue Lake Trail 172. At Trail 172 hikers have two choices: Hike south to Trail 054 and then left (east) to the lower trailhead at Big John Flat (about 4.7 miles), or head north to Blue Lake (6.7 miles) or to Mud Lake on Trail 217 (1.9 miles). Mud Lake is adjacent to FR 123, the Forest Service road used to access the upper Big John Flat Trailhead. —*Contributed by the Fishlake National Forest, Beaver Ranger District*

(Note: Since this hike covers an area with three different trailheads and route options of various lengths, no key points are provided.)

33 Fish Lake Mountains

An overnighter to the Fish Lake Hightop. The hiking is scenic along a high, glaciated plateau, with excellent views of southern Utah from the top.

Start: The trailhead just past Pelican Overlook.
Distance: 13 miles point to point.
Difficulty: Moderate.
Trail surface: Forest trail.
Seasons: Late spring through fall.
Land status: National forest.
Nearest town: Richfield.
Fees and permits: No fees or permits required.

Maps: USGS Fish Lake and Mount Terrill quads; National Geographic Trails Illustrated Fish Lake North and Central Capitol Reef Map.
Trail contacts: Loa/Teasdale Ranger District, Fishlake National Forest, P.O. Box 129, Loa, UT 84747; (435) 836-2811; www.fs.fed.us/r4/fishlake.

Finding the trailhead: Take Highway 25 north from Highway 24 about 13 miles west of Loa. Drive another 10 miles—the last 5 miles with beautiful Fish Lake on your right—and, as the road nears the southwest side of Widgeon Bay, turn left toward Pelican Overlook. The trailhead is about a mile farther at a loop at the end of the road. Caution—the road is a little rough for passenger cars; high-clearance vehicles are recommended.

For the shuttle option, drive about 3 miles beyond the Pelican Overlook turnoff to the Tasha Equestrian Campground. *DeLorme: Utah Atlas & Gazetteer:* Page 27 A6.

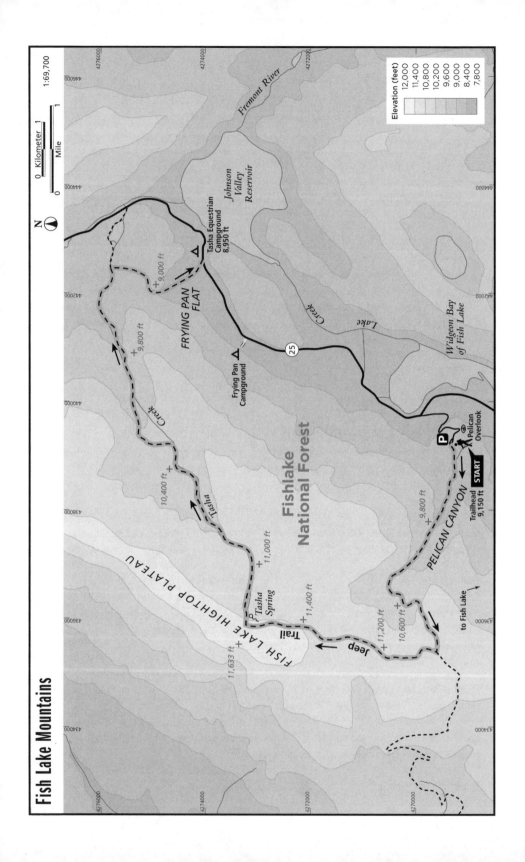

Fish Lake Mountains

1:69,700

Elevation (feet)

| 12,000 |
| 11,400 |
| 10,800 |
| 10,200 |
| 9,600 |
| 9,000 |
| 8,400 |
| 7,800 |

N

0 Kilometer 1

0 Mile 1

Fremont River

Johnson Valley Reservoir

Tasha Equestrian Campground 8,950 ft

+ 9,000 ft

FRYING PAN FLAT

+ 9,800 ft

Frying Pan Campground

25

Creek

Lake

Widgeon Bay of Fish Lake

Creek

10,400 ft +

Tasha

P

Pelican Overlook

9,800 ft +

PELICAN CANYON

Trailhead 9,150 ft

START

Fishlake National Forest

+ 11,000 ft

Tasha Spring

FISH LAKE HIGHTOP PLATEAU

Trail

Jeep

+ 11,400 ft

11,200 ft +

10,600 ft +

to Fish Lake

11,633 ft +

The Hike

The Fish Lake Hightop—a long, narrow, and glaciated plateau—lies just west of Fish Lake, one of the state's largest natural lakes. It offers an excellent overnight hike, climbing through aspen, spruce, and fir to the plateau at more than 11,200 feet.

The recommended 13-mile route begins at Pelican Overlook, climbs to the plateau, then traverses north and descends Tasha Creek to Frying Pan Flat. A car shuttle is required. Of course an out-and-back hike to the Hightop, returning to Pelican Point, is possible and, indeed, popular.

Beginning at about 9,150 feet, the trail climbs steadily up Pelican Canyon for about 2.5 miles before making a steep but short ascent to the plateau. Once on top, the trail makes a gradual, 0.75-mile climb to a jeep trail used mostly by hunters during fall.

Turn right (north) and hike another 2.5 miles to the junction at Tasha Spring. You climb gradually among scrubby subalpine fir to more than 11,400 feet. There are plenty of campsites on top, but consider using a stove for your cooking rather than burning the little bit of wood you may find.

Views are exceptional from the Hightop. On a clear day you can see the Henry Mountains, the LaSals, the Abajos, and the Four Corners area to the east and the many Great Basin ranges to the west.

From early July to mid-September, you may see domestic sheep on the Hightop, but they are loosely herded and therefore not particularly noticeable.

At the Tasha Spring junction, turn right (east). The spring offers a welcome water source after several miles along the dry, glaciated plateau. Be sure to treat all water used for drinking and cooking.

The 5.5-mile, 2,100-foot descent to the Tasha Creek junction is gradual, and the trail parallels Tasha Creek most of the way. At the junction turn right (south), climb a low ridge, and then descend into Frying Pan Flat. The Tasha Equestrian Campground and Highway 25 are at the southeast end of the flat, 1.5 miles from the junction.

Under the Fishlake National Forest Plan, published in 1986, the entire Hightop, from Tasha Creek north to Daniels Pass, is being managed as a nonmotorized recreation area, except during the winter months, when snowmobiles are allowed.
—*Originally contributed by Dave Hall*

Key Points

0.0 Start at the trailhead just past Pelican Overlook.

3.5 Reach the jeep trail on top of the plateau. Turn right (north).

6.0 Arrive at the Tasha Spring junction. Turn right (east).

11.5 Arrive at the junction at Tasha Creek. Turn right (south).

13.0 Arrive at the Tasha Equestrian Campground and Highway 25.

34 Fish Creek Lake

A day hike to the 11,000-foot Boulder Top plateau with opportunities for world-class fishing. The hike is along the Fish Creek section of the Great Western Trail, the trail system that traverses 4,455 miles through Arizona, Utah, Idaho, Wyoming, and Montana. More than 1,600 miles of Great Western Trail exist in Utah, encompassing many of the popular trails in the state as it threads its way through deserts, canyons, meadows, and forests.

Start: Great Western Trail 001 trailhead.
Distance: 11 miles out and back.
Difficulty: Moderate.
Trail surface: Forest trail.
Seasons: June through October.
Land status: National forest.
Nearest town: Torrey.
Fees and permits: No fees or permits required.

Maps: USGS Blind Lake quad; National Geographic Trails Illustrated Fish Lake North and Central Capitol Reef Map.
Trail contacts: Fremont River Ranger District, Dixie National Forest, P.O. Box 129, Loa, UT 84747; (435) 836-2811; www.fs.fed.us/dxnf and www.fs.fed.us/r4/fishlake.

Finding the trailhead: Drive south from Torrey on Highway 12—known locally as the Boulder Mountain Highway—for about 6 miles. Designated as one of the ten most scenic highways in America, it boasts spectacular views along its 32-mile length. Turn right onto Forest Road 179. Follow this dirt road another 5 miles to a junction with Forest Road 520. The trailhead is on your left (south) just past this junction. *DeLorme: Utah Atlas & Gazetteer:* Page 28 C1.

The Hike

The Fish Creek section of Great Western Trail 001 takes you onto Boulder Mountain from its northern edge. The entire 50,000-acre Boulder Top plateau is dotted with a profusion of beautiful little mountain lakes with descriptive names like Bakeskillet, Horseshoe, and Halfmoon. It also is home to mountain lakes with some of the best fishing in the world.

From the trailhead, you follow a very steep and rocky four-wheel-drive road (signed as GREAT WESTERN TRAIL) for about 2 miles to a junction. Bear left (south) to stay on the Great Western Trail. After passing through a narrow canyon, the trail skirts an easily missed and unexpected treasure: A small waterfall, nearly dry by midsummer, cascades down a rocky staircase, draped in moss and wildflowers. Leaving the waterfall, you then finish your climb onto the rocky meadows near Beef and Little Beef Meadows.

Take some time to enjoy the breathtaking views and wildflower-carpeted meadows on Boulder Top, then retrace your steps the 2.5 miles to the trail junction. Turn left (west) onto Wildcat Trail 140 and hike a little over a mile to Fish Creek Lake

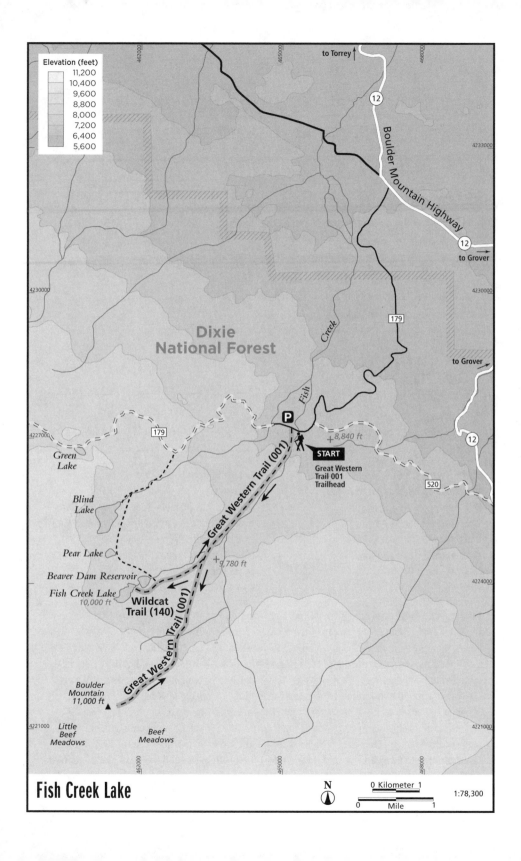

Fish Creek Lake

(one of the north slope lakes classed by the Utah Division of Wildlife Resources as world-class fisheries).

Wildcat Trail 140 continues northwest past Pear and Blind Lakes, also excellent for fishing, and eventually intersects FR 179 near Green Lake. In fact, this part of the trail is one of the most popular areas in the national forest because of the fishing. If you crave solitude, it's best to backtrack to the Great Western Trail and the trailhead. —*Originally contributed by Joe Colwell*

Key Points

0.0	Start at the signed Great Western Trail 001 trailhead.
2.0	Bear left (south) at the junction.
4.5	Reach the rocky Beef and Little Beef Meadows. Turnaround point.
7.0	Return to the trail-road junction. Turn left (west).
8.0	Reach Fish Creek Lake. Turnaround point.
11.0	Arrive back at the trailhead.

35 Fish Creek

A moderate hike up a tributary of the Price River. The Fish Creek drainage is a 25,560-acre semiprimitive, roadless area known for its solitude and good fishing.

Start: Lower Fish Creek Trailhead.
Distance: 10 miles point to point.
Difficulty: Easy to moderate.
Trail surface: Forest trail.
Seasons: May through October.
Land status: National forest.
Nearest town: Scofield.

Fees and permits: No fees or permits required.
Maps: USGS Scofield Reservoir and C Canyon quads; Northeastern Utah Multipurpose Map.
Trail contacts: Price Ranger District, Manti-LaSal National Forest, 599 West Price River Drive, Price, UT 84501; (435) 637-2817; www.fs.fed.us/r4/mantilasal.

Finding the trailhead: Drive south from Provo and up Spanish Fork Canyon on U.S. Highway 89/6. Five miles past Soldier Summit, turn right onto Highway 96 toward Scofield Reservoir. Continue 16 miles to the town of Scofield. Go to the westernmost north-south street in town and follow it north around the west side of the reservoir. After about 4 miles, Forest Road 123 branches off to the left and heads up the south side of Fish Creek for 1.5 miles before ending at the Fish Creek Campground and Trailhead. The access road to the campground is not maintained and becomes impassable after a heavy rainstorm. *DeLorme: Utah Atlas & Gazetteer:* Page 46 C2.

To leave a vehicle at the upper trailhead, drive back to Scofield and continue south on Highway 96. Turn right (west) onto Highway 264 and drive to its junction with Highway 31. Turn right (north) onto Skyline Drive and drive about 14 miles to the signed trailhead. *DeLorme: Utah Atlas & Gazetteer:* Page 46 B1.

Fish Creek

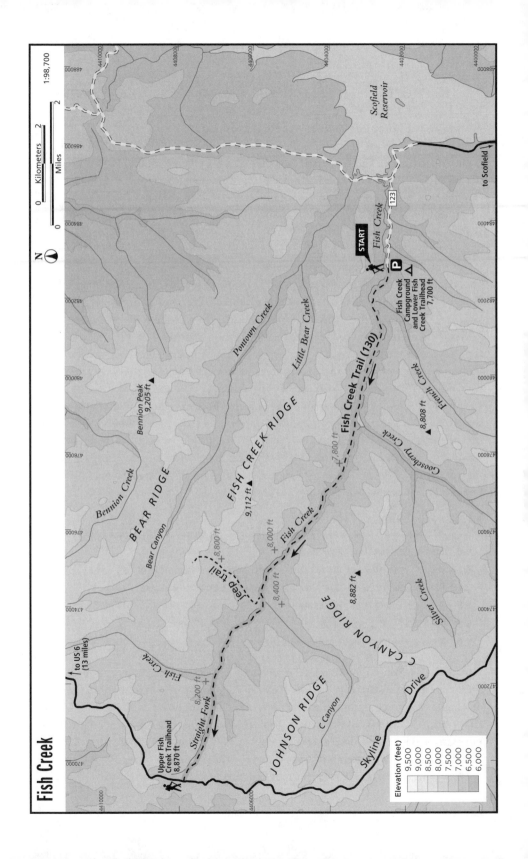

Elevation (feet)
9,500
9,000
8,500
8,000
7,500
7,000
6,500
6,000

1:98,700

0 Kilometers 2

0 Miles 2

N

START

Fish Creek Trail (130)

Fish Creek Campground and Lower Fish Creek Trailhead 7,700 ft

Scofield Reservoir

123

to Scofield

Fish Creek

French Creek

Gooseberry Creek

8,808 ft

8,882 ft

7,800 ft

8,000 ft

8,400 ft

8,800 ft

Jeep trail

Straight Fork

8,200 ft

Fish Creek

Upper Fish Creek Trailhead 8,870 ft

to US 6 (13 miles)

Bennion Creek

Bennion Peak 9,205 ft

Pontown Creek

Little Bear Creek

BEAR RIDGE

Bear Canyon

FISH CREEK RIDGE

9,112 ft

C CANYON RIDGE

Slinket Creek

JOHNSON RIDGE

C Canyon

Skyline Drive

The Hike

The Fish Creek Trail is a National Recreation Trail and offers a relatively moderate hike, gaining 1,100 feet from the trailhead to Skyline Drive, about 10 miles in. There is lush river bottom vegetation and some fine fishing.

The view from the trailhead is a good indication of the terrain you'll see traveling up the drainage. The broad, flat canyon bottom is filled with willows, and meandering Fish Creek is often obstructed with beaver dams.

The trail begins on the west side of the campground and winds up the south side of the canyon for 0.75 mile before reaching French Creek. This first segment of the trail is one of the best on the hike. The trail climbs from 7,700 feet through a cool and shady aspen-fir forest—a relief on a hot summer day.

As you hike pay attention to the willow-choked stream below. Beaver and deer abound at dusk, and it's sometimes possible to spot a moose, a member of an introduced herd. Unfortunately, many of these magnificent animals have been lost to poachers. Also notice the many bird species in the dense willow stands.

At French Creek the trail crosses the stream and continues on the north side of the canyon. From here, travel is in direct sun on a hot, dry sagebrush hillside. The trail does not continue up the cooler, forested slope, because generations of anglers have beaten a path on the north side of the canyon, closer to the creek.

About 2 miles up the canyon from French Creek, a tributary enters from the southwest. This is the Gooseberry Creek–Silver Creek drainage. About 3 miles farther, the trail crosses Fish Creek and follows its south side, passing C Canyon on the left (southwest) in less than a mile. Shortly after, the trail crosses back to the north side of Fish Creek and then reaches the confluence with Straight Fork. Follow Straight Fork northwest for 2 miles to Skyline Drive.

Key Points

0.0 Start at the lower Fish Creek Trailhead.

0.75 French Creek enters on the left (southwest). Cross to the north side of Fish Creek.

2.75 The Gooseberry Creek-Silver Creek drainage enters from the southwest.

6.5 C Canyon enters from the southwest.

8.0 Confluence with Straight Fork.

10.0 Arrive at the upper Fish Creek Trailhead.

Options: The Fish Creek drainage offers a variety of long-distance options if you shuttle a car. For instance, at the C Creek drainage, you can continue up C Canyon or explore the upper tributaries of Fish Creek. Skyline Drive is about 5 miles up either drainage. Alternatively, you can go north from C Creek 1.5 miles on a trail to Fish Creek Ridge and drop down another 0.75 mile into Pontown/Bear Creek, traveling downstream about 6 miles to a dirt road at the mouth of Pontown Canyon.
—*Originally contributed by Linda and Rick Van Wagenen*

36 San Rafael River

A long day hike or overnighter along the San Rafael River in the Glen Canyon geologic formations. The seclusion of the region and its unusual beauty offer a unique experience.

Start: Fuller Bottom Trailhead.
Distance: 15 miles point to point.
Difficulty: Moderate with bushwhacking, route finding, and river crossings.
Trail surface: Trail, wash bottom.
Seasons: Spring and fall. Watch for high runoff in late May and flash-flood potential July through September.
Land status: Bureau of Land Management (BLM) wilderness study area.
Nearest town: Castle Dale.

Fees and permits: No fees or permits required.
Maps: USGS Bottleneck Peak and Sids Mountain quads; Northeastern and Southeastern Utah Multipurpose Maps.
Trail contacts: Price Field Office, Bureau of Land Management, 125 South 600 W., Price, UT 84501; (435) 636-3600; www.blm.gov/utah/price (a brochure about this hike is available on the Web page).

Finding the trailhead: To reach the upstream river crossing and the beginning of your hike, drive east from Highway 10 on a dirt road 2 miles north of Castle Dale. (This road, known as the Green River Cutoff, meets combined U.S. Highway 6/191 to the east, northwest of Green River.) After about 13 miles, you reach Buckhorn Well—a tank, pump house, and water trough. From this junction, turn right (south), then bear right and follow the signs toward the San Rafael River to Fuller Bottom. It's 5.4 miles to the river crossing. You have to pass through two gates along the way; leave the gates as you found them, and be sure to respect private property. This road can be rough following bad weather. High-clearance vehicles are recommended. Contact the BLM office in Price for the latest report. Park on the high terrain on the north side of the river.

To shuttle a car to the San Rafael Bridge Recreation Site for the point-to-point trip, continue east past Buckhorn Well for 2 miles and turn right (southeast) toward the river. Descend Buckhorn Wash for about 9 miles to the river. The recreation site is on your left just after you cross the river. *DeLorme: Utah Atlas & Gazetteer:* Page 39 B4.

The Hike

Numerous washes and the San Rafael River have cut a path through the thick sandstone layers in the Glen Canyon Series of the San Rafael Swell. Panoramas can be viewed from the top of the swell as you drive in and out of the region, and unique riparian habitat exists in the washes and canyon bottoms.

From the beginning of your hike at the Fuller Bottom Trailhead to the finish at the San Rafael Bridge Recreation Site southeast of Buckhorn Well, you will lose less than 200 feet in elevation over about 15 miles. The canyon walls will tower higher and higher above you as the river cuts deeper into the San Rafael Swell.

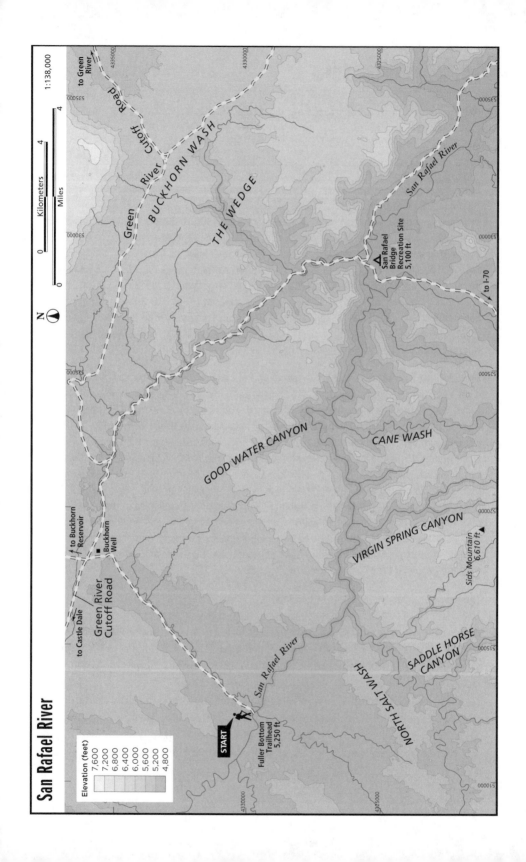

San Rafael River

Elevation (feet)
7,600
7,200
6,800
6,400
6,000
5,600
5,200
4,800

1:138,000

N

Kilometers
0   4   4

Miles
0   4

to Castle Dale

to Buckhorn Reservoir

Green River Cutoff Road

Buckhorn Well

Green River Cutoff Road

BUCKHORN WASH

THE WEDGE

to Green River

San Rafael River

San Rafael Bridge Recreation Site
5,100 ft

to I-70

San Rafael River

GOOD WATER CANYON

CANE WASH

VIRGIN SPRING CANYON

Sids Mountain
6,610 ft

SADDLE HORSE CANYON

NORTH SALT WASH

START

Fuller Bottom Trailhead
5,250 ft

San Rafael River

Day hikes and out-and-back overnighters are possible from the trailhead. Carry your own water unless you take the proper steps to purify river water. Also, prepare to get wet (old running shoes or lightweight canvas boots are recommended), since numerous river crossings are necessary. An inner tube or small inflatable raft would aid crossing in high water. Life preservers are recommended for small children, although this might be a less-than-enjoyable and difficult hike for most kids.

From the trailhead, follow the river downstream. Notice the river cutting through various geologic layers—specifically, the Carmel (top), Navajo, Kayenta, Wingate, and Chinle formations.

Four miles downstream, North Salt Wash enters from the southwest. If you have time, this canyon offers interesting exploring. In Saddle Horse Canyon—4 miles up North Salt Wash from the San Rafael River—you will find a giant monolith and small wetland areas. Ascents of Sids Mountain can be made from this canyon. Sids Mountain, with its high point at 6,610 feet, is 1,200 feet above the river. There are overlooks of Virgin Spring Canyon, the Wedge, and, of course, the San Rafael River.

Continuing downstream on the San Rafael for another 2.5 miles, you reach Virgin Spring Canyon entering from the south. This canyon also offers interesting possibilities for exploration. The route has a difficult spot after about a mile, and inexperienced hikers might have some trouble here.

Numerous cottonwood groves along the river provide pleasant campsites. Be sure to leave them as you found them, because the area gets more use each year.

Wildlife is abundant along the river. Especially interesting in the San Rafael region are the numerous amphibians, including the Woodhouse's, red-spotted, and spadefoot toads. Also look for the speckled dace (a fish). The toads breed in areas that are not accessible to the dace. The Woodhouse's and red-spotted toads breed in the same springs, but at different times. Look for the dace in isolated pools up side washes—far from the populations in the river.

Three and a half miles downstream from Virgin Spring Canyon, Good Water Canyon enters from the north. Just around the corner—half a mile away—Cane Wash joins the San Rafael. This is a long canyon, originating 15 miles to the south. Its interesting geology and many springs provide a rewarding side excursion.

The rest of the route after Cane Wash is on a well-used trail on the south side of the river. Hike about 4.5 miles to the river crossing and the end of your trip at the recreation site. —*Originally contributed by Peter Hovingh*

Key Points

- **0.0**   Start at the Fuller Bottom Trailhead.
- **4.0**   North Salt Wash enters from the southwest.
- **6.5**   Virgin Spring Canyon enters from the south.
- **10.0**   Good Water Canyon enters from the north.
- **10.5**   Cane Wash enters from the south.
- **15.0**   Arrive at the San Rafael Bridge Recreation Site.

37 Lower Black Box

A wet day hike or overnighter through the Lower Black Box of the San Rafael River, located within the Mexican Mountain Wilderness Study Area.

Start: The road closure at the wilderness study area boundary.
Distance: 11-mile lollipop loop.
Difficulty: Extremely strenuous (not recommended for children).
Trail surface: Wading and swimming in the San Rafael River.
Seasons: Early summer and fall.
Land status: Bureau of Land Management (BLM) wilderness study area.

Nearest town: Castle Dale.
Fees and permits: No fees or permits required.
Maps: USGS Spotted Wolf Canyon and Drowned Hole Draw quads; Southeastern Utah Multipurpose Map.
Trail contacts: Price Field Office, Bureau of Land Management, 125 South 600 W., Price, UT 84501; (435) 636-3600; www.blm.gov/utah/price.

Finding the trailhead: Drive east from Highway 10 on a dirt road 2 miles north of Castle Dale. (This road, known as the Green River Cutoff, meets combined U.S. Highway 6/191 to the east, northwest of Green River.) After about 13 miles you reach Buckhorn Well—a tank, pump house, and water trough. Continue east past Buckhorn Well for 2 miles and turn right (southeast) toward the river. Descend Buckhorn Wash for about 9 miles to the San Rafael River. Follow the road south along the river another 13 miles to Sinkhole Flat and a signed junction. Turn left here. (The trailhead also can be easily accessed from Interstate 70. Take exit 129 to the northeast 5.5 miles to the signed junction at Sinkhole Flat.) After about 2 miles turn left again, passing up the road to Jerrys Flat. About 3 miles farther along, a 10-mile loop begins around Jackass Benches. Take the right fork of the loop, and at 3.6 miles look for a faint road heading to the east. Drive about 2.5 miles to the road closure at the wilderness study area boundary. *DeLorme: Utah Atlas & Gazetteer:* Page 39 C5.

The Hike

The Lower Black Box of the San Rafael River provides one of the more interesting river hikes in the state. The San Rafael area has not received the attention other rivers have. Therefore, chances are you won't be running into many other hikers.

The trip involves about a 2.3-mile hike down to the river, another 2.5 miles along the rim on the east side of the river, and then a 4-mile hike/wade through the Lower Black Box. The entire trip can be done in a day, or you can backpack to the river and camp near Sulphur Spring.

Roads to the trailhead are seasonal and can present problems following bad weather. Call the BLM to check on conditions. Also, the BLM reports that road signs are occasionally vandalized and are slow to be replaced. Follow your maps carefully.

Be sure to check water conditions. The trip should not be attempted in late spring when water may be cool and very high. Flash floods can be a problem, so get

Lower Black Box

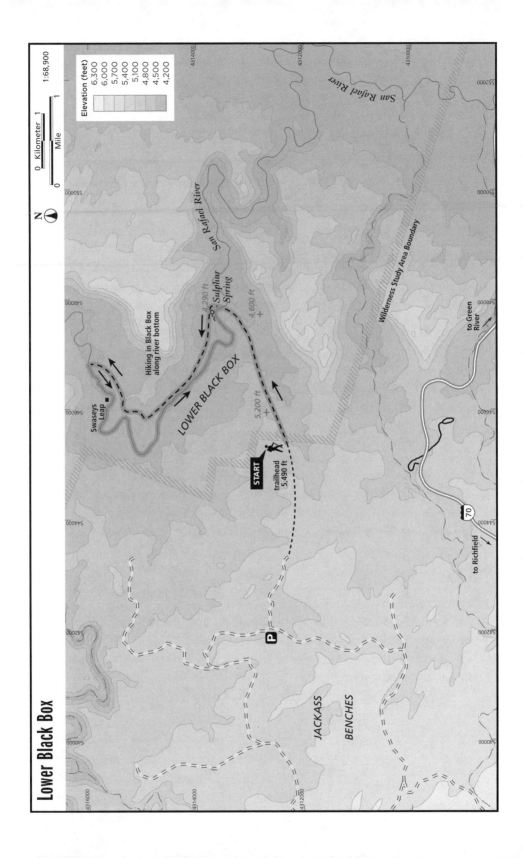

a good weather forecast and take along river survival gear. A trip in early fall is beautiful. Packing in water is recommended, unless proper purification methods are used.

A good camping spot exists at the river half a mile downstream from Sulphur Spring. If you camp here, you can hike upstream along the east side the following morning and then hike/float down through the Lower Black Box, arriving back at your camp.

The hike along the east side of the San Rafael is not a difficult one. Cross the river at Sulphur Spring and follow a path to the northwest, keeping the river to your left. After about 2.4 miles—half a mile upstream from Swaseys Leap—descend to the river at the cottonwood trees.

Here you begin the hike and wade through the Lower Black Box. Take precautions. You should be prepared to hike in the river (dry bank hiking is rare), often in extremely cold water that is chest deep or deeper. The first 1.5 miles below Swaseys Leap contain steep boulder drops. Plastic liners or dry bags in your pack are recommended, and a life jacket can help through the deeper sections of river.

The 4-mile hike through the Box is spectacular as you cut deeper and deeper into sandstone layers. You will pass under Swaseys Leap, a bridge over the upper end of the canyon. The bridge was used as a crossing for sheep, and several tales have developed around it. One story has it that one of the Swasey brothers acquired his brother's flock of sheep by jumping the gap with his horse and winning a bet. The story is also told that the Wild Bunch, on the run after a bank robbery, eluded a posse by leaping the gap.

Toward the end of the hike, you reach Sulphur Spring, a warm springs along the river. Copper sulfate is forming in one of the springs.

If you're camping, continue another half mile below Sulphur Spring to reach your campsite. If you spend another night here after your trip through the Box, you may want to hike a few miles downstream the next day. The scenery is spectacular as the river cuts through the San Rafael Reef. —*Originally contributed by Peter Hovingh*

Key Points

0.0 Start at the wilderness study area road closure.

2.3 Arrive at Sulphur Spring. Cross the river and follow a path to the northwest.

4.7 Descend to the river to begin the hike/wade downstream.

8.7 Arrive back at Sulphur Spring.

11.0 Arrive back at the road closure.

38 Upper Black Box

A hike/float through the Upper Black Box of the San Rafael River. This route offers canyoneering adventure in a striking canyon setting.

Start: The flats above Lockhart Box.
Distance: 13 miles point to point.
Difficulty: Extremely strenuous (not recommended for children).
Trail surface: Wading and swimming in the San Rafael River.
Seasons: Early summer and fall.
Land status: Bureau of Land Management (BLM) wilderness study area.
Nearest town: Green River.

Fees and permits: No fees or permits required.
Maps: USGS Devils Hole, Mexican Mountain, Drowned Hole Draw quads; Northeastern and Southeastern Utah Multipurpose Map.
Trail contacts: Price Field Office, Bureau of Land Management, 125 South 600 W., Price, UT 84501; (435) 636-3600; www.blm.gov/utah/price.

Finding the trailhead: The most popular access point starts near the Lockhart Box. Drive west of Green River on Interstate 70 for about 27 miles. Take exit 129 and drive north for about 18 miles to the San Rafael Bridge Recreation Site. Drive across to the north side of the swinging bridge and continue southeast for about 7.5 miles to Lockhart Box. A vehicle can be shuttled 5 miles farther to the end of the road, near the takeout point at Mexican Bend. *DeLorme: Utah Atlas & Gazetteer:* Page 39 B5.

The Hike

The Black Boxes of the San Rafael River are located on BLM-administered lands in the northeastern part of the San Rafael Swell. These canyon segments possess spectacular scenery and geology, and provide a unique and challenging adventure. The narrow, deeply incised canyons meander through the Coconino sandstone, the oldest exposed formation in the swell.

The canyons can be hiked if water flows are less than 60 to 75 cubic feet per second (cfs). Twenty-five cfs is preferable, although a lot of swimming and wading will still be necessary. Recommended flows for tubing are 60 to 75 cfs. Life jackets and inner tubes are advised regardless of the flow. You can measure the river's depth midstream under the swinging bridge near the San Rafael Bridge Recreation Site. To minimize the risks of high water, the maximum depth should not exceed 25 inches. Obtain current flow information by calling (801) 539–1311 or going online at www.usgs.gov.

Allow a minimum of twelve hours to complete the 13-mile section from Lockhart Box to Mexican Bend. There are a few benches in the upper portion of the canyon that would be suitable for an overnight bivouac.

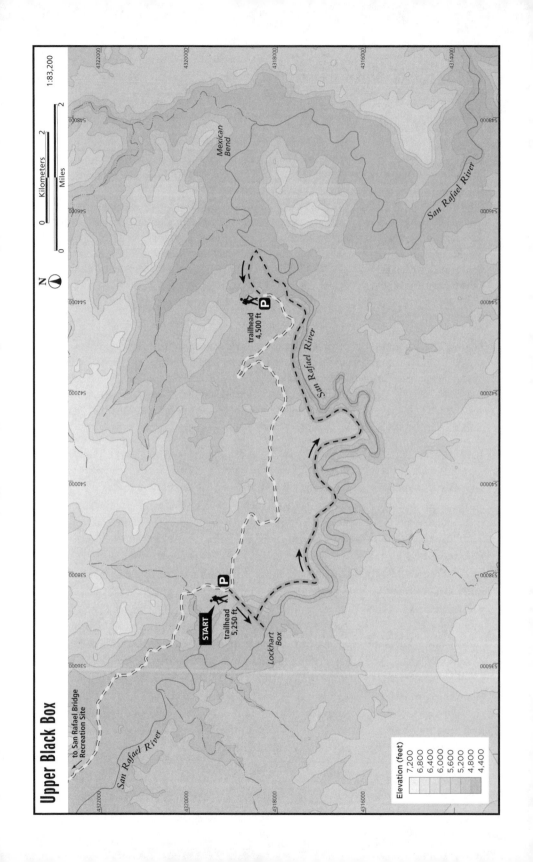

Upper Black Box

1:83,200

N

Kilometers

Miles

Elevation (feet)

7,200
6,800
6,400
6,000
5,600
5,200
4,800
4,400

San Rafael River

to San Rafael Bridge
Recreation Site

START

trailhead
5,250 ft

P

Lockhart
Box

San Rafael River

trailhead
4,500 ft

P

Mexican
Bend

San Rafael River

From the flats above Lockhart Box, walk in a southwesterly direction for 0.5 mile along an old stock trail and descend to the river.

The rapids in the Upper Black Box increase in frequency and difficulty as you progress downstream. There are several large boulder fields that require some scrambling. The river disappears into the rocks in some places, requiring scouting or portages. About three-quarters of the way through the canyon, there is a large rockfall. Use a 20-foot section of rope to negotiate this stretch.

The last few miles are flat water, which you will need to swim. The canyon ends at Mexican Bend. Exit here and follow the first drainage back to the road and your waiting vehicle. —*Originally contributed by the BLM*

Key Points

0.0 Start at the flats above Lockhart Box.

0.5 Descend to the river at Lockhart Box. Hike/wade downstream.

13.0 Arrive at Mexican Bend.

Honorable Mentions

Central Utah

| Delano Peak

The Tushar Mountains, east of Beaver, don't have the reputation of the spectacular Wasatch Range near Salt Lake. Therefore, few hikers realize there are higher peaks in the Tushars—most notably 12,169-foot Delano Peak. This part of the Fishlake National Forest offers high-alpine scenery and excellent opportunites for day hikes or overnight backpacking trips. The Tushar Mountains were at one time home to one the state's largest deer herds. There are three approaches to Delano Peak (and Mount Holly, 11,985 feet, to the southeast), ranging in distance from 1.5 to 6 miles. All can be hiked individually or as part of a longer loop hike, necessitating a car shuttle. Portions of the routes are along existing trails, although once you're above timberline, you'll be traversing your own trail much of the way.

For the longer hike, take Highway 153 about 18 miles east of Beaver to Elk Meadows Ski and Summer Resort. Continue another mile on Highway 153 past Elk Meadows to the beginning of Trail 175, which leaves the highway on your left (northeast). The trailhead is not signed, but you should be able to spot the blazes on trees.

A second, more primitive approach to Delano Peak begins from Big John Flat Road (Forest Road 123). Drive about 16 miles east of Beaver on Highway 153 and turn left (north) onto FR 123. Follow this dirt-and-gravel road (not recommended for low-clearance vehicles) 3.6 miles north to the flat. Keep to the right and proceed another 1.8 miles to the trailhead. (You should be about half a mile past Griffith Creek.) The trail begins on an old jeep road that has been closed and posted with a NO MOTORIZED VEHICLE sign.

The third and easiest route to Delano Peak is to approach from farther north. Continue on FR 123 past this trailhead and drive about 3 miles to the ridgeline above Mud Lake. As the road crosses through the ridgetop, watch for the Forest Service radio repeater just to your right. Park here and travel cross-country to Delano Peak, about 2 miles to the south. For more information contact Beaver Ranger District, Fishlake National Forest, P.O. Box E, Beaver, UT 84713; (435) 438–2436; www.fs.fed.us/r4/fishlake. *DeLorme: Utah Atlas & Gazetteer:* Page 26 B3. *—Originally contributed by Tim Randle*

J Bullion Canyon Trail System

The upper Bullion Canyon drainage encompasses some of the most wild and scenic country in the Fishlake National Forest. It is a land filled with wildflowers, crystal-clear creeks, and towering peaks. This high-mountain paradise is crisscrossed by a series of trails first upturned by wildlife and later used by Indians, gold miners, and forest rangers. The trails consist of five periodically maintained and relatively well-signed routes. A 10- to 12-mile loop hike can be made by linking together four of the trails. A brochure titled *Hiking and Horseback Travel in the Upper Bullion Canyon Drainage* has information and a map and is available from the Beaver Ranger District.

To access the Bullion Pasture Trailhead, drive 16 miles east of Beaver on Highway 153 to Forest Road 123. Turn left and drive north, passing Big John Flat and Mud Lake, to the trailhead at Bullion Pasture below Mount Belknap. High-clearance vehicles are recommended on this road. For more information contact Beaver Ranger District, Fishlake National Forest, P.O. Box E, Beaver, UT 84713; (435) 438–2436; www.fs.fed.us/r4/fishlake. *DeLorme: Utah Atlas & Gazetteer:* Page 26 B3.

K Boulder Top Trails

Boulder Mountain, south of Torrey, is one of the less publicized wonders of southern Utah. It ascends to more than 11,000 feet, starting at Capitol Reef National Park and climbing from piñon-juniper slickrock canyons, through ponderosa pine forests, aspen hillsides, and spruce-fir forests, up 500-foot basalt cliffs onto the subalpine meadows and forests of Boulder Top. The views from the Boulder Mountain Highway (Highway 12) are spectacular enough to gain it recognition as one of the ten most scenic highways in America. The views from the rim of Boulder Top, 2,000 feet higher, are even more spectacular. The LaSal Mountains east of Moab, the Henry Mountains, the San Rafael Swell, Navajo Mountain, Monument Valley, and even the Kaibab Plateau (north rim of the Grand Canyon) in Arizona can all be seen in the breathtaking panorama. Four major trails are easily accessed from Highway 12 and travel short but steep distances to Boulder Top. The trail to Bowns Point is the shortest at 1 mile.

All four trails are accessed from Highway 12. Drive about 14 miles north from Boulder Town to Forest Road 554 and turn left (west) for 1 mile to the Great Western Trail (Bowns Point) access trailhead on your left. The 1-mile climb to Bowns Point, at the southeast point of Boulder Top, offers the most panoramic views.

To reach the Behunin Point Trail, continue north on Highway 12 for 6 miles and turn left (west) onto Forest Road 247 (Pleasant Creek Trail 158). Almost 2 miles on an unimproved four-wheel-drive road brings you to the trailhead of Behunin Point Trail 117, which takes off to the left, roughly following Behunin Creek and climbing 4 miles to Boulder Top.

For Meeks Lake, continue on FR 247 for 0.5 mile to the trailhead for Meeks Lake Trail 118 on your right. Trail 118 connects with Great Western Trail 001 and Rim Trail 005.

Two miles farther north on Highway 12, Chokecherry Point Trail leaves the highway and accesses Boulder Top via Forest Road 177. For more information contact Fremont River Ranger District, Dixie National Forest, P.O. Box 129, Loa, UT

84747; (435) 836–2811; www.fs.fed.us/dxnf and www.fs.fed.us/r4/fishlake. *DeLorme: Utah Atlas & Gazetteer:* Page 28 C1. —*Originally contributed by Joe Colwell*

L Slickrock Trail

Boulder Mountain is a scenic "island in the desert" that borders the western boundary of Capitol Reef National Park. The fantastic slickrock wilderness of the park gradually ascends onto a flat piñon- and juniper-covered bench before climbing onto the summit of Boulder Top at more than 11,000 feet in elevation. The 25-mile Slickrock Trail 120 follows the original wagon road that once connected Grover to Boulder Town. The well-marked trail maintains a general elevation of about 7,600 feet but ascends and descends several drainages as it follows the base of the Navajo sandstone escarpment—the top of which is modern Highway 12 (a designated National Forest Scenic Byway rated as one of the ten most scenic drives in the United States). You hike across areas of slickrock Navajo sandstone, old-growth ponderosa pine, and piñon-juniper forests. Interesting geology along the trail includes black basalt boulders sitting in grand profusion on white sandstone.

There are numerous access points from Highway 12 to the Slickrock Trail. You could choose one of the Forest Service campgrounds along the highway—Oak Creek, Pleasant Creek, or Singletree, or the undeveloped campground at Lower Bowns Reservoir, 4 miles east of the highway on Forest Road 181—to use as a base camp to explore the Slickrock Trail. Or you can hike the entire trail north to south with a vehicle shuttle. To access the north end of the trail, take Highway 12 southeast of Grover about 0.5 mile to its junction with Miners Mountain Road. Turn left (east) and drive 2 miles to the Slickrock Trail 120 trailhead. The first section of trail to Happy Valley is designated as shared use (off-road vehicles are allowed); from there to the Teasdale Ranger District boundary is horse and foot use only. For more information contact Fremont River Ranger District, Dixie National Forest, P.O. Box 129, Loa, UT 84747; (435) 836–2811; www.fs.fed.us/dxnf and www.fs.fed.us /r4/fishlake. *DeLorme: Utah Atlas & Gazetteer:* Page 28 C1. —*Originally contributed by Joe Colwell*

M Left Fork of Huntington Creek

The trail along the Left Fork of Huntington Creek is a National Recreation Trail in a 31,100-acre semiprimitive roadless area. It follows the right (north) side of the river, gaining about 800 feet in 5.8 miles to an optional trailhead on Miller Flat Road. As you begin the gentle climb, notice Seeley Mountain (10,360 feet) to the west and the several 10,000-foot peaks of Candland Mountain to the north and west. The stream channel flows over sedimentary formations that make up the Wasatch Plateau—interbedded layers of sandstone, shale, and limestone. The predominant life-forms of the area are typical of the Canadian and Hudsonian life zones—aspen, Douglas fir, white fir, and spruce-fir forests. The patient and discerning hiker may see mule deer, elk, and beaver, as well as a variety of small mammals and birds. Black bear, mountain lion, coyote, and bobcat also frequent the drainage but are rarely seen. Rainbow and cutthroat trout are the most common species in the stream. Brown and eastern brook trout inhabit the lower portions of the Huntington.

To reach the trailhead, drive 20 miles south of Price to Huntington on Highway 10. Turn right (northwest) onto Highway 31 at a sign indicating Huntington Canyon and Cleveland Reservoir. Continue northwest up Huntington Canyon about 18 miles. A sign at the fork of the river identifies the Forks of Huntington Campground and the Left Fork of Huntington Creek Trailhead to the left (west). Drive up the Left Fork Road about 0.5 mile to the end of the campground and the trailhead. For more information contact Price Ranger District, Manti-LaSal National Forest, 599 West Price River Drive, Price, UT 84501; (435) 637–2817; www.fs.fed.us/r4/mantilasal. *DeLorme: Utah Atlas & Gazetteer:* Page 46 D2. —*Originally contributed by Linda and Rick Van Wagenen*

N Thompson Canyon

The Book Cliffs have never been a popular hiking area—a real mystery to those few hikers who have traveled through this rugged and beautiful country. In fact, most people think of the Book Cliffs only as the 800-foot cliff along the route between Price and Green River. The Book Cliffs have much, much more to offer. Elk, deer, and a healthy population of mountain lions inhabit the area, although your chances of spotting a lion are minimal. Desert bighorn sheep have been spotted in Rattlesnake Canyon to the northwest. And you'll probably spot a number of hawks and eagles along the hike. Thompson Canyon, east of Green River, puts you on the doorstep of millions of acres of splendid backcountry. This 13-mile overnighter takes you from about 6,000 feet along the creek bottom to the top of Thompson Canyon at more than 8,000 feet. The Book Cliffs have few maintained hiking trails. Canyon bottoms and ridgelines provide excellent walking terrain, but all hikers should carry the appropriate topographic maps and know how to use them.

To reach the trailhead, drive east of Green River on Interstate 70. After about 25 miles, turn left into the little town of Thompson Springs. Drive through town and into Thompson Canyon on a good, graded road. In about 4 miles, just after a developed rock art site on the left, the road splits—the right fork heading up Sego Canyon, the left up Thompson. Drive up Thompson Canyon for about 3 miles until the end of the maintained county road at a developed water site for the town of Thompson Springs. Look for a parking place here because the road becomes less used beyond this point. (Keep in mind that you are on private property in this part of the canyon, so respect the owner's rights.) For more information contact the Moab Field Office, Bureau of Land Management, 82 East Dogwood, Moab, UT 84532; (435) 259–2100; www.ut.blm.gov. *DeLorme: Utah Atlas & Gazetteer:* Page 40 B2. —*Originally contributed by Bill Hargraves*

Southern Utah: The National Parks, Pine Valley Mountains, BLM Wilderness, Escalante River, Henry Mountains, and Grand Gulch Area

39 Pine Valley Mountains

A moderately difficult two-day loop hike in the Pine Valley Wilderness. The range is located in the extreme southwest corner of the state and offers backcountry solitude in rugged country.

Start: Whipple Trailhead.
Distance: 17-mile loop.
Difficulty: Strenuous.
Trail surface: Rocky forest trail.
Seasons: Midsummer through fall.
Land status: Wilderness area, national forest.
Nearest town: Enterprise.

Fees and permits: The Pine Valley Recreation Area charges a $2.00-per-car fee to park.
Maps: USGS Signal Peak and Grass Valley quads; Pine Valley Wilderness Map.
Trail contacts: Pine Valley Ranger District, Dixie National Forest, 196 East Tabernacle, St. George, UT 84770; (435) 688-3246; www.fs.fed.us/dxnf.

Finding the trailhead: From Interstate 15 in Cedar City, take Highway 56 west about 30 miles to Newcastle. Turn left and drive southwest about 9 miles to the junction of Highway 18 near Enterprise. Turn left and continue another 15 miles to Central, turning left again. The town of Pine Valley is 8 miles up the road. Turn left at the Pine Valley Church and continue the final 3.5 miles to the Whipple Trailhead in the Pine Valley Campground and Recreation Area. *DeLorme: Utah Atlas & Gazetteer:* Page 17 C4.

The Hike

The Pine Valley Mountains rise 3,500 feet from the floor of the Colorado Plateau and Great Basin to 10,000-foot peaks forested by virgin Engelmann spruce. Water is one of the most valuable resources in the range. The Pine Valleys are a major source for the Ash Creek, Virgin River, and Santa Clara River drainages. This mountain island surrounded by desert offers wildlife habitat for a large cougar population, mule deer, golden eagle, and beaver.

The loop hike—about 17 miles total—involves considerable altitude change and should only be attempted by hikers in good condition.

All drinking water obtained along the trail should be treated. It's a good idea to fill your water bottles with fresh water (available at the recreation area) before starting the hike.

From the trailhead at 7,050 feet, the Whipple Trail ascends almost 5 miles to Whipple Valley at 9,100 feet. The trail is well defined and easy to follow. About halfway along, you cross Hop Canyon, the only water source before Whipple Valley (usually dry by August 1, earlier in dry years). The 2,000-foot elevation gain only represents the net difference on the topo map. The hike goes up and down quite a bit along the way, including two significant climbs out of Hop Canyon.

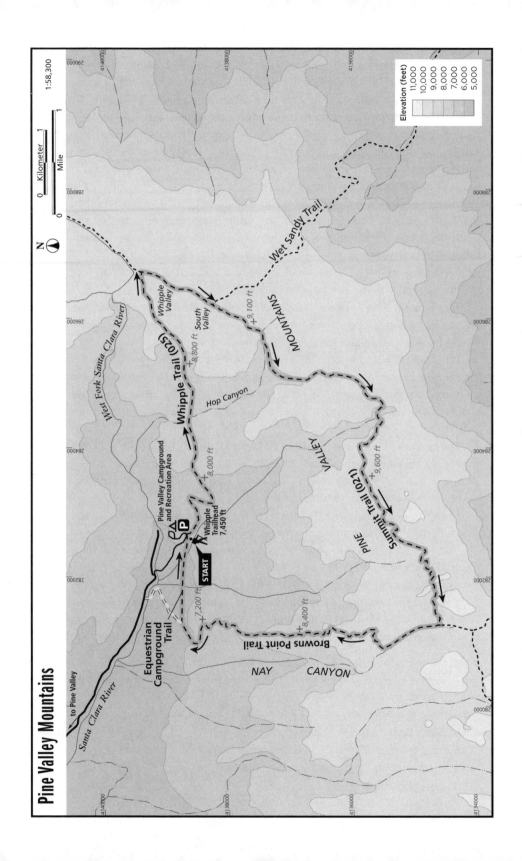

Pine Valley Mountains

Elevation (feet)

11,000
10,000
9,000
8,000
7,000
6,000
5,000

1:58,300

N

0   Kilometer   1

0   Mile   1

Santa Clara River

to Pine Valley

West Fork Santa Clara River

Whipple Valley

Whipple Trail (025)

+ 8,800 ft   South Valley

+ 9,100 ft

MOUNTAINS

Hop Canyon

+ 8,000 ft

Pine Valley Campground
and Recreation Area

Whipple Trailhead
7,450 ft

START

+ 7,200 ft

Equestrian
Campground
Trail

PINE   VALLEY

Summit Trail (021)

+ 9,600 ft

Browns Point Trail

+ 8,400 ft

NAY   CANYON

Wet Sandy Trail

A trail sign showing directions and destinations along the Summit Trail indicates that you have reached Whipple Valley. Whipple Valley has water only in spring and early summer. A tributary of the Left Fork of the Santa Clara River runs through the middle of the valley, and water stands among the grass and clumps of flowers on the valley floor. During this time of year, the standing water can extend from the tree line at the edge of the valley to the streambanks, so be cautious. All that water early in the year and the steel shoes of a horse or the lugged soles of a hiker's boots can lead to serious trail erosion.

Turn right (south) at the junction with the Summit Trail. Continue on the Summit Trail 1 mile to South Valley. The Wet Sandy Trail heads left (southeast) at the southeast corner of the valley, but you should continue south on the Summit Trail into the trees.

Cross a stream (Hop Canyon) within a mile. If you find water, stock up. It's about 6.5 difficult miles to the Browns Point Trail.

The Summit Trail between South Valley and the Browns Point Trail snakes its way up and down a long series of switchbacks that cross a number of ridges—hard on the lungs going up and tough on the knees coming down.

The country here has large aspen, Engelmann spruce, and Douglas fir. Early in summer the northern slopes still have snowbanks that provide a welcome handful of moisture. The trail is blazed all the way, but some of the older blazes may be difficult to locate. Occasionally you may have to backtrack 100 feet or so to find one you missed.

The Summit Trail meets the Browns Point Trail in Nay Canyon at 9,600 feet. Turn right (north) into Nay Canyon and take advantage of the water here, as the Browns Point Trail heads up the east side of the canyon and then descends the ridge to the north—away from the creekbed.

From the ridge at close to 10,000 feet, you switchback down about 3,000 feet. Again, finding the blazes along this 3-mile stretch may be difficult.

The recreation area is in view most of the way down. At the base of the ridge, the trail leaves the wilderness area. Turn right (east) onto the Equestrian Campground Trail and hike about 1.5 miles to the trailhead.

This hike traverses only a fraction of the 192 miles of trails in the Dixie National Forest. Stop by the Heritage Center Visitor Center in Pine Valley or the district office in St. George for maps and more information. —*Originally contributed by Mark McKeough*

Key Points

0.0 Start at the Whipple Trailhead.

5.0 Arrive at Whipple Valley. Turn right (south) onto the Summit Trail.

6.0 Reach South Valley. Bear right (south).

12.5 Junction with the Browns Point Trail. Turn right (north).

15.5 Junction with the Equestrian Campground Trail. Turn right (east).

17.0 Arrive back at the trailhead.

40 Kolob Arch

A long day hike or overnighter into the Kolob Canyons section of Zion National Park. Along the way you'll enjoy dramatic views of the Finger Canyons of the Kolob and massive Kolob Arch, and delightful campsites along Timber and La Verkin Creeks.

Start: La Verkin Creek Trailhead at Lee Pass.
Distance: 14.4 miles out and back.
Difficulty: Moderately strenuous.
Trail surface: Dirt, rock, and sand trail.
Seasons: Late spring through fall.
Land status: National park.
Nearest town: Cedar City.
Fees and permits: A $20-per-vehicle entrance fee ($10 on foot or bicycle), valid for seven days, is charged to enter the park. A free backcountry permit is required for overnight trips and is available at the Kolob Canyons or Zion Visitor Center.
Maps: USGS Kolob Arch quad; National Geographic Trails Illustrated Zion National Park Map.
Trail contacts: Superintendent, Zion National Park, SR 9, Springdale, UT 84767; (435) 772-3256; www.nps.gov/zion; or Kolob Canyons Visitor Center at (435) 586-9548.

Finding the trailhead: Drive southwest from Cedar City on Interstate 15 for 18 miles to exit 40 (Kolob Canyons). Turn left (east) into the park and drive about 4 miles, passing Kolob Canyons Visitor Center, to Lee Pass (6,060 feet), where a parking area is provided. *DeLorme: Utah Atlas & Gazetteer:* Page 17 B5.

The Hike

The Kolob Canyons section of Zion National Park, long known for its outstanding scenery, was designated as Zion National Monument in 1937. In 1956 it was added to Zion National Park. John D. Lee lived for a while below the pass bearing his name (where you find the trailhead) following the Mountain Meadows Massacre on September 11, 1857.

The 14.4-mile round trip to Kolob Arch makes a moderate overnight trip or a fairly strenuous day hike. A backcountry permit is required for overnight trips. Due to heavy use, a zone system restricts the number of campers in the Kolob Arch area. The area between the Kolob Arch Trail and Hop Valley Trail junctions shows the heavy impact of too much camping use. Please make your camp away from this area if possible. Permits can be obtained at the Kolob Canyons Visitor Center just off exit 40 on I–15.

Because the National Park Service is concerned for the safety of hikers and preservation of the natural ecosystem, pets are not permitted on trails. This also makes it easier to see deer and other wildlife. Cougars have been reported in the area and could be dangerous to pets brought illegally on the hike.

Those wishing to cook should bring backpacker stoves—open fires are not allowed. Plan to use one gallon of water per person per day while in the backcountry, particularly during summer months when afternoon temperatures can reach

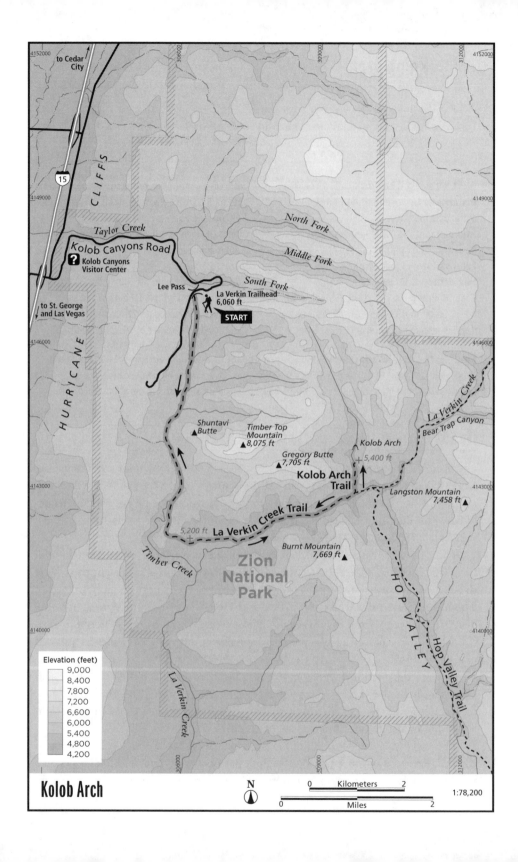

to Cedar City

CLIFFS

15

Taylor Creek

North Fork

Middle Fork

Kolob Canyons Road

? Kolob Canyons
Visitor Center

Lee Pass

South Fork

La Verkin Trailhead
6,060 ft

START

to St. George
and Las Vegas

HURRICANE

La Verkin Creek

Bear Trap Canyon

Shuntavi
▲Butte

Timber Top
Mountain
▲8,075 ft

Gregory Butte
▲7,705 ft

Kolob Arch

+ 5,400 ft

**Kolob Arch
Trail**

Langston Mountain
7,458 ft ▲

5,200 ft **La Verkin Creek Trail**

Timber Creek

Burnt Mountain
7,669 ft ▲

**Zion
National
Park**

HOP VALLEY

La Verkin Creek

Hop Valley Trail

Elevation (feet)

9,000
8,400
7,800
7,200
6,600
6,000
5,400
4,800
4,200

Kolob Arch

N

0   Kilometers   2

0   Miles   2

1:78,200

more than one hundred degrees Fahrenheit. Timber Creek and La Verkin Creek are perennial sources of water, so you do not have to carry your entire supply. Just be sure to purify all surface water. And remember that everything you pack in should come back out with you.

There are several potential problems to consider if you decide to take this trip at other than the "best season." The Kolob Canyons Road is occasionally closed from early November to Easter each year due to snow and loose rocks on the road. This would add 7 miles to the hike (3.5 miles each way), because you have to park at the locked gate at the bottom of Hurricane Cliffs and walk to and from Lee Pass and the La Verkin Trailhead. High water during spring runoff makes crossing La Verkin Creek difficult and hazardous. Snowstorms during winter and early spring can complicate your trip by making the steep sections of the trail slippery and/or muddy.

The view from the trailhead is worth the trip for everyone, but for the backpacker, it is only the beginning. The trail rapidly drops about 500 feet and reaches Timber Creek in just more than a mile. There are good campsites under large cottonwoods along Timber Creek. In the next 2.5 miles, you have commanding views of Timber Top Mountain (8,075 feet) and Shuntavi Butte to the east of the trail.

The route leaves Timber Creek and climbs to a ridge covered with juniper and piñon pine. The trail gradually descends about 400 feet in the next mile to La Verkin Creek. This is a good place to enjoy the splashing waters and dramatic views up La Verkin Creek. The towering canyon walls to the northeast culminate in Gregory Butte at 7,705 feet. This feature was named for Herbert E. Gregory, a prominent twentieth-century geologist of the region. To the southeast are Neagle Ridge and Burnt Mountain (7,669 feet), which was struck by lightning and burned in August 1978.

From here, it is easy going as you travel upstream (northeast) for the next 2 miles to the Kolob Arch Trail junction. You pass several good campsites near a stream flowing off the north slopes of Neagle Ridge and Burnt Mountain. As you hike past Burnt Mountain, stay alert for a major canyon opening to the north just past Gregory Butte.

Kolob Arch is nearby, so this is a good place to enjoy the views up and down La Verkin Creek and savor the wilderness beauty. You are in the Kayenta formation (lower Jurassic) for the entire hike, except for the floodplain alluvium of sand and gravel found along the stream channels. The surrounding cliffs are Navajo sandstone, out of which Kolob Arch has been formed.

Turn left (north) at the Kolob Arch Trail sign. You may wish to follow the trail on the east side of the creek or return to the streambed in a short distance, which some consider easier. For variety, take the alternate route on your return.

About a half mile from the junction, a small stream comes in from a canyon to the left (west) below Kolob Arch, which can be seen high on the canyon wall above. Because of erosion problems, hiking the side stream and steep slope below the arch is prohibited.

Photography is best in the morning—a good reason to make this an overnight trip. For safety, hikers should camp above the high-water mark in drainages and along rivers.

Kolob Arch is one of the largest freestanding arches on the North American continent. Its span was conservatively measured at 290 to 310 feet by Fred Ayres and A. E. Creswell in 1953. New measurements done in 1984 by two teams placed the span at 310 feet and 292 feet, respectively. Accurate measurement is difficult, because the arch is 700 feet above the canyon, and its legs are remnants of the former cliff.

Those who wish to stay longer in this area may want to take side trips to the falls in Beartrap Canyon farther up La Verkin Creek or into Hop Valley to the south. Reach Hop Valley via the Hop Valley Trail junction, a quarter mile east of the Kolob Arch Trail junction.

Make sure you are rested and have plenty of drinking water for the return trip to Lee Pass. You must regain the 800 feet of elevation you lost coming into the area. Avoid the climb out of Timber Creek on hot summer afternoons, if possible. This south-facing slope can be much hotter than other portions of the hike and is more enjoyable before noon—another reason to camp out.

Detailed information on other hiking objectives within Zion is available daily all year at the Zion Visitor Center, located a mile north of Springdale or the Kolob Canyons Visitor Center. Uniformed personnel can suggest a variety of trips to fit your interests, skill, and available time for each season of the year. —*Originally contributed by Victor Jackson*

Key Points

0.0 Start at the La Verkin Creek Trailhead at Lee Pass.

1.1 The trail quickly drops to Timber Creek.

6.7 Turn left (north) onto the Kolob Arch Trail.

7.2 Arrive at the Kolob Arch viewpoint.

7.7 Return to the junction with the La Verkin Creek Trail. Turn right (west).

14.4 Arrive back at the trailhead.

41 Under-the-Rim Trail

A two- to three-day backpack in Bryce Canyon National Park. This is a remote hike through the base of the older sections of Bryce Canyon, with distant panoramic views, geologic features, abundant wildlife, and marked transitions in vegetation.

Start: Bryce Point Trailhead.
Distance: 22.9 miles point to point.
Difficulty: Moderate to strenuous.
Trail surface: Canyon trail, rocky and sandy areas.
Seasons: Late spring through fall.
Land status: National park.
Nearest town: Tropic.
Fees and permits: A $20-per-vehicle entrance fee ($10 on foot or bicycle), valid for seven days, is charged to enter the park (includes unlimited use of park shuttles in summer). A

$5.00 backcountry permit is required for all overnight hiking and is available at the park visitor center.
Maps: USGS Bryce Point, Tropic Reservoir, and Rainbow Point quads; National Geographic Trails Illustrated Bryce Canyon National Park Map.
Trail contacts: Superintendent, Bryce Canyon National Park, P.O. Box 17001, Bryce Canyon, UT 84717; (435) 834-5322; www.nps.gov/brca.

Finding the trailhead: From Highway 12, southeast of Panguitch and west of Escalante, drive 3 miles south on Highway 63 into Bryce Canyon National Park. Stop at the visitor center on the right. You must obtain a backcountry permit and register for one or more of the twelve primitive campsites along the trail. No more than fourteen consecutive days can be spent on the Under-the-Rim Trail. After stopping here drive south another 1.5 miles and turn left toward the Bryce Point parking area and trailhead, which is another 2 miles ahead. *DeLorme: Utah Atlas & Gazetteer:* Page 19 A4.

To leave a car at Rainbow Point, drive about 15.5 miles past the Bryce Point turnoff. The Rainbow Point Trailhead is at the end of the road on the east end of the loop parking lot. *DeLorme: Utah Atlas & Gazetteer:* Page 18 B3.

The Hike

There are two trailheads for the Under-the-Rim Trail—Bryce Point and Rainbow Point—as well as four connecting trails back to the rim along the trail's length. Bryce Canyon officials recommend that you hike from north to south, beginning at Bryce Point and finishing the 22.9-mile trail at Rainbow Point. Shuttling a car is recommended.

Keep in mind that open fires are not permitted due to fire danger and slow vegetative recovery. Also, pets are not allowed on any of the trails in the park. Finally, park regulations require that you carry out all trash. Don't bury it.

If you're hiking in late summer, thunderstorms are frequent. Avoid isolated trees and viewpoints during storms: Lightning frequently strikes objects along the rim. Flash floods are also possible.

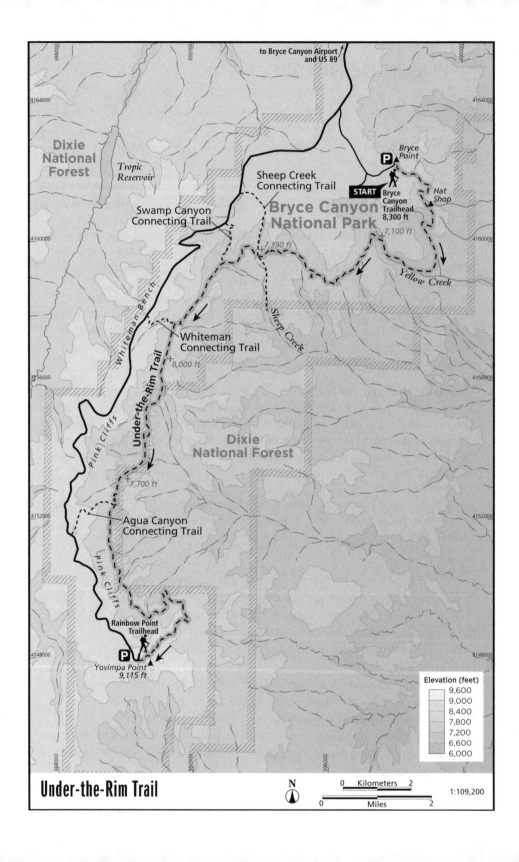

Under-the-Rim Trail

N

0   Kilometers   2

0   Miles   2

1:109,200

The trail at Bryce Point starts at about 8,300 feet. The descent into the canyon is not a continuous one. There is quite a bit of elevation change as the trail winds around eroding limestone fins and through gullies and ravines. The trail cuts into the Claron formation (the predominant geologic formation in the park) and the other crossbedded sandstones. The ancient, nearly horizontal strata of the Claron represent Cretaceous geology (sixty million years old) and a time when nonoxidating freshwater lakes covered the Bryce Canyon area. More recently, regional faulting and volcanic activity, as well as the erosional forces of wind, water, and freezing temperatures, formed the landscape seen today. The Hat Shop, about 2 miles down the trail, is an excellent example of the differential weathering that can occur when these erosional agents work on dissimilar rock types.

Continuing past the Hat Shop, the trail begins a rugged 650-foot descent about 1.5 miles to Yellow Creek. Ponderosa pines give way to Gambel oak as you pass the first campsite near the creek. You may be able to fill water bottles here, but don't count on it. Carry your own supply and be prepared to treat any water you find.

Depending on the season, cactus blooms may be seen. Similarly impressive is the view back toward the rim, where the Pink Cliffs rise to towering heights. About a mile past the junction with Yellow Creek, the trail heads into denser vegetation and topographic diversity.

The Sheep Creek and Swamp Canyon areas—9.4 and 10.5 miles from the trailhead—offer good "halfway" points for overnight hikers. A side trip up the Swamp Canyon Connecting Trail to the rim of the canyon may be rewarding. Hawks, falcons, and hummingbirds flourish in this area. Keep your eyes and ears open. Perhaps you'll spot a Cooper's hawk amid the trees.

From the Whiteman Connecting Trail south, the solitude of the area increases. Vegetation becomes denser, giving way to spruce, fir, and groves of aspen. Trail conditions vary from ball-bearing limestone and wide, dry drainages to loose sandy hills. You will find a greater density of seasonal springs and water sources. Toward evening, the native wildlife seeks these watering sites. Mule deer may wander right into camp. If you're lucky, you could even spot more secretive mammals. The ringtail cat, black bear, and cougar occasionally leave sign but are seldom seen.

The second half of the trip begins the ascent to the highest point in the park. The climb is rather arduous but well worth the effort, for it provides magnificent vistas back (northwest) toward the rim of the Pink Cliffs, south across the plateaus toward the Grand Canyon, southwest toward Coral Pink Sand Dunes, and southeast toward the Grand Staircase–Escalante area.

The hike concludes by contouring around the Pink Cliffs and then climbing to 9,115 feet at Rainbow Point.

If you're not too tired upon ending your hike, or if you allow another day in the park, you may want to hike some of the day trails, where you will encounter the pinnacles and formations of the amphitheater for which Bryce is famous. —*Originally contributed by Heidi Herendeen*

Key Points

0.0 Start at the Bryce Point Trailhead.

9.4 Junction with the Sheep Creek Connecting Trail. Continue straight (west).

10.5 Junction with the Swamp Canyon Connecting Trail. Continue straight (south).

12.1 Junction with the Whiteman Connecting Trail. Continue straight (south).

16.5 Junction with the Agua Canyon Connecting Trail. Continue straight (south).

22.9 Arrive at Rainbow Point.

42 Hackberry Canyon

A two- or three-day backpack in the Paria-Hackberry Wilderness Study Area in the Grand Staircase–Escalante National Monument. Hackberry is a highly scenic canyon with numerous side canyons to explore, interesting geology, Sam Pollock Arch, and Watson's Cabin, an early homestead.

Start: Round Valley Draw Trailhead.
Distance: 21 miles point to point.
Difficulty: Moderate.
Trail surface: Wash bottom.
Seasons: Spring or fall.
Land status: Bureau of Land Management (BLM) wilderness study area.
Nearest town: Cannonville.
Fees and permits: A free backcountry permit for overnight backpacking is required and is available at the Kanab, Cannonville, and Escalante Visitor Centers.
Maps: USGS Slickrock Bench and Calico Peak quads; Southwestern Utah Multipurpose Map.
Trail contacts: Grand Staircase-Escalante National Monument, 190 East Center Street, Kanab, UT 84741; (435) 644–4680; www.ut.blm.gov/monument.

Finding the trailhead: Access is by seasonal roads, which may be impassable when wet. From Cannonville on Highway 12 (about 8 miles east of Bryce Canyon National Park), take Cottonwood Canyon Road southeast for about 7 miles to the entrance of Kodachrome Basin State Park. Continue east for 6.7 miles to Round Valley Draw and turn right (south) onto the "Rush Beds" dirt road. Drive about 1.7 miles to an undeveloped parking area and trailhead. To access Hackberry from the south via U.S. Highway 89, drive east from Kanab to mile marker 18 and turn left (north) onto Cottonwood Road. Continue about 27 miles to the Round Valley Draw turnoff on the left, about 3 miles past the Grosvenor Arch intersection on the right. *DeLorme: Utah Atlas & Gazetteer:* Page 19 B5.

Hiking Hackberry's full length requires spotting a vehicle at the mouth of the canyon, located on Cottonwood Road 12.2 miles south of the Round Valley Draw turnoff (14.4 miles north of US 89). *DeLorme: Utah Atlas & Gazetteer:* Page 19 C5.

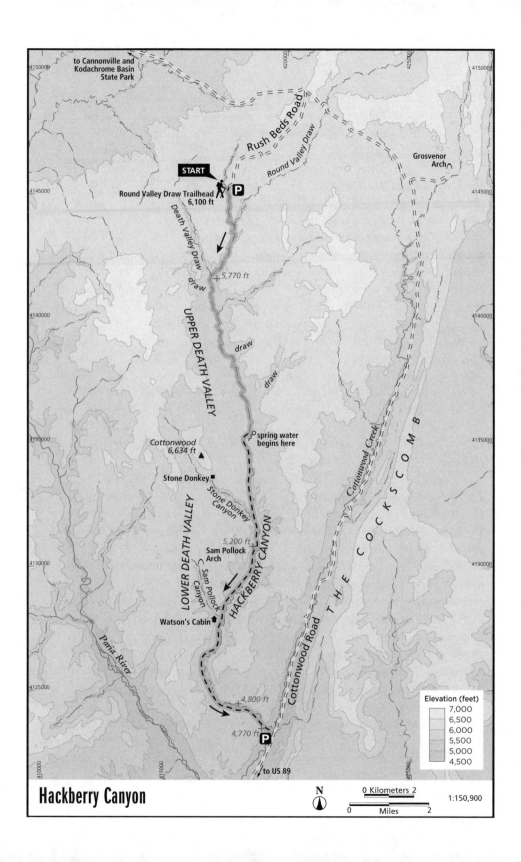

to Cannonville and
Kodachrome Basin
State Park

Rush Beds Road

Round Valley Draw

Grosvenor
Arch

START

Round Valley Draw Trailhead
6,100 ft

P

Death Valley Draw

5,770 ft

UPPER DEATH VALLEY

draw

draw

draw

Cottonwood Creek

THE COCKSCOMB

spring water
begins here

Cottonwood
6,634 ft

Stone Donkey

Stone Donkey Canyon

LOWER DEATH VALLEY

HACKBERRY CANYON

5,200 ft

Sam Pollock Arch

Sam Pollock Canyon

Watson's Cabin

Cottonwood Road

Paria River

4,800 ft

4,770 ft

P

to US 89

Elevation (feet)

7,000
6,500
6,000
5,500
5,000
4,500

Hackberry Canyon

N

0 Kilometers 2

0 Miles 2

1:150,900

The Hike

Hackberry Canyon offers a variety of scenery as it cuts through the White and Vermilion Cliffs. The upper portion of the hike, Round Valley Draw, is narrow, typical of canyons cut into the Navajo sandstone. Farther south, just before the canyon turns east and cuts through the East Kaibab Monocline (Cockscomb), it forms a valley bounded by the colorful formations making up the Vermilion Cliffs, and also exposes the banded Chinle formation. There are interesting side canyons, and the country above the canyons offers excellent opportunities for exploration. The area receives very little use, which enhances the sense of discovery.

From the trailhead at about 6,100 feet, you descend to about 4,770 feet at the mouth of the canyon. The first 1.5 miles of the route through Round Valley Draw is in a narrow slot canyon that presents some hazards and obstacles not found in the lower canyon. You will need to climb down a 20-foot pour-off at the head of the draw, as well as several 6- to 8-foot pour-offs. Consider carrying a 35-foot length of rope or webbing to lower your pack through these sections.

At 2.75 miles from the trailhead, you reach the junction with Hackberry Canyon. Continue south along the sandy wash bottom. Less than 0.5 mile farther, a major side canyon enters from the left (east) and makes a good side hike. There are a number of falls, but you can climb around them. This canyon opens into a large basin with scattered ponderosa pine. It is very scenic and provides access to the rim for a view of the surrounding country. The first opportunity for water is about 7 miles below this canyon, so carry what you need to get to this point. Be sure to treat all water for drinking and cooking.

About a mile below where you first find water is an old livestock trail to the west rim. The trail starts from the top of a high, sandy bench covered with cobbles. The bench is identified by a wire fence.

About a mile farther, again to the west, is the next tributary canyon, Stone Donkey. The name comes from a rock feature north of the canyon. This interesting canyon narrows to a slot a few feet wide toward its upper end. Two storage sheds and a corral mark the mouth of Stone Donkey Canyon.

About 1.75 miles below Stone Donkey Canyon is a large rockfall. In October 1987 a huge slab fell away from the right (west) canyon wall and broke into large fragments that completely filled the canyon. The rockfall temporarily dammed the creek, creating a small lake that extended about 100 yards upstream. The creek has since worked through the debris and drained most of the lake. Stay to the east side of the canyon for the best route over the rockfall.

As Hackberry Canyon begins to widen another 1.75 miles downstream, the side canyon containing Sam Pollock Arch enters from the right (west). This spectacular arch is about 1.5 miles from Hackberry. You will encounter a 20-foot waterfall along the way, but you can pick a route around it on the north side. Use caution, and don't attempt if you're not comfortable with rock scrambling.

About a half mile below Sam Pollock Canyon, also on the west side of Hackberry, is Watson's Cabin, an early homestead. At this point you have dropped 1,100 feet from the trailhead.

Three miles below, the canyon jogs east and exits the Cockscomb through a gorge about 2 miles long. The steep canyon walls in this last section may require walking in the shallow flowing wash. You meet Cottonwood Road at the end of this narrow section.

Hackberry Canyon is located in the Paria-Hackberry Wilderness Study Area, which encompasses the Paria River and a large section of the White Cliffs. It contains many interesting canyons, arches, and rock forms. The scenery is outstanding, and a variety of hiking opportunities are available, ranging in difficulty from easy day hikes to extended trips into more remote areas of the backcountry.

Key Points

0.0   Start at the Round Valley Draw Trailhead.

2.75   Junction of Hackberry Creek and Round Valley Draw. Continue south.

12.25   Reach the mouth of Stone Donkey Canyon.

14.0   Rockfall.

15.75   Canyon leading to Sam Pollock Arch.

16.25   Pass Watson's Cabin.

21.0   Arrive at Cottonwood Road.

Option: You can bypass the difficult slot portion of upper Round Valley Draw by turning off Cottonwood Road 1 mile before the "Rush Beds" dirt road onto Road 419A, a Grand Staircase–Escalante National Monument administrative road that is closed to motorized and mountain bike traffic but open to hiking. The road connects with Hackberry Creek in about 3.5 miles; it's a little more than 1 mile from there to the Hackberry Creek–Round Valley Draw junction. —*Originally contributed by Bill Booker*

43 Lower Muley Twist Canyon

A day hike with overnight options through part of the Waterpocket Fold. You hike through a deep canyon in a remote, lightly used wilderness with splendid vistas, gaining a historical perspective on the Mormon pioneers who passed through this area in the late 1800s.

Start: Lower Muley Twist Trailhead off Burr Trail Road.
Distance: 6 miles point to point.
Difficulty: Moderate.
Trail surface: Sandy canyon floor.
Seasons: Spring (early April through mid-May) and fall (early October through late November).
Land status: National park.
Nearest town: Boulder.

Fees and permits: A $5.00-per-vehicle entrance fee, valid for seven days, is charged to enter the park. A free backcountry permit is required for overnight use.
Maps: USGS Wagon Box Mesa and The Post quads; National Geographic Trails Illustrated Glen Canyon and Capitol Reef Map.
Trail contacts: Superintendent, Capitol Reef National Park, HC 70 Box 15, Torrey, UT 84775-9602; (435) 425-3791; www.nps.gov/care.

Finding the trailhead: Take Notom-Bullfrog Road south from Highway 24 near the east border of Capitol Reef National Park. After about 35 miles, turn right (west) onto Burr Trail Road and continue another 2 miles to the Lower Muley Twist Trailhead on the left. The Burr Trail was first used to move cattle across the Waterpocket Fold.

For a shuttle hike, drive another 2.3 miles south past the Burr Trail Road turnoff on Notom-Bullfrog Road to The Post. Park here or bear right onto a dirt spur road for another 0.7 mile. The road ends at the signed trailhead for Lower Muley Twist. *DeLorme: Utah Atlas & Gazetteer:* Page 28 D3.

The Hike

The Lower Muley Twist hike passes through a representative portion of the 100-mile-long eroded uplift called the Waterpocket Fold, most of which lies within Capitol Reef National Park. The canyon offers many opportunities for side trips and off-trail exploring.

There are several possible hikes in the canyon. You may choose an out-and-back day hike starting from the trailhead on the Burr Trail Road, a day or overnight hike from the same trailhead to The Post on the Notom-Bullfrog Road, or an extended overnighter farther into Muley Twist Canyon.

If you choose the overnight option, get a permit at the Highway 24 visitor center in Capitol Reef National Park. Fires are not permitted. Check at the visitor center for other backcountry regulations as well as updates on road and trail conditions.

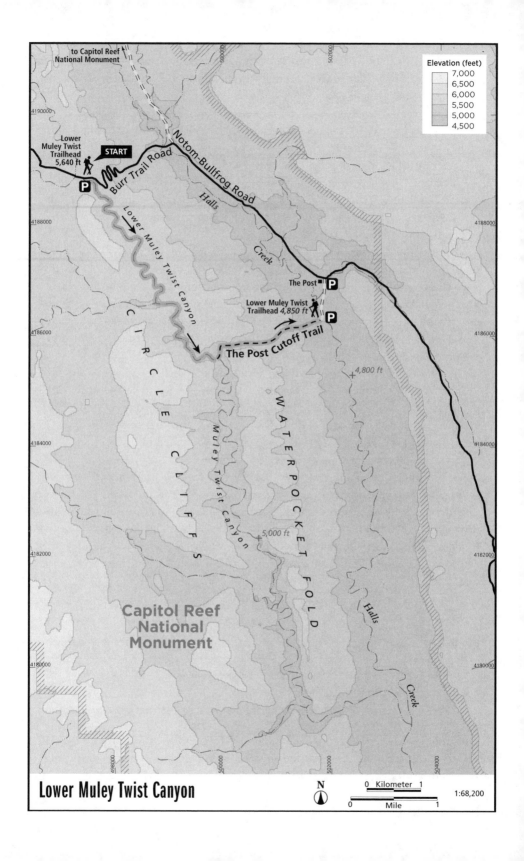

to Capitol Reef
National Monument

Lower
Muley Twist
Trailhead
5,640 ft

START

Burr Trail Road

Notom-Bullfrog Road

Halls

Creek

Lower Muley Twist Canyon

The Post

Lower Muley Twist
Trailhead 4,850 ft

The Post Cutoff Trail

C I R C L E

C L I F F S

Muley Twist Canyon

W A T E R P O C K E T   F O L D

4,800 ft

5,000 ft

Halls

Creek

Capitol Reef
National
Monument

Elevation (feet)
7,000
6,500
6,000
5,500
5,000
4,500

4190000

4188000

4186000

4184000

4182000

4180000

Lower Muley Twist Canyon

N

0   Kilometer   1

0   Mile   1

1:68,200

From the Burr Trail parking area at about 5,640 feet, begin a descent into Lower Muley Twist Canyon. The canyon winds tortuously through its entire length, enough to "twist a mule" pulling a wagon.

Carry at least one gallon of water per person, especially in summer. There are no reliable water sources in the area. And during June, July, and August, temperatures often rise to more than one hundred degrees Fahrenheit.

The canyon narrows in some areas while widening in others. For the most part, the slickrock canyon walls are white Navajo sandstone colored by streaks of desert varnish and lichens. The red sandstone is from the Kayenta and Wingate formations. It is the Wingate that has been undercut in the canyon, forming "sandstone caves" and high arching overhangs.

About 4 miles down Muley Twist, after descending approximately 300 feet, you reach the junction with a cutoff trail to The Post on the left (east). (Day hikers without a shuttle could backtrack to the trailhead at this point for an 8-mile round trip.) Turn left and hike the 2 miles to the lower trailhead (2.7 miles to The Post), climbing up and over the Waterpocket Fold. If you keep going south through Muley Twist, it is 8 more miles to Halls Creek, the continuation of Charles Hall's road to the old Colorado River crossing.

In 1880 Charles Hall operated the Hole-in-the-Rock ferry, which was first established by Mormon pioneers. Business at the crossing was slow; not many cared to face such an arduous overland journey and nearly impossible descent to the river. Hall found a less hazardous Colorado River crossing and river approach about 35 miles upriver from Hole-in-the-Rock at a place today called Halls Crossing.

To reach the crossing, travelers struggled east from Escalante on the Hole-in-the-Rock Trail, then turned into Harris Wash. They then crossed the Escalante River and ascended a short distance into the narrow canyon of Silver Falls Creek.

After reaching a mesa, the pioneers dropped into a funnel between two cliffs, descending 1,000 feet into a winding, deep canyon, today called Lower Muley Twist Canyon. In 1882 this canyon heard the rumble of wheels and braying of mules as a company moved through the narrow gorge to San Juan County, then a Mormon mission.

Today little evidence remains of the pioneers' passage, but you can retrace their journey.

Key Points

0.0   Start at the Lower Muley Twist Trailhead off Burr Trail Road.

4.0   Junction with The Post cutoff trail. Turn left (west).

6.0   Arrive at the Lower Muley Twist Trailhead off Notom-Bullfrog Road and your vehicle.

Option: For an overnight trip, continue south through the canyon from the cutoff trail to The Post for 8 miles. Near the end of Muley Twist, the canyon suddenly narrows and heads directly east. As the narrows open, you see sheer cliffs, the east rim of the Strike Valley formed by Halls Creek. Turn left (north) and hike 5 miles back to The Post, ascending about 300 vertical feet along the way. The land here is parched and dry. You can hike along Halls Creek or follow an old jeep road. You pass reminders of use by stockmen over the years—bleached bones of range cattle, cowboy campsites, and trampled wash banks.

If you've left a car at The Post, your hike is over. For those parked at the Burr Trail Road trailhead, you must decide whether to walk the Notom-Bullfrog Road north and then up the Burr Trail Road switchbacks (4.3 miles) to the trailhead or return via the cutoff trail west and then north up Lower Muley Twist (6 miles). —*Originally contributed by George Davidson*

44 Swett Canyon

A desert canyon hike to Hoskinnini Monument and Lake Powell. The hike through the Little Rockies, southeast of the Henry Mountains, features spectacular slickrock geology and solitude.

Start: The parking area off Highway 276 where it crosses Swett Creek.
Distance: 15 to 17 miles (depending upon the current level of Lake Powell) out and back.
Difficulty: Moderately strenuous.
Trail surface: Rocky creekbed (no constructed trail).
Seasons: Spring and fall.
Land status: Bureau of Land Management (BLM) wilderness study area and national recreation area.

Nearest town: Hanksville.
Fees and permits: No fees or permits required.
Maps: USGS Mount Holmes quad; National Geographic Trails Illustrated Glen Canyon and Capitol Reef Area Map; Southeastern Utah Multipurpose Map.
Trail contact: Henry Mountains Office, Bureau of Land Management, P.O. Box 99, Hanksville, UT 84734; (435) 542-3461; www.ut.blm.gov.

Finding the trailhead: Drive 23 miles southeast from Hanksville on Highway 95 to Highway 276. Turn right (south) onto Highway 276; Mount Holmes is straight ahead. About 14 miles from the Highway 95-276 junction, before Highway 276 swings to the southwest, away from and past Mount Holmes, you cross Swett Creek where a large culvert allows the creek to pass under the road. Parking is limited, but there is space for two cars on the east side of the road. *DeLorme: Utah Atlas & Gazetteer:* Page 29 4D.

The Hike

The Little Rockies area, part of a 38,700-acre BLM wilderness study area tucked away in Utah's slickrock country, offers an excellent backpacking experience. The two main peaks, Mount Holmes (7,930 feet) and Mount Ellsworth (8,235 feet),

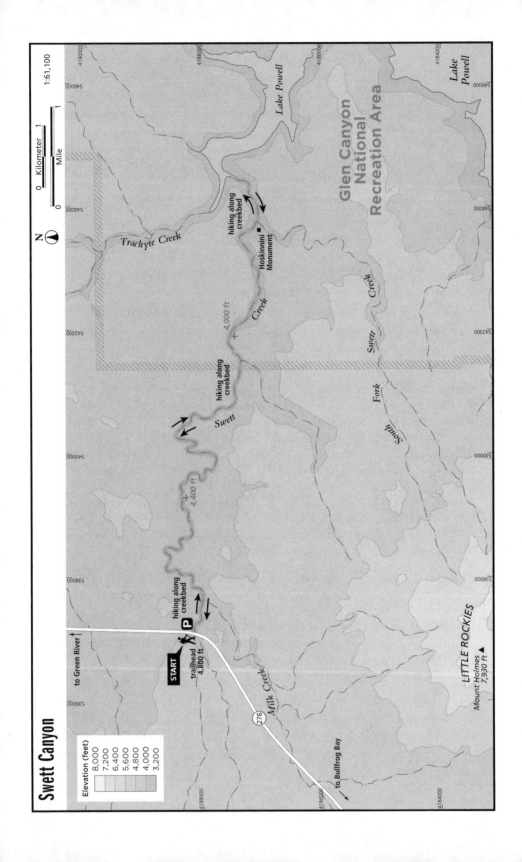

Swett Canyon

Elevation (feet)
8,000
7,200
6,400
5,600
4,800
4,000
3,200

N

0 Kilometer 1
0 Mile 1

1:61,100

to Green River

START
trailhead
4,800 ft

P

hiking along
creekbed

to Bullfrog Bay

276

Milk Creek

4,400 ft

Swett

hiking along
creekbed

Creek

4,000 ft

Trachyte Creek

hiking along
creekbed

Hoskinnini
Monument

Swett
Creek

South
Fork

Glen Canyon
National
Recreation Area

Lake Powell

Lake
Powell

LITTLE ROCKIES

Mount Holmes
7,930 ft

twist and spire 3,000 feet above the valley floor to form a rugged outline against the desert sky.

This hike winds through remote and seldom-traveled country. There is little chance you will encounter many other hikers. From the trailhead at the Highway 276–Swett Creek junction, you descend about 1,100 feet to the shores of Lake Powell.

Begin the hike by making your way from the road down to the creek bottom. Look closer at the 15-foot culvert under the roadway. The size of this giant culvert is an indication of the expected size of the hundred-year flood of Swett Creek.

Travel in the narrow canyon is between sandstone walls and over granitic stones and boulders in the streambed. Immense pressures from intrusive volcanic magma called a laccolith formed the Little Rockies and the Henry Mountains directly to the northwest. The laccolith is the source of much of the granitic rock found in the bottom of the river channels. Because of this granite, sturdy hiking boots are recommended for the canyon. Even though you may get wet, your feet will be more comfortable in boots.

Swett Canyon is usually dry except for isolated pockets of water, which are not dependable. During a thunderstorm, however, the creek turns into a raging torrent, and the hike should never be attempted at this time.

No trail exists through the narrow, winding canyon except for the rocky creekbed. Hiking conditions in the canyon can change with each season, ranging from an easy walk to a rock scramble. Flash-flood activity can move or remove rocks from the narrow canyon, also changing the conditions.

About a half mile before reaching Lake Powell—7 miles down the canyon—look for Hoskinnini Monument. Hoskinnini was a Navajo chief who lived in Monument Valley and visited the area. The monument is a large rock monolith standing 400 feet high.

Campsites in the canyon are limited, and a good foam pad is advised. Firewood is very scarce, so use your backpacker stove.

As with other canyon hikes, be conscious of the weather. The high, narrow slick-rock walls are an excellent channel for flash floods. Contact the BLM's Henry Mountains Office in Hanksville before making your trip. —*Originally contributed by Tim Randle*

Key Points

0.0 Start at the parking area where a culvert allows Swett Creek to pass under Highway 276.

7.0 Pass Hoskinnini Monument.

7.5–8.5 Reach the shores of Lake Powell. Turnaround point.

15.0–17.0 Arrive back at the parking area.

45 Egypt–Twentyfive Mile Wash

This loop hike offers a diverse desert canyon hiking experience. The hike can vary in duration, depending on the number and length of side trips taken, but requires a minimum of two long days. The recommended and more leisurely trip, with time for exploring, takes four to five days.

Start: Egypt Trailhead in the Grand Staircase-Escalante National Monument.
Distance: 20-mile loop.
Difficulty: Strenuous due to length and hiking through water and dense vegetation.
Trail surface: Slickrock, sand, wash bottoms.
Seasons: Spring and fall.
Land status: National recreation area, national monument (Bureau of Land Management).
Nearest town: Escalante.
Fees and permits: A free backcountry use permit is required for overnight trips, and is available at any monument visitor center and at the self-registration box at the Egypt Trailhead.
Maps: USGS Sunset Flat and Egypt quads; Southeastern Utah Multipurpose Map; National Geographic Trails Illustrated Canyons of the Escalante Map.
Trail contacts: Escalante Interagency Visitor Information Center, Box 225, Escalante, UT 84726; (435) 826-5499; www.ut.blm.gov/monument or www.nps.gov/glca.

Finding the trailhead: Drive east from Escalante on Highway 12 for 5 miles to Hole-in-the-Rock Road. Turn right and drive 15 miles to The Egypt turnoff. Turn left onto Egypt Road. Within 3.5 miles Egypt Road crosses the upper portion of Twentyfive Mile Wash. Continue another 5.5 miles and bear right. Egypt Trailhead is 1 mile farther. This road is usually passable for vehicles with moderate clearance, but check with the Escalante Interagency Visitor Information Center for current road conditions. *DeLorme: Utah Atlas & Gazetteer:* Page 20 B2.

The Hike

The 20-mile loop hike begins on Egypt Bench, high above the Escalante River, and descends about 1,000 feet via Fence Canyon into the Escalante River's canyon, continuing downriver to the confluence of Twentyfive Mile Wash. The route then snakes up Twentyfive Mile Wash, exits from the wash to the north, and concludes with a cross-country trek over slickrock back to the Egypt Trailhead. Out-and-back options, rather than the full loop hike, are possible.

Several locations along this hike can be extremely hazardous during flash floods, so get an up-to-date forecast and watch the weather. You will be hiking in water along a good portion of this trek, so use footwear that stands up to wet conditions and provides sufficient ankle support. Army-surplus "jungle boots" are ideal.

Water availability varies considerably from season to season. Check conditions with the Escalante Interagency Visitor Information Center when you obtain your

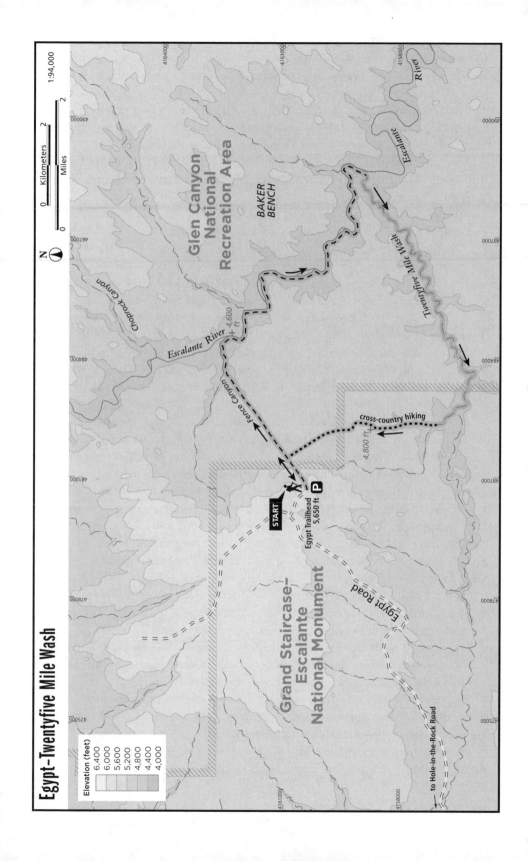

Egypt–Twentyfive Mile Wash

1:94,000

Elevation (feet)

6,400
6,000
5,600
5,200
4,800
4,400
4,000

Grand Staircase–
Escalante
National Monument

Glen Canyon
National
Recreation Area

BAKER
BENCH

Chopock Canyon

Escalante River

+ 4,600 ft

Fence Canyon

Twentyfive Mile Wash

Escalante River

cross-country hiking

+ 4,800 ft

START

Egypt Trailhead
5,650 ft

Egypt Road

to Hole-in-the-Rock Road

free backcountry permit. Boil all surface water, adding iodine or using an appropriate filtering technique. Fence Canyon, only a mile long, has a small stream flowing most of the year.

From the trailhead at about 5,650 feet, descend the bench over slickrock, using an old stock trail. Head northeast toward Fence Canyon and its two upper arms. Skirt the north rim of Fence Canyon's southern arm here. You will be hiking cross-country on slickrock and sand. Just before you reach the junction of the two arms, the stock trail descends into Fence Canyon. The distance from the trailhead to the junction is about 2 miles.

Hike in the wash bottoms whenever possible. In doing so, human traces will be erased during high water. Camping in wash bottoms, however, can be dangerous. Fires are not permitted, so use your backpacker stove. Fires cause considerable damage; their ash and charcoal remains, not to mention rock rings, last for decades.

It is only half a mile to the mouth of Fence Canyon and the Escalante River. The mouth of the river is at about 4,600 feet—1,000 feet below the trailhead. You descend less than 200 feet over the next 5.5 miles before leaving the Escalante at Twentyfive Mile Wash.

Prior to your hike down the Escalante, you might enjoy the side trip upstream about a mile to Choprock Canyon, which enters from the east. The route offers interesting hiking in narrow, deeply incised canyons. Do not, however, hike here when bad weather threatens.

Since the hike down the Escalante follows the canyon bottom, you will be walking in and out of knee-deep water. River levels vary. Wash bottoms and the river canyon are heavily vegetated. The dense vegetation also can make passage difficult. Cottonwood, willow, Russian olive, and tamarisk predominate here.

One mile downstream, an old stock trail leads up and out the left (east) side of the canyon to Baker Bench. This canyon makes an interesting side trip. In only a short distance, you'll climb to an excellent view of the Escalante River below.

Twentyfive Mile Wash is another 4.5 miles downstream. Before you reach it, however, there will be fine hiking along the Escalante. There are numerous benches and excellent campsites.

About half a mile before Twentyfive Mile Wash, a canyon enters from the left (north) side of the Escalante. The river then bends around to the right. Twentyfive Mile Wash enters from the right (west) just beyond the bend.

The lower 2 miles of Twentyfive Mile Wash are narrow and winding. The wash drains a large area and is subject to flash flooding. The lower portion of this canyon provides little opportunity to climb to higher ground, so use caution.

You might explore some of the small side canyons off the lower portion of Twentyfive Mile Wash. Some of these canyons are deep, shady, and lush and offer interesting photographic opportunities. Watch for poison ivy.

About 6 miles up Twentyfive Mile Wash, a side canyon leads into the wash from the right (north). It is the first large canyon upstream (half a mile) from the Glen

Canyon National Recreation Area boundary sign. This route is extremely brushy, with deep beaver ponds to wade. A better route is to continue west beyond this side canyon about 0.75 mile to where you can exit Twentyfive Mile Wash on the right (north). Once you have exited Twentyfive Mile, hike cross-country over sand and slickrock, using Egypt Bench as your landmark, until you reach the steep slickrock route that leads up to the trailhead. —*Originally contributed by Jay Wells*

Key Points

0.0 Start at the Egypt Trailhead on Egypt Road.

2.0 Descend to the junction of Fence Canyon.

2.5 Arrive at the mouth of Fence Canyon and the Escalante River. Turn right (downstream).

3.5 Pass an old stock trail leading east to Baker Bench.

8.0 Twentyfive Mile Wash enters from the right (west) after a right-hand bend in the Escalante River.

14.0 Exit Twentyfive Mile Wash on the right (north).

20.0 Arrive back at the Egypt Trailhead.

46 Main Moody Canyon

A long day hike or overnight backpack into remote and spectacular side canyons of the Escalante River in the Glen Canyon National Recreation Area. Special attractions include solitude, spectacular desert varnish walls, and the possibility of seeing desert bighorn sheep.

Start: The parking area near the end of Moody Creek Road.
Distance: 12.6 miles out and back.
Difficulty: Moderately strenuous but without technical difficulties.
Trail surface: Wash bottom.
Seasons: Spring and fall.
Land status: National recreation area.
Nearest town: Boulder.
Fees and permits: A free backcountry use permit is required for overnight trips.
Maps: USGS Horse Pasture Mesa and Scorpion Gulch quads; Southeastern Utah Multipurpose Map; National Geographic Trails Illustrated Canyons of the Escalante Map.
Trail contacts: Escalante Interagency Visitor Information Center, Glen Canyon National Recreation Area, Box 225, Escalante, UT 84726; (435) 826-5499; www.nps.gov/glca or www.ut.blm.gov/monument.

Finding the trailhead: Follow Burr Trail Road east from Boulder for 19 miles and turn right (south) onto the Wolverine Loop road. Continue south on this road for 20 miles to Moody Creek Road. (You can also follow Burr Trail Road 33 miles east of Boulder to the second access road for the Wolverine Loop.) These two roads eventually intersect and continue south into Moody Creek. The road descends into the dry wash of Main Moody Canyon and follows it for about 3

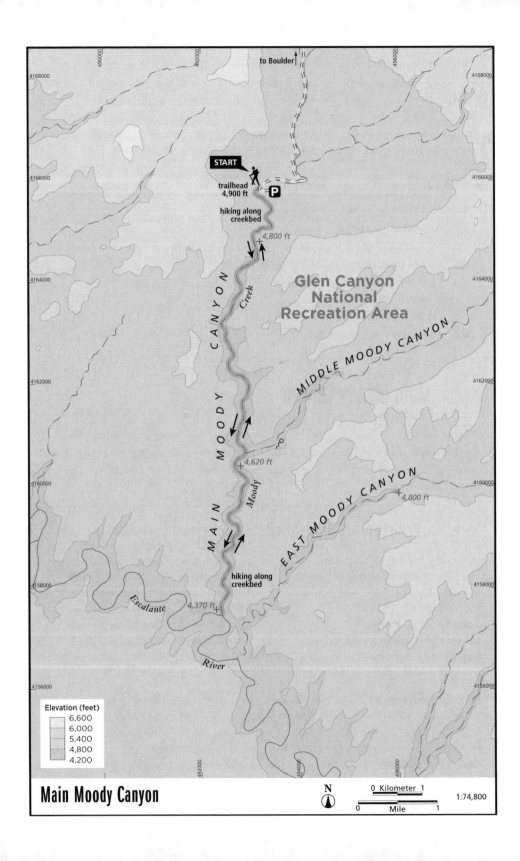

to Boulder

START
trailhead
4,900 ft

hiking along
creekbed

4,800 ft

Glen Canyon
National
Recreation Area

Creek

MAIN MOODY CANYON

MIDDLE MOODY CANYON

4,620 ft

Moody

EAST MOODY CANYON

4,800 ft

hiking along
creekbed

Escalante

4,370 ft

River

Elevation (feet)

6,600
6,000
5,400
4,800
4,200

Main Moody Canyon

N

0 Kilometer 1

0 Mile 1

1:74,800

miles, heading south at first. After turning and following the canyon west for about 0.75 mile, the road leaves the canyon and turns due east. Just after the road leaves the canyon, there is a parking area where the hike begins. The road is generally passable for vehicles with high clearance (road conditions vary and are subject to the weather). Check on the condition of the roads before making the trip. *DeLorme: Utah Atlas & Gazetteer:* Page 28 D1 and page 20 A2.

The Hike

Moody Canyon should be attempted only by hikers who are comfortable with and prepared for remote desert backpacking. Water may be nonexistent except at the Escalante River, and you will probably be the only person for miles around—especially in the off-season. Despite (or possibly because of) its remote nature, the Escalante country receives more and more use each year. If you decide to camp on this hike, do your part to preserve this unique and fragile wilderness by camping with as little impact as possible.

The hike begins in a dry, rocky streambed in spacious upper Main Moody Canyon. In spring Indian paintbrush, red and blue penstemon, purple aster, and evening primrose are among the colorful wildflowers that abound.

About 4 miles from the parking area, Middle Moody Canyon enters the main canyon from the left (east). The Escalante River is about 2.3 miles farther down the canyon.

Canyon walls loom over you during much of the hike to the Escalante, with huge, deep red Wingate sandstone boulders and rock rubble along the way. You descend about 600 feet from the trailhead to the Escalante.

Excellent campsites exist at the mouth of Moody Canyon. Unless recent rains have filled the pools of Moody Creek, the Escalante is your only water source, so purify the water. If you pack in a collapsible one-gallon water container, the silted water can settle in it as you make camp.

You could easily spend a lifetime in the remarkable Escalante country without seeing but a portion of its treasures. When you visit this area, respect it—for your own safety and for its continued beauty.

Key Points

0.0 Start from the parking area where Moody Creek Road turns due east.

4.0 Middle Moody Canyon enters from the left (east).

6.3 Arrive at the Escalante River. Turnaround point.

12.6 Arrive back at the parking area.

Option: From the base camp, it is about 1.5 miles downstream to the mouth of East Moody Canyon. Be prepared to do some scrambling on the Escalante River's banks as you approach East Moody. If you are hiking in the early morning or evening, notice the splendid canyon wall reflections in the river. You may see deer along the river, and coyotes' special rendition of canyon music may pierce the evening air.

East Moody is narrow near its mouth, making boulder-hopping necessary to hike up the canyon. About 2 miles from the mouth, observe the skyward-reaching walls covered with desert varnish. The mood changes here with the day's changing light. Reflected light from the opposite wall intensifies the colors and provides some excellent photographic opportunities. Pools from recent rains offer excellent reflection shots.

About 3 miles farther upstream, the canyon broadens. At the base of the cliff, you may see desert bighorn sheep, reintroduced by the Division of Wildlife Resources. Golden eagles and canyon wrens are common. You may also see cougar tracks at some of the water holes, but it will be a unique experience, indeed, if you spot one of these secretive cats. —*Originally contributed by John George*

47 Upheaval Dome

This hike—part loop, part out-and-back overnighter—is in the Island in the Sky District of Canyonlands National Park, 23 miles southwest of Moab. The route offers the only access to the radically distorted and colorful rock interior of Upheaval Dome, as well as outstanding views of canyon country and the Green River.

Start: From the Upheaval Dome parking lot.
Distance: 18.3-mile lollipop loop.
Difficulty: Strenuous.
Trail surface: Rocky trail, loose talus in spots.
Seasons: Spring and fall.
Land status: National park.
Nearest town: Moab.
Fees and permits: A $10.00-per-vehicle entrance fee ($5.00 on foot or bicycle), valid for seven days, is charged to enter the park. A

$15 overnight backpack permit also is required; call (435) 259-4351.
Maps: USGS Upheaval Dome quad; National Geographic Trails Illustrated Island in the Sky District Canyonlands National Park Map; Canyonlands National Park Map.
Trail contacts: Superintendent, Canyonlands National Park, 2282 Southwest Resource Boulevard, Moab, UT 84532; (435) 719-2313; www.nps.gov/cany.

Finding the trailhead: Take Highway 313 southwest from U.S. Highway 191 (about 10 miles north of Moab). Continue about 17 miles into Canyonlands National Park. The Island in the Sky Visitor Center is 2 miles farther. Rangers there can advise you as to current trail conditions and regulations. About 6 miles from the visitor center, turn right (west) and drive 5.5 miles northwest to the Upheaval Dome parking lot. *DeLorme: Utah Atlas & Gazetteer:* Page 30 A1.

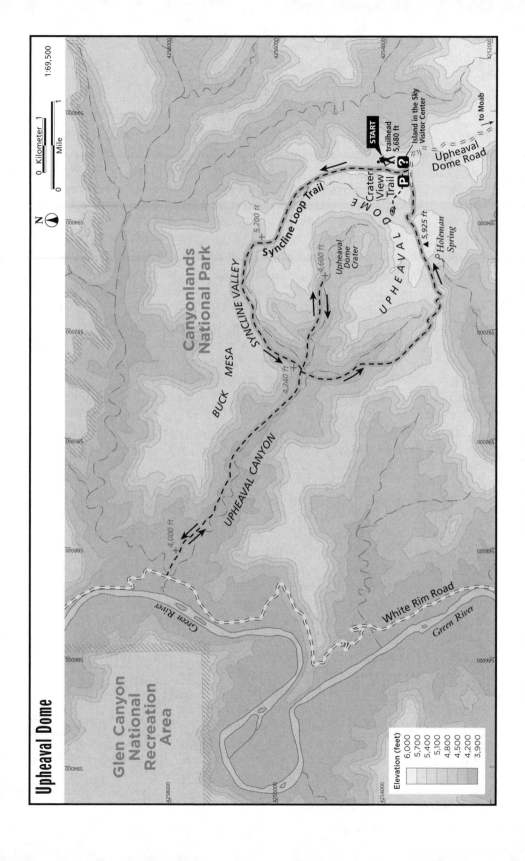

Upheaval Dome

1:69,500

N

Elevation (feet)
- 6,000
- 5,700
- 5,400
- 5,100
- 4,800
- 4,500
- 4,200
- 3,900

Glen Canyon National Recreation Area

Green River

Canyonlands National Park

BUCK MESA

SYNCLINE VALLEY

UPHEAVAL CANYON

Syncline Loop Trail

Crater View Trail

UPHEAVAL DOME

Upheaval Dome Crater

Holeman Spring

Island in the Sky Visitor Center

Upheaval Dome Road

to Moab

White Rim Road

Green River

START
trailhead
5,680 ft

P

5,925 ft

+ 5,200 ft

+ 4,600 ft

+ 4,240 ft

+ 4,000 ft

0 Kilometer 1

0 Mile 1

The Hike

The overnight trip around Upheaval Dome and northwest to the Green River and back involves hiking in fairly rough terrain. Be sure to have at least one gallon of water per person per day for your hike. No potable water is available along any of the hiking trails.

A permit is required for all overnight stays in the backcountry. Canyonlands National Park charges a nonrefundable reservation fee of $15 for each backpacking permit (which covers a group up to the park's limit of seven). All permits can be reserved in advance (call 435–259–4351) or are available to walk-ins on a first-come, first-served basis at a visitor center.

Pick up a copy of the *Crater View Trail Guide* at the parking lot. By hiking this half-mile trail first, you'll have a better understanding of Upheaval Dome and its geology. Returning from the Crater View Trail, you can take the Syncline Loop Trail in either direction to begin your adventure around Upheaval Dome. This description follows a counterclockwise trek.

Heading around the eastern side of the dome, the trail descends 1,300 feet in 4.9 miles through Syncline Valley to Upheaval Canyon. At the junction of Syncline Valley and Upheaval Canyon, turn left (southeast, upstream in the normally dry wash) and hike 1.5 miles into the interior of the basin at the center of the dome. Here, at about 1,300 feet below the Crater View Trail overlook, you may be able to see other park visitors gazing down upon you.

It's an otherworldly experience. Geologists still don't know for sure what caused this medley of rock to dome up in the first place. Possibly the crater is the result of an impact by an ancient meteorite. Another popular theory states that the layers of rock were forced up by a salt plug pushing from below. In the heat of summer, the crater is an oven; it can be very warm in other seasons as well.

Retrace your steps and head northwest toward the Green River, 3.5 miles downstream via Upheaval Canyon. After an initial 400-foot descent, the canyon opens into a huge desert flatland called Upheaval Bottom. Halfway across the bottom you intersect White Rim Road (a four-wheel-drive road), a 100-mile loop that circles the entire Island in the Sky mesa. Campsites are available here.

Just beyond the road, a wide band of willow, cottonwood, and tamarisk thickets borders the river. Buried in the vegetation, but not difficult to find, is an old cowboy line camp corral and cabin. Following the wash will lead you to the river. Remember to treat any water for drinking.

Don't be surprised at the scarcity of wildlife and vegetation. The canyon country is a harsh environment, and its inhabitants require large areas of land to survive. Desert bighorn sheep, mule deer, coyotes, bobcats, and the elusive cougar all inhabit this land. Many smaller mammals, birds, and reptiles also call this country home.

The 3.4-mile return trip around Upheaval Dome along its western side is strenuous. (As an alternative, you could retrace your steps through the Syncline Valley.)

The loose talus slope can cause poor footing, and one short section of trail traverses a ledge above a high cliff. The National Park Service has installed railings along the ledge for assistance, but be careful—you're on your own. Allow sufficient time and water to make this trip a safe one.

Key Points

0.0 Start at the Upheaval Dome parking area.

4.9 Junction of the Syncline Loop Trail and Upheaval Canyon. Turn left (southeast).

6.4 Reach the basin at the center of the dome. Turnaround point.

11.4 Arrive at the Green River. Turnaround point.

14.9 Junction of the Syncline Loop Trail and Upheaval Canyon. Turn right (south) onto the Syncline Loop Trail.

18.3 Arrive back at the parking area.

Option: The 8.3-mile loop around Upheaval Dome can be done in one day (six to eight hours). Add another 3 miles if you want to hike into the center of the dome and back out. —*Originally contributed by Dave May*

48 Dark Canyon

The Dark Canyon Wilderness, south of Canyonlands National Park, offers beautiful forest and desert scenery, Indian ruins, and peace and solitude. This five- to seven-day trip is for experienced backpackers.

Start: The trailhead at the end of Woodenshoe Road.
Distance: 40-mile loop backpack.
Difficulty: Moderately difficult. Map-reading skills are required.
Trail surface: Wash bottom.
Seasons: Late spring to early summer, and fall.
Land status: Wilderness area.
Nearest town: Blanding.
Fees and permits: No fees or permits are required. Hikers are encouraged to inquire about current weather and water conditions before starting, and to sign in at the trailhead registers.

Maps: USGS Woodenshoe Buttes, Poison Canyon, Warren Canyon, and Black Steer Canyon quads; National Geographic Trails Illustrated Manti-LaSal National Forest Map.
Trail contacts: Monticello Ranger District, Manti-LaSal National Forest, P.O. Box 820, Monticello, UT 84535; (435) 587-2041; www.fs.fed.us/r4/mantilasal. The lower portion of Dark Canyon (which is not part of this loop) is managed by the Monticello Field Office, Bureau of Land Management, P.O. Box 7, Monticello, UT 84535; (435) 587-1510; www.blm.gov/utah/monticello.

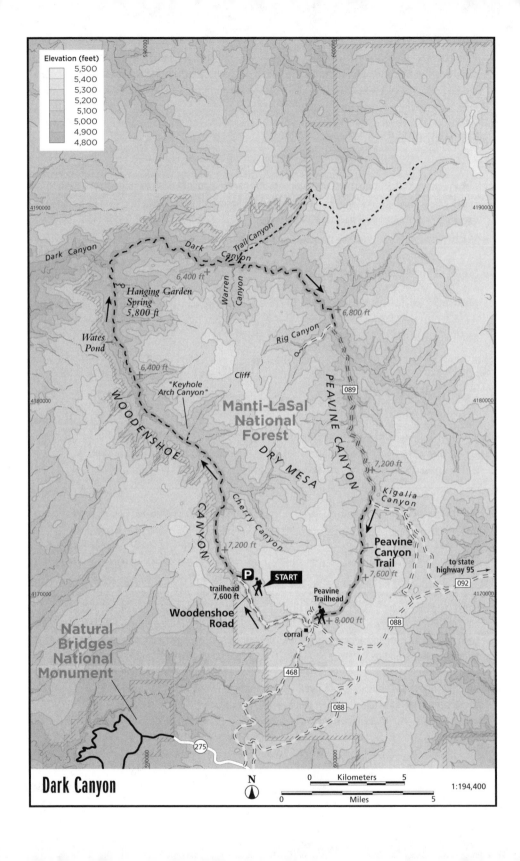

Elevation (feet)
5,500
5,400
5,300
5,200
5,100
5,000
4,900
4,800

Dark Canyon

Dark Canyon

Dark Trail Canyon Canyon

6,400 ft

Warren Canyon

Hanging Garden Spring 5,800 ft

Wates Pond

6,400 ft

Rig Canyon

Cliff

"Keyhole Arch Canyon"

Manti-LaSal National Forest

6,800 ft

089

PEAVINE CANYON

7,200 ft

WOODENSHOE

DRY MESA

Kigalia Canyon

Cherry Canyon

7,200 ft

CANYON

Peavine Canyon Trail

7,600 ft

to state highway 95

092

P

START

trailhead 7,600 ft

Peavine Trailhead

8,000 ft

088

Woodenshoe Road

corral

Natural Bridges National Monument

468

088

275

Dark Canyon

N

0 Kilometers 5

0 Miles 5

1:194,400

Finding the trailhead: From Blanding, drive south on U.S. Highway 191 and then west on Highway 95 toward Natural Bridges National Monument. Turn north off Highway 95 onto the Natural Bridges Road (Highway 275). After about a mile, turn right and follow the graded road (San Juan County Road 228) to Little Maverick Point and through Bears Ears Pass. About 2 miles north of the Bears Ears, turn left at a junction onto Forest Road 081. Look to your right for a fence line a short distance from the junction. Alongside this fence line is the Peavine Trailhead, with a bulletin board and a register box. Leave a vehicle or a bike here for a shuttle hike. If you only have one vehicle, at the end of the hike you will need to walk from here to the starting trailhead. To reach the start of this loop hike, continue down the road for about 2 miles and turn right onto Woodenshoe Road, which ends in about a mile. Park at the end of the road, where you will find a three-panel kiosk, a vault toilet, and a register box.

In early spring the route described above may be impassable. An alternative route would be to head west of Blanding on Highway 95 as above; about 20 miles from Blanding, however, turn right (north) at the large Forest Service sign indicating South Cottonwood Road. Continue through a creek crossing and up to a junction. Take the right-hand road (South Elk's Road, or Forest Road 092) toward Milk Ranch Point. Drive about 30 miles, past Milk Ranch Point and Arch Canyon Overlook. You will pass the junction north of Bears Ears Pass and see the Peavine Trailhead along the fence line on your right. The rest of the directions are the same. *DeLorme: Utah Atlas & Gazetteer:* Page 22 A1.

The Hike

This loop hike in the canyons surrounding Dry Mesa—Woodenshoe, Dark, and Peavine—measures about 40 map miles, but with side excursions it can easily be extended to twice that. The Dark Canyon area is rich in biological, geological, archaeological, and historical perspectives and remains in a relatively pristine state. The Dark Canyon Wilderness, designated in 1984, encompasses 45,000 acres. The lower portion of Dark Canyon is part of the 62,000-acre BLM Dark Canyon Primitive Area.

Hikers in Dark Canyon should be experienced in map reading and able to carry at least a full day's water supply (one gallon or more per person), in addition to food and equipment for a five- to seven-day trip. Water may be available from springs, seeps, and intermittent streams, but you should not count on it. (Be sure to treat any water you do find.) The hike is a relatively dry one and can be stressful for persons unaccustomed to desert hiking and summer temperatures that can reach one hundred degrees Fahrenheit. Fall daytime temperatures can be in the mid- to low nineties, with nighttime temperatures dropping into the forties.

Although the hike does not require technical climbing equipment, the route is rugged and undeveloped. Beginning at about 8,000 feet on the plateau and rimrocks of Cedar Mesa sandstone, you descend 2,200 feet to the sandy, dry streambed in the calcareous layers of the Hermosa formation.

Spring is the best time to attempt this route, although hikers make the trip throughout the year. Thunderstorms occur in summer and early fall, but the canyon bottoms are relatively broad, so flash-flood danger is not as severe as elsewhere in canyon country. However, there have been flooding problems in early spring. Some snow accumulates on the plateau in winter but does not present any problems in the canyon, although access to the Dark Canyon area is limited when winter moisture arrives.

From the parking area, follow the trail into Woodenshoe Canyon through the hiker maze in the fence. The trail is fairly well established and marked with cairns. The hiking is relatively easy, descending gradually along the canyon bottom.

About 4 miles from the trailhead, Cherry Canyon enters from the right (southeast). There is good camping here, and water is plentiful a short distance up Cherry. Unfortunately, a summer 2003 fire involving more than 3,000 acres burned nearly the entire drainage, causing sedimentation problems and an increase of flash-flood runoff. Still, hiking among the small pools in the streambed is fascinating.

You can find cliff dwellings about a mile down Woodenshoe beyond the mouth of Cherry Canyon. Three well-preserved petroglyphs are on the walls above the dwellings. Remember that these remnants of ancient culture are nonrenewable resources, which are protected by federal law. Please make sure that your exploration results in minimum impact.

In another mile, an unnamed canyon enters from the east. Look for an arch shaped like a keyhole.

The tracks of wildlife mix with traces of ancient civilizations. The sandy streambeds reveal tracks of cougar, bear, deer, raccoon, and ringtail cat, along with smaller tracks of rodents. More than sixty species of mammals are present in the area. Brilliantly colored lizards sun themselves on rocks, and a variety of birds find an ideal habitat in these canyons.

From "Keyhole Arch Canyon," the sandy streambed continues northwest with occasional large rocks in wash areas. The canyon walls become steeper and higher. About 2.5 miles farther down the canyon is a small seep, and approximately 3 miles farther you'll see Wates Pond, an excellent camping spot.

The canyon leads due north from Wates Pond. You descend stream-worn steps of bedrock with embedded fossils. Occasionally the trail wanders away from the streambed through scrub oak and juniper. The area is strewn with brilliant lithic chips of chert and agate.

About a mile before Woodenshoe Canyon meets Dark Canyon, a spring trickles down from the east canyon wall. This is a good water source known as Hanging Garden. Just beyond, Dark Canyon descends to the left (west) toward the Colorado River. An old sign marks the junction. That route, however, is for another trip. To complete this loop, turn right (east) into upper Dark Canyon.

From the junction at about 5,800 feet, you climb gradually to the next good campsite—6 miles up the canyon, just 1 mile beyond the spot where Trail Canyon and Warren Canyon enter from the north and south, respectively. Lithic chips, pottery shards, sand dunes, and water make for an interesting and comfortable camp.

For the next several miles, you traverse sagebrush flats. At the point where Rig Canyon enters Dark Canyon—about 5 miles from Trail Canyon—human intrusions (lumber, fences, a road, and a corral) begin to appear. There are signs and an old corral at this junction. (Note: About 2 miles up Rig Canyon is a spring and old oil-drilling camp.)

Continue southeast past Rig Canyon another mile to Peavine Canyon. Leave upper Dark Canyon here and head south on Forest Road 089 into Peavine. In about 5 miles the road jogs to the southeast into Kigalia Canyon. Bear right (southwest) onto the Peavine Canyon Trail. Peavine Canyon is beautiful, with lush vegetation because of its good water supply in the upper canyon.

Hike south on the Peavine Canyon Trail for about 5 miles to the trailhead along FR 081. If you spotted a car here, your hike is over. Otherwise, you must hike the 3 miles back to the trailhead.

This canyon loop around Dry Mesa offers rugged terrain, beautiful scenery, and solitude. Shorter trips in the area are possible, but a week in this splendid backcountry is time not soon forgotten. —*Originally contributed by Flo Krall, Ramona Allen, and Bob Stack*

Key Points

0.0 Start at the trailhead at the end of Woodenshoe Road.

4.0 Pass Cherry Canyon on the right. Continue northwest.

6.0 Pass "Keyhole Arch Canyon." Continue northwest.

11.5 Wates Pond.

15.0 Hanging Garden spring.

16.0 Junction of Woodenshoe Canyon and Dark Canyon. Turn right (east).

21.0 Pass Trail Canyon on the left and Warren Canyon on the right.

26.0 Pass Rig Canyon on the right.

27.0 Turn right onto FR 089 into Peavine Canyon.

32.0 Junction with Kigalia Canyon. Bear right onto the Peavine Canyon Trail.

37.0 Arrive at Peavine Trailhead along FR 081.

40.0 Arrive back at the trailhead at the end of Woodenshoe Road.

49 Bridges Loop

An enjoyable day hike to three huge natural sandstone bridges, involving easy walking and no unusual hazards. You'll also see Ancestral Puebloan ruins, pictographs and petroglyphs, a wide range of vegetation types, and spectacular cliff and canyon scenery.

Start: Sipapu Bridge Trailhead.
Distance: 8.6-mile loop.
Difficulty: Moderate.
Trail surface: Dry streambed.
Seasons: Spring and fall.
Land status: National monument.
Nearest town: Blanding.
Fees and permits: A $6.00-per-vehicle entrance fee ($3.00 on foot or bicycle), valid

for seven days, is charged to enter the national monument.
Maps: USGS Moss Back Butte and Kane Gulch quads; National Geographic Trails Illustrated Dark Canyon/Manti-LaSal National Forest Map.
Trail contacts: Superintendent, Natural Bridges National Monument, HC 60 Box 1, Lake Powell, UT 84533; (435) 692-1234; www.nps.gov/nabr.

Finding the trailhead: Drive south on U.S. Highway 191 from Blanding and turn west onto Highway 95. Follow Highway 95 west. Turn northwest onto Highway 275 and drive 5 miles to Natural Bridges National Monument. Three-quarters of a mile after the visitor center, just inside the monument boundary, is the beginning of 8-mile-long Bridge View Drive. Turn right onto the one-way loop and continue about 1.75 miles to the Sipapu Bridge Trailhead. (You pass Sipapu Overlook along the way.) You can also leave a vehicle at the Owachomo Trailhead for a one-way shuttle, shortening the hike by about 2.5 miles. If only one car is available, however, a maintained trail leads from the road above Owachomo Bridge back to Sipapu. *DeLorme: Utah Atlas & Gazetteer:* Page 22 A1.

The Hike

The Bridges Loop is a superb day trip suitable for experienced hikers and reasonably active families. The trail follows White Canyon and Armstrong Canyon past three natural bridges and several Ancestral Puebloan ruins. The only appreciable elevation change involves climbing into and out of the canyons; these stretches are steep but short.

Camping in the monument (except in the developed campground) and overnight parking on Bridge View Drive are prohibited. Nearly all hikers make the loop in a counterclockwise direction because it is easier. Also, since the loop has an alternate access point near the halfway point (Kachina Bridge), the trip can be easily modified.

Follow the trail to the White Canyon streambed near Sipapu Bridge. This first stretch is only about 0.6 mile, but you descend more than 400 vertical feet in the process. The trail to the base of the bridge has ladders, stairs, switchbacks, and short,

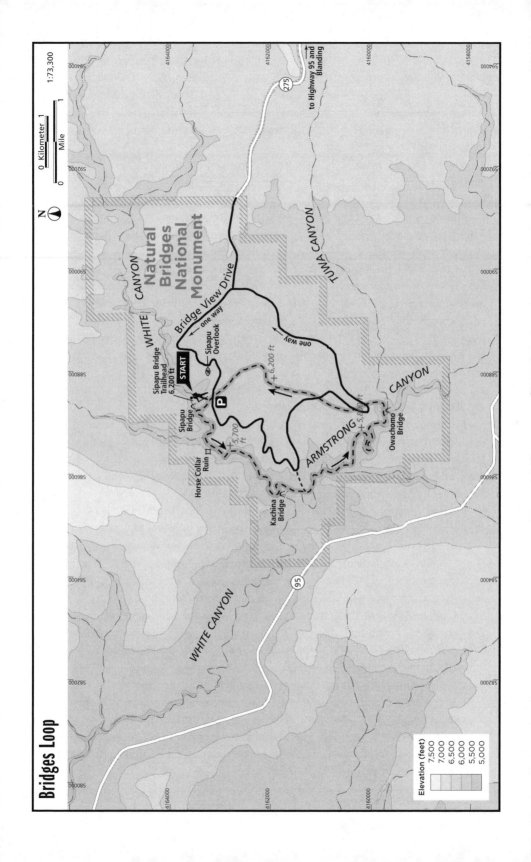

Bridges Loop

Elevation (feet)
7,500
7,000
6,500
6,000
5,500
5,000

1:73,300

0 Kilometer 1

0 Mile 1

N

Natural Bridges National Monument

WHITE CANYON

TUWA CANYON

ARMSTRONG CANYON

WHITE CANYON

Bridge View Drive

one way

one way

Sipapu Overlook

START

Sipapu Bridge Trailhead 6,200 ft

P

Sipapu Bridge 5,700 ft

Horse Collar Ruin

+ 5,700 ft

+ 6,200 ft

+ 5,800 ft

Owachomo Bridge

Kachina Bridge

to Highway 95 and Blanding

275

95

steep sections of slickrock. If you looked at the bridge from the Sipapu Overlook before dropping down into the canyon, you will be astonished at how large the bridge is up close. It's a common canyon country and desert phenomenon. Natural features are often larger than they appear to be from a distance. The lack of familiar objects of known size precludes an accurate size estimate, and the brain consistently underestimates.

The rock of the Natural Bridges area is a crossbedded sandstone known as Cedar Mesa sandstone. It is of Permian age, more than 225 million years old. Long after the land here began its slow rise from an ancient seabed, two small streams formed on the western slopes of Elk Ridge and made meandering channels across the flat land. They gradually entrenched themselves while the land underwent new uplift. As the land continued to rise, the streams cut even deeper channels—known today as White and Armstrong Canyons. Every stream attempts to make a straight channel with an even grade from its source to its mouth. Any obstacles, such as hills or large rock masses, are gradually worn away. Thus, these winding streams constantly tried to straighten their courses. During floods, silt-laden waters were thrown with great force against the walls of the meanders. In several places a fin of rock around which the stream wound was so thin that over many centuries a hole was gradually bored, and a natural bridge was born. The stream continued to cut its channel and, with the aid of other processes of erosion, enlarge the opening. Eventually the old meander was left high and dry as a "fossil" streambed.

Most of the natural bridges in the United States are in the Four Corners region of the Southwest, where favorable materials and conditions for bridge making exist. Rainbow Bridge, south of Natural Bridges National Monument, on Lake Powell, is the world's largest. Sipapu Bridge is the largest bridge in Natural Bridges National Monument and is nearly as large as Rainbow Bridge.

Leaving Sipapu, walk down the canyon (west and south) in or along the streambed. There is no developed and maintained trail, so follow the drainage.

Not far from Sipapu, on a broad ledge sheltered by an alcove on your right, Horse Collar Ruin is worth a stop. It is an Ancestral Puebloan village, which was abandoned more than 700 years ago but is still in good shape. Remember, these sites are irreplaceable. Don't enter the structures, climb on them, rub the mortar, or wiggle rocks. The National Park Service and Bureau of Land Management have found that "innocent vandalism" damages these ancient treasures more than malicious effort. That's because only a few nuts want to destroy them, but thousands of us want to touch them. The result is less dramatic, but inevitably the same—destruction of the art and architecture left by the previous owners of this real estate.

Another 2.3 miles downstream from Sipapu, Kachina Bridge spans the canyon in massive grandeur. More Ancestral Puebloan ruins are on the right just beyond the bridge, and rock art is visible on the near abutments. Most of the ancient dwellings are in positions exposed to winter sun but sheltered from the hottest summer sun, a very effective use of passive solar energy.

Immediately beyond Kachina, White Canyon bears right (west) and, on your left (southeast), Armstrong Canyon enters. Head up Armstrong Canyon. There's usually a nice pool at the foot of a dry falls near the mouth of Armstrong. It's a great place to frolic in the cool water, but it's also in plain view of a heavily visited overlook on the canyon rim. You may want to be discreet.

Continue up Armstrong Canyon about 3 miles, following the streambed, until you get to Owachomo Bridge. This very old, thin, and delicate bridge does not span Armstrong Canyon; it parallels it. Owachomo's evolution has been very different from that of the other bridges. Although unlikely, it is possible to walk right by Owachomo without seeing it. A very short distance up the canyon, you will encounter a fairly large pool at the junction of Armstrong and Tuwa Canyons. Tuwa enters from the left (east). Depending on the quantity and temperature of the water in the pool, it can be a very pleasant swimming hole. If you get to the pool without seeing Owachomo, however, you've gone a little too far.

At Owachomo Bridge climb the short but steep trail north up to the park road on the mesa top. Cross the road and continue on the trail about 2 miles back to the Sipapu Trailhead. This portion of the hike travels through the "pygmy forest" of piñon and juniper, typical of most of the area for miles around. On spring trips you may encounter wildflowers. In any season birds, small animals, and the occasional deer can be seen. Be meticulous about staying on the trail. A very delicate soil/lichen/plant community covers much of the area. Walking across a patch of this cryptogamic crust can create a long-lasting disturbance. —*Originally contributed by Dave May*

Key Points

0.0 Start at the Sipapu Bridge Trailhead.

0.6 Reach Sipapu Bridge.

2.9 Reach Kachina Bridge. Bear left toward Armstrong Canyon.

5.9 Reach Owachomo Bridge.

8.6 Arrive back at the trailhead.

50 Fish Creek and Owl Creek Loop

A multiday loop backpack in two spectacular desert canyons. Both Owl Canyon and Fish Canyon are quite deep and narrow, with an abundance of stark, scenic beauty. During the hike you'll pass Nevill's Arch, two unnamed arches, and a few Ancestral Puebloan cliff dwellings and rock-art sites.

Start: The trailhead off San Juan County Road 253.
Distance: 17-mile loop.
Difficulty: Strenuous.
Trail surface: Wash bottom (no maintained trail).
Seasons: Spring and fall.
Land status: Bureau of Land Management (BLM).
Nearest town: Blanding.
Fees and permits: Day-use permits cost $2.00 per person per trip. Overnight permits are $8.00 or $5.00 (depending on season)
and are available on a first-come, first-served basis at the Kane Gulch Ranger Station between 8:00 A.M. and noon. Advance reservations are available during peak seasons.
Maps: USGS Snowflat Spring Cave, South Long Point, and Bluff NW quads; National Geographic Trails Illustrated Grand Gulch Plateau Map; Southeastern Utah Multipurpose Map.
Trail contacts: Monticello Field Office, Bureau of Land Management, P.O. Box 7, Monticello, UT 84535; (435) 587-1510; www.blm.gov/utah/monticello.

Finding the trailhead: From Highway 95 east of Natural Bridges National Monument and west of Blanding, drive south on Highway 261. In about 4 miles you pass the Kane Gulch Ranger Station on your right. Drive another mile and turn left onto CR 253. After about 5 miles on this road, you arrive at the parking area and trailhead at a reclaimed drill hole. *DeLorme: Utah Atlas & Gazetteer:* Page 22 B2.

The Hike

This wonderful canyon trek is becoming a popular backpack for hikers of all ages. The area is experiencing increased visitation as a result of overcrowding in Grand Gulch—just to the west on the other side of Highway 261. Keep this in mind while you hike. More hikers, of course, means more impact on the land. Do your part by "walking softly"—keep a clean camp, use your backpacker stove, respect the privacy of other hikers, and, above all, do not climb on any Ancestral Puebloan archaeological sites. The BLM is finding that innocent but frequent hiker impacts on these ruins can do as much harm as isolated cases of malicious damage.

Fish Creek and Owl Creek offer an environment quite different from Grand Gulch. While piñon, juniper, and yucca vegetate the gravel and dirt bottoms in Grand Gulch, hiking in Fish and Owl is along a slickrock streambed in the upper canyon areas and along sand-cemented gravel near the junction. Vegetation ranges from yucca, prickly pear, piñon, and juniper to the spectacular ponderosa pine and manzanita groves in upper Fish Creek.

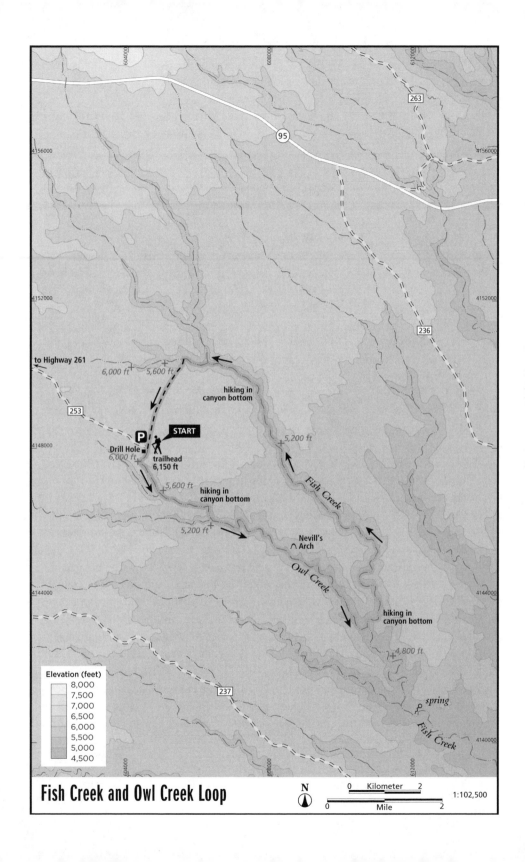

Fish Creek and Owl Creek Loop

Elevation (feet)
8,000
7,500
7,000
6,500
6,000
5,500
5,000
4,500

N

0   Kilometer   2

0   Mile   2

1:102,500

The loop hike can be done in either direction, but the trailhead is closer to Owl Creek, and BLM cairns lead a quarter mile south to this canyon, so most hikers enter Owl Creek and exit through Fish Creek to the north.

The 7-mile hike from the trailhead to the Fish-Owl junction descends more than 1,300 feet. At the junction you begin regaining this elevation. It's another 10 miles back to your car.

Follow the BLM cairns into Owl Canyon. You will shinny down sandstone, pass a small Ancestral Puebloan site, and become immersed in the canyon. Two pour-offs have to be navigated before you reach fresh water at the first canyon split—about 1.5 miles from the rim.

At both pour-offs, cairns mark a path on the left side. At the bottom of the second, you'll find a good campsite for the first night. Camping is permitted in well-used campsites only, and no fires are allowed in the canyons. You'll find a spring here, as well as several side canyons worthy of exploration. Nevill's Arch, an impressive sandstone feature, juts out from the north side of the main canyon about 5 miles into the hike.

Except for the pools, Owl Creek is usually dry between this spot and the middle of Fish Creek, about 9 miles away. Plan accordingly for the waterless stretch ahead. (It can be wetter during the spring snowmelt.)

Upon reaching the Fish-Owl junction, turn left (north) and begin winding up Fish Creek. This beautiful canyon has 500-foot walls dotted with many Ancestral Puebloan sites, with hiking primarily on ledged slickrock, which creates many pools filled with hanging gardens.

About 7 miles up Fish Creek is a major junction. Take the left (west) fork and continue 0.5 mile to a spring. A good campsite exists here, not far from the trail out of the canyon to the top. This is a good place to base yourself for a day or two in order to explore the upper reaches of Fish Creek. Here towering ponderosa pines reach for the canyon rim, and dense patches of manzanita carpet what little terrain is not slickrock.

If you encounter rain, by all means go hiking, but as with other canyon hikes, check with the BLM field office or the Kane Gulch Ranger Station for an extended forecast. Avoid hiking in narrow canyons if the weather looks bad, and don't camp in a wash bottom. If you're prepared for it, however, a storm in canyon country can be a delightful experience. The canyons turn silver as countless cascading rivulets pour over the rims, down slickrock walls, and into the streambed.

The climb out begins at the spring on the south wall of Fish Creek's Left Fork. The steep, 600-foot climb requires a slow, steady pace. There are no dangerous exposures, and at the top several places just under the rim allow you to climb out. Take one of these routes and then locate the well-used trail at the canyon edge that heads south 1.5 miles to your car at the trailhead. —*Originally contributed by Bruce Hucko*

Key Points

0.0 Start at the trailhead off CR 253, at the old drill hole.

7.0 Reach the junction of Owl and Fish Creeks. Turn left (north).

15.5 Climb out of Fish Creek's canyon.

17.0 Arrive back at the trailhead.

51 Arch Canyon

A little-known box canyon on Bureau of Land Management and Forest Service land suitable for a long day hike or two- to four-day backpacking trip, using the extra time to explore the numerous side canyons. Although Arch Canyon receives little use compared with the better-known Grand Gulch and Dark Canyon Primitive Areas, it offers outstanding scenery and numerous ruins; also, it is comparatively easy to get to by car.

Start: The mouth of Arch Canyon.

Distance: 18 miles out and back.

Difficulty: Moderate.

Trail surface: Wash bottom.

Seasons: Late spring and early fall.

Land status: Bureau of Land Management (BLM), national forest.

Nearest town: Blanding.

Fees and permits: No fees or permits required.

Maps: USGS South Long Point and Hotel Rock quads; National Geographic Trails Illustrated Grand Gulch Plateau Map.

Trail contacts: For the lower canyon, Monticello Field Office, Bureau of Land Management, P.O. Box 7, Monticello UT 84535; (435) 587-1510; www.blm.gov/utah/monticello. For the upper canyon, Monticello Ranger District, Manti-LaSal National Forest, P.O. Box 820, Monticello, UT 84535; (435) 587-2041; www.fs.fed.us/r4/mantilasal.

Finding the trailhead: Drive south from Blanding on U.S. Highway 191 to Highway 95. Turn right (west) and drive 14 miles to Comb Wash Road. It's a right (north) turn just after the highway crosses the Comb Ridge, a rock wall several hundred feet high and about 20 miles long. Drive up the west side of the wash for 2.5 miles to where the road turns east to cross the wash. Park here, in a grove of giant cottonwoods. *DeLorme: Utah Atlas & Gazetteer:* Page 22 B2.

The Hike

The high, forested massif of Abajo Peak and the rest of the Blue Mountains are drained by numerous canyons, many of which are not only fascinating to explore but also difficult to reach by road. For this reason, the area offers more solitude than other, better-known parts of Utah's redrock country. In addition, spring snowmelt in the mountains above ensures a steady flow of water in many canyons, making

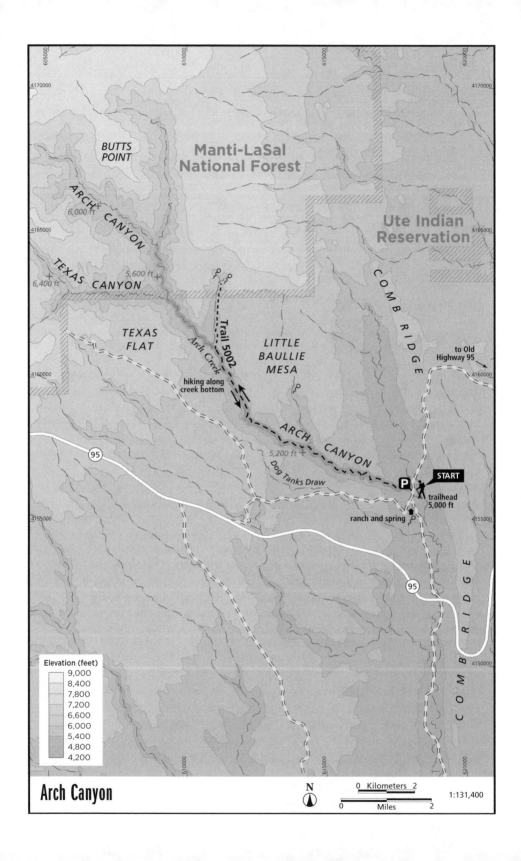

BUTTS
POINT

Manti-LaSal
National Forest

Ute Indian
Reservation

ARCH CANYON

6,000 ft

TEXAS CANYON

6,400 ft

5,600 ft

TEXAS
FLAT

Trail 5002

Arch Creek

hiking along
creek bottom

LITTLE
BAULLIE
MESA

COMB RIDGE

to Old
Highway 95

ARCH CANYON

5,200 ft

Dog Tanks Draw

95

P

START

trailhead
5,000 ft

ranch and spring

95

COMB RIDGE

Elevation (feet)

	9,000
	8,400
	7,800
	7,200
	6,600
	6,000
	5,400
	4,800
	4,200

Arch Canyon

N

0   Kilometers   2

0   Miles   2

1:131,400

desert backpacking less of a chore than usual. The Ancestral Puebloan Indians found the area ideal, and most south-facing alcoves contain evidence of their culture, from petroglyphs and three-bushel granaries to multilevel apartments and kivas. You can help preserve these sites by not climbing on walls or camping in alcoves with ruins. Of course, all artifacts are protected by state and federal antiquities acts.

Arch Canyon is a 12-mile-long box canyon that climbs gradually from 5,000 feet at the trailhead to 8,000 feet at its upper reaches, northeast of Bears Ears. Several tributaries of 4 to 6 miles make the hiking possibilities quite varied. A number of deep pools in the stream make for good swimming and wading early in summer, and several tiny waterfalls occur where rock strata come together. Campsites are easy to find all along the canyon. Few fire scars exist here, so use discretion when choosing a spot for your kitchen. A backpacker stove is recommended.

Water is available year-round from Arch Creek, but treatment is recommended. Also, deerflies can be numerous in summer. Take along a good insect repellent, even in late spring.

Arch Canyon has a floor of red, sandy soil that supports a heavy growth of sage-brush, yucca, piñon pine, juniper, cactus, and wildflowers. Most of these bloom in May and June, when there is plenty of water in the ground.

Enter the canyon through its narrow outlet in the sandstone wall and be sure to close the stock gate behind you. Immediately inside the entrance is a cluster of ruins that the BLM has tried to protect from trampling cattle with a chain-link fence. Fortunately, the destruction extends only this far—the rest of the canyon has been left alone, and grazing does not appear to be heavy.

After about 3 miles of gentle hiking, the first tributary canyon enters from the right (north). Near its head, about 1.5 miles upstream, you'll find a spring and a ruin. The next tributary also enters from the right, another 4 miles farther up the main canyon. As you approach, the walls become steeper and higher, with more precipitous and photogenic rock formations. In late spring wildflowers abound along here, particularly the sego lily, lupine, penstemon, and desert paintbrush, not to mention the extravagant pincushion, claret cup, and prickly pear cacti. This second tributary also contains a cliff dwelling and springs near its head, 1.5 miles to the north. At the mouth of the second tributary, you will have climbed nearly 500 feet from the trailhead.

Almost 2 miles farther, after you've entered the Manti-LaSal National Forest, Texas Canyon joins Arch Canyon from the left (west) in a beautiful grove of ponderosa pine. Several excellent camping spots exist nearby, and directly opposite, on the canyon's northeast wall, is a massive circular arch that catches the full light of the evening sun. While the rock behind the arch remains in shadow, the arch seems to swell up out of the canyon wall, as if it had just been cast in molten gold.

Texas Canyon heads due west for 2 miles and then forks. It has many exciting rock formations and is well worth exploring. Arch Canyon also forks into Butts Canyon about a mile above its junction with Texas. Both branches have numerous steep alcoves and castellated buttresses, which offer interesting possibilities for climbs and photographs. You could easily spend a week in the Arch Canyon system and never waste a minute. —*Originally contributed by John Tallmadge*

Key Points

0.0 Start at the mouth of Arch Canyon.

3.2 Reach the first tributary canyon on the right (north).

7.2 Reach the second tributary canyon on the right (north).

9.0 Arrive at the junction with Texas Canyon. Turnaround point.

18.0 Arrive back at the trailhead.

52 Mule Canyon

An easily accessible day hike or overnighter in Mule Canyon, one of the canyons of the Grand Gulch Plateau.

Start: Where San Juan County Road 263 crosses Mule Canyon.
Distance: 8 miles out and back.
Difficulty: Easy.
Trail surface: Wash bottom.
Seasons: Spring and fall.
Land status: Bureau of Land Management (BLM).
Nearest town: Blanding.
Fees and permits: Day-use permits cost

$2.00 per person per trip and are available at the trailhead or at the Kane Gulch Ranger Station between 8:00 A.M. and noon.
Maps: USGS South Long Point and Hotel Rock quads; National Geographic Trails Illustrated Grand Gulch Plateau Map.
Trail contacts: Monticello Field Office, Bureau of Land Management, P.O. Box 7, Monticello, UT 84535; (435) 587–1510; www.blm.gov/utah/monticello.

Finding the trailhead: Drive south from Blanding on U.S. Highway 191 to Highway 95. Turn right (west) and drive 19 miles to dirt CR 263 (old Highway 95), which exits to the north. This road is about half a mile east of a stabilized roadside ruin called Mule Canyon Indian Ruins and 1 mile west of the Highway 95–Mule Canyon junction. In 0.25 mile this dirt road crosses Mule Canyon. Park here to begin your hike. *DeLorme: Utah Atlas & Gazetteer:* Page 22 B2.

The Hike

Mule Canyon offers an easily accessible canyon trip. Hikers of all ages enjoy the Cedar Mesa sandstone, Indian ruins, and solitude. You can hike in Mule Canyon during any season, although caution is advised in winter due to potentially icy conditions. Access may also be limited during this season.

Highway 95 crosses Mule Canyon west of Blanding, just south of where Mule and the North Fork join. Day hikes and overnighters are excellent in both of these

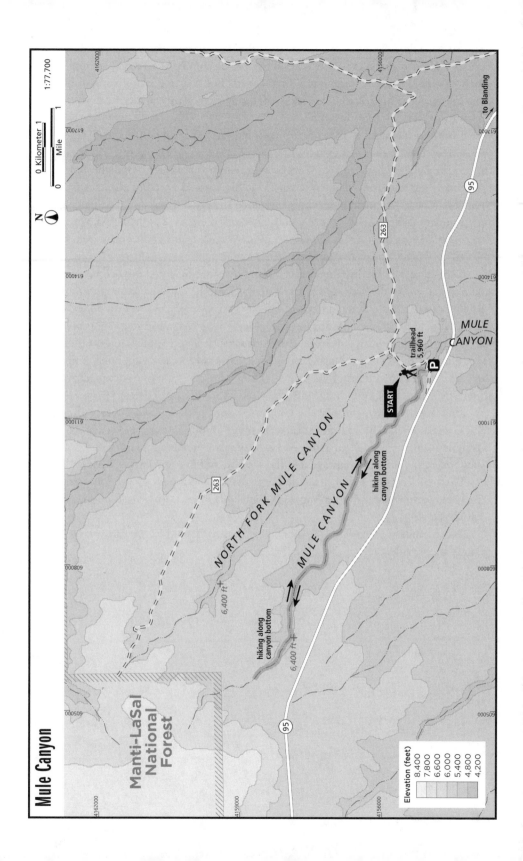

Mule Canyon

Manti-LaSal National Forest

NORTH FORK MULE CANYON

MULE CANYON

263

263

hiking along canyon bottom

hiking along canyon bottom

6,400 ft

6,400 ft

START

trailhead
5,960 ft

P

MULE CANYON

to Blanding

95

95

N

1:77,700

0 Kilometer 1

0   Mile   1

Elevation (feet)

8,400
7,800
6,600
6,000
5,400
4,800
4,200

canyons. Mule Canyon carves its way south of Highway 95; however, deep pour-offs (dry waterfalls) make hiking more difficult there. The North Fork of Mule Canyon, also an excellent hike, is three quarters of a mile farther up the dirt road. You may want to try this hike another time.

From the trailhead at about 5,960 feet, the canyon meanders about 7 miles to 7,600 feet. The first 4 miles feature little elevation change, making this trip ideal for young or inexperienced hikers. The canyons along this stretch wind through the pinkish white sandstone of the Cedar Mesa, highlighted by relict Douglas fir and ponderosa pine. The many beautiful seeps along the canyon walls support patches of red monkey flower, shooting star, columbine, and the rare canyon orchid. You may see mule deer, as the canyon serves as a migratory area, and occasionally predators. Watch for birds of prey soaring above the canyon.

Occasionally a cliff dwelling shows among the trees. Splendid opportunities exist here to appreciate the crafts of the late Pueblo II and III cultures, although unfortunately pottery shards, flint, and other artifacts have been carried off by hikers who ignored the value of the outdoor museum. Remember that all artifacts are protected by federal antiquities laws; do your part by leaving artifacts where you find them.

Many of the cliff dwellings have a long "defensive wall" with holes pointing toward different directions of the canyon. These ports, according to some archaeoastronomers, may have been built with the solstices in mind.

One site in the canyon may be connected with present Zuni puberty rites. As the sun sets during the summer solstice, it shines through a port and sends a beam of light below a petroglyph representing a woman. A Zuni legend says, "A light shown through the port impregnated the woman and the twins were born."

These sites combine rock art, building structure, and modern Zuni ethnography for a fascinating perspective on Ancestral Puebloan culture. —*Originally contributed by Fred Blackburn*

(Note: Since you may hike as short or as long as desired in the canyon, no Key Points are provided.)

53 Marching Men and Tower Arch

An easy day hike into a wonderland of sandstone formations located 22 miles from Moab. Points of interest include the uniquely eroded sandstone "marching men," Tower Arch, and a historical inscription left by the man who first suggested that this area be preserved.

Start: Klondike Bluffs parking area.
Distance: 6-mile loop.
Difficulty: Moderate.
Trail surface: Sandy and rocky trail, dirt road.
Seasons: Fall and spring.
Land status: National park.
Nearest town: Moab.
Fees and permits: A $10.00-per-vehicle entrance fee ($5.00 on foot or bicycle), valid for seven days, is charged to enter the park. No permit is required to day hike.

Maps: USGS Klondike Bluffs quad; National Geographic Trails Illustrated Arches National Park Map.
Trail contacts: Superintendent, Arches National Park, P.O. Box 907, Moab, UT 84532; (435) 719-2299; www.nps.gov/arch.

Finding the trailhead: Enter Arches National Park near Moab from U.S. Highway 191. Stop at the visitor center just off the highway and ask about road conditions to Klondike Bluffs. The Salt Valley Road is generally passable to two-wheel-drive vehicles. Heavy rains, however, can make the road impassable to any vehicle, so be certain to check on road conditions. Drive about 17 miles into the park to the dirt Salt Valley Road—on your left after driving through most of the park. Follow this road for 7.7 miles to a junction, where a sign points you to the left to the Klondike Bluffs parking area, 1.3 miles farther. *DeLorme: Utah Atlas & Gazetteer:* Page 40 D2.

The Hike

Arches National Park offers a number of "major attractions" served by developed trails, but each of these destinations also features opportunities for informal side trips or extensions. Additionally, many very pleasant places are not served by trails but are still easily accessible.

This is rugged-looking country, but it is also very delicate. Irresponsible hikers can leave long-lasting scars. Avoid wandering through patches of biological soil crust—low-lying, nonflowering plants. Big, black, and bumpy when mature, this important crust is nearly invisible in its early developmental stages. Providing nutrients for higher plants and helping hold the sand in place are critical roles for this important but often ignored plant community. Help preserve this delicate ecosystem by walking only on the trails, staying on slickrock, or following sandy washes.

This hike to Marching Men and Tower Arch is an easy 6-mile loop through Klondike Bluffs, an area of slickrock and beautifully eroded sandstone. The elevation changes less than 300 feet. Most of the route is on four-wheel- or two-wheel-drive dirt roads, but traffic is minimal.

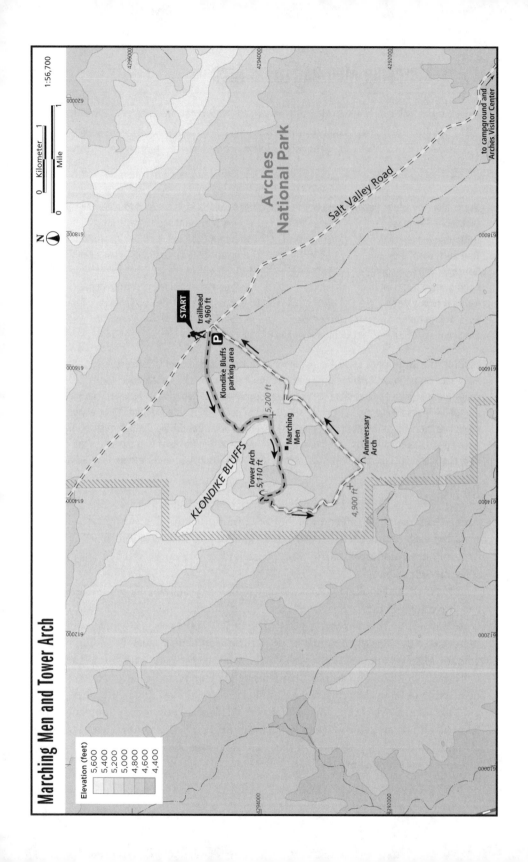

Marching Men and Tower Arch

Elevation (feet)
5,600
5,400
5,200
5,000
4,800
4,600
4,400

N

1:56,700

0   Kilometer   1

0   Mile   1

Arches
National Park

START
trailhead
4,960 ft

Klondike Bluffs
parking area

Salt Valley Road

5,200 ft

Marching
Men

Anniversary
Arch

4,900 ft

KLONDIKE BLUFFS

Tower Arch
5,110 ft

to campground and
Arches Visitor Center

Along the foot trail is a row of towering monoliths called the Marching Men, an impressive stone arch, a historic inscription, and much more. Usually hikers make the trip to see Tower Arch, but that's just an excuse to get into this fabulous backcountry.

A developed trail leads from the parking area over the east end of the bluffs, passes through a maze of elaborately eroded sandstone figures, and reaches Tower Arch after about 1.7 miles.

Tower Arch spans an opening more than 45 feet high and about 100 feet long. A nearby sandstone "tower" is the reason for the name. The rock in which this arch—and others in the park—has formed was deposited as sand about 150 million years ago during the Jurassic period. This 300-foot layer, called the Entrada sandstone, is believed to have been laid down mainly by wind. Its characteristics suggest that it accumulated in a vast coastal desert. In time it was buried by new layers and hardened to rock.

The rock then uplifted, twisted, and severely cracked several times. Later, after erosion stripped away the overlying layers, the sandstone was exposed to weathering, and the formation of arches began. Water entering cracks in the sandstone dissolved some of the cementing material, and running water and wind removed the loose sand. Cracks widened into narrow canyons separated by fins. More rapid weathering of softer areas in some of these vertical walls resulted in undercutting. The quarrying by water and frost persisted, perforating the fins, enlarging the perforations, and smoothing their contours until large, graceful arches were the final creation.

One of the Tower Arch abutments bears a 1922 carved inscription recording the presence of Alex Ringhoffer and his family in the area. While carving on rocks today is considered vandalism, this historic note is an important record of early discovery in the area. Ringhoffer was a prospector so impressed by the Tower Arch area (which he called Devils Garden) that he recommended to the Rio Grande Railroad that they develop it as a tourist attraction. Ringhoffer's suggestion led to a series of events that resulted in President Hoover's 1929 proclamation establishing Arches National Monument. The original proclamation covered two small areas, one of them being Devils Garden. The area Ringhoffer called Devils Garden, however, was not included. Confusion during the late 1920s resulted in the inadvertent transfer of the name to another location and to the exclusion of the originally proposed site from the monument. It was forty years before Ringhoffer's Devils Garden was added to the monument, and by that time (1969), it was called Klondike Bluffs.

From Tower Arch, the trail continues north for 0.25 mile. At this point you turn south and join the four-wheel-drive road that continues a little more than 3.5 miles south then northeast back to the Salt Valley Road. Here you are about a third of a mile from your parked vehicle. Walking this stretch of road is generally enjoyable; traffic is very light, and you're likely to have it to yourself.

Tower Arch is the usual attraction for most hikers, but the entire Klondike Bluffs area is a great place for fascinating exploring. Unstructured wandering amid eroded sandstone rock gardens, discovery of slickrock potholes—teeming with unusual critters at certain times of year—and observations of diverse vegetation can be an exercise in serendipity.

Watch for wildlife. The species here are characteristic of the sparse piñon-juniper forest communities of the Great Basin Desert. Larger mammals—deer, coyotes, kangaroo rats, and foxes—are present, but are most active at dusk and dawn. You may, however, see birds, ground squirrels, rabbits, and small reptiles.

This hike is a perfect introduction to the Arches backcountry. After completing it, you'll want to begin plans for your next trip. —*Originally contributed by Dave May*

Key Points

0.0 Start at the Klondike Bluffs parking area.

1.7 Reach Tower Arch on your right.

5.7 Arrive at Salt Valley Road. Turn left (northwest).

6.0 Arrive back at the parking area.

54 Negro Bill Canyon

A delightful day hike in a slickrock canyon in the Negro Bill Wilderness Study Area. The hiker-only trail winds through the canyon to Morning Glory Arch, the sixth largest natural bridge in the United States.

Start: Negro Bill Canyon Trailhead.
Distance: 4 miles out and back to Morning Glory Arch.
Difficulty: Easy to moderate.
Trail surface: Sand/dirt trail.
Seasons: Spring and fall.
Land status: Bureau of Land Management (BLM) wilderness study area.
Nearest town: Moab.

Fees and permits: No fees or permits required.
Maps: USGS Moab and Rill Creek quads; National Geographic Trails Illustrated Arches National Park Map.
Trail contacts: Moab Field Office, Bureau of Land Management, 82 East Dogwood, Moab, UT 84532; (435) 259-2100; www.ut.blm.gov.

Finding the trailhead: Drive 2 miles northwest of Moab on U.S. Highway 191 and turn right onto Highway 128, just south of the Colorado River. Follow the meanders of the river for about 3 miles to the mouth of Negro Bill Canyon on the right. Park in the dirt parking area (which also serves as a parking area for mountain bikers exiting the Porcupine Rim Trail). The hike begins on the left side of the parking area at a signed trailhead at about 4,000 feet. The canyon climbs gradually from here. *DeLorme: Utah Atlas & Gazetteer:* Page 40 D3.

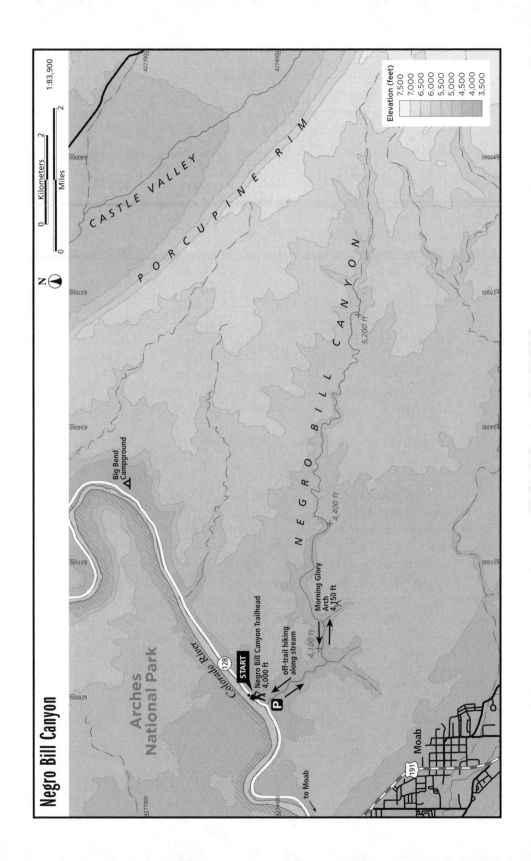

Negro Bill Canyon

1:83,900

N

Elevation (feet)
7,500
7,000
6,500
6,000
5,500
5,000
4,500
4,000
3,500

Kilometers

Miles

CASTLE VALLEY

P O R C U P I N E   R I M

N E G R O   B I L L   C A N Y O N

5,200 ft

Big Bend
Campground

Arches
National Park

Colorado River

128

START

Negro Bill Canyon Trailhead
4,000 ft

off-trail hiking
along stream

4,100 ft

Morning Glory
Arch
4,150 ft

4,400 ft

P

Moab

191

to Moab

The Hike

This lovely little canyon was one of the most controversial sites in southeastern Utah, an early battleground of the Sagebrush Rebellion. In June 1979 Negro Bill Canyon was the center of a land management battle. Local antienvironmental and antifederal activists—part of the Sagebrush Rebellion—used a county bulldozer to demolish a modest dirt barrier the Bureau of Land Management had built to keep vehicles from damaging the canyon while it was being considered for possible wilderness status. The BLM replaced the barrier a few weeks later, but angry Grand County commissioners held a formal meeting and declared that the road up the canyon belonged to the county. That same day county officials used the bulldozer again to plow through the new barrier. Then the county reportedly spread gravel on the lower part of the road to "improve it," making it an improved way and thus not suitable for a roadless area.

The federal government filed suit in U.S. district court over the incident. The result was a negotiated settlement, and today the canyon is part of the Negro Bill Wilderness Study Area.

It's a fine place for beginning hikers and children, with Morning Glory Arch just off the canyon's main section only 2 miles from the trailhead.

The well-marked trail follows the canyon bottom, crossing the stream several times. Usually you can hop this perennial stream, but there may be some crossings where your feet get wet.

Pink and gray cliffs rise above the talus slopes, from which sprout abundant vegetation. Not far from the trailhead, a pink boulder sits in the middle of the stream, just up from a small waterfall. Along this section the cliff faces are close together, smooth or rippled, streaked and rough, often gouged by deep cracks or caves. They are laced with bands of bushes.

Wildlife is abundant. You may see garter snakes and frogs along the stream, lizards are everywhere, and hawks soar above the pink sandstone walls and knobs. Big tea green crayfish live in some of the stream's larger pools.

About a half mile from the trailhead, look for a beautiful alcove in the left (north) wall. In fall the thick vegetation is spectacular. The alcove has a sandy floor and sheer cliffs that glow salmon and orange. You can almost always find a shady nook in this spot.

At a large spine of rocks, a little more than a mile into the canyon, a major side canyon enters from the right (south). This canyon has some interesting hiking, although thick vegetation makes the going tough in spots. You encounter rough slickrock terrain that requires scrambling at times. The route parallels cliffs, drops into water pockets, and crosses boulder-strewn stretches. You may find an enormous cottonwood tree in a box canyon in this area.

In another 0.5 mile turn right (southeast) into another side canyon. Hike for 0.4 mile and look for Morning Glory Arch, a 243-foot-long rock span, set back against the cliff above a spring and a small pool. It is hard to distinguish from the rock wall until you are almost under it. Turn around here or continue exploring the main canyon as far as you'd like. —*Originally contributed by Joe Bauman*

Key Points

0.0   Start from the parking area at the mouth of Negro Bill Canyon.

1.1   A side canyon enters from the right (south).

1.6   Another side canyon enters from the right (southeast). Turn right.

2.0   Arrive at Morning Glory Arch. Turnaround point.

4.0   Arrive back at the parking area.

Honorable Mentions

Southern Utah

○ Canaan Mountain

Canaan Mountain offers the backcountry enthusiast some of the most scenic and diverse hiking experiences in southern Utah. Hikers should be proficient in back-country navigation and map reading, since only the access routes to the mountain-top are readily followed. Canaan Mountain, an ecologically intact escarpment surrounded on three sides by 1,800- to 2,200-foot cliffs, boasts terrain similar to Zion National Park, with which it shares a common border. Piñon and ponderosa pine, juniper, aspen, manzanita, Gambel oak, sagebrush, and western wheatgrass are the principal vegetation types on Canaan. Mule's-ears, sand dropseed, and poa are secondary species. Maple and fir species are found on cooler sites within large crevices that cut into the heart of the mountain. On the talus slopes below the rims, littleleaf mountain mahogany and juniper are major plant species, with Oregon grape, Gambel oak, and shrubbery maples clinging aggressively to the steep, heavily bouldered terrain. The major trailheads developed by the BLM are Squirrel Canyon on the south side of the mountain and Eagle Crags to the north. The most popular route originates at Squirrel Canyon, 2 miles north of Colorado City, Arizona, and traverses the mountain to just south of Rockville, Utah (about 16 miles, depending on the route). From the Squirrel Canyon Trailhead, either the Squirrel Canyon Trail or the Water Canyon Trail will take you to the top. You can take a shorter loop hike, starting and finishing at Squirrel Canyon via Water Canyon, or you can spot a car at the Eagle Crags Trailhead near Rockville to hike the entire route.

To reach the Squirrel Canyon Trailhead, head southeast from Hurricane on Utah Highway 59 for about 24 miles to Hildale, just before the Arizona border. On the northeast end of town, follow a dirt road north 1.5 miles to the trailhead in Short Creek Canyon. There is a small parking lot. To spot a car on the north end of the mountain, take Utah Highway 9 to Rockville, south of Zion National Park. At the east end of town, head south on the paved road and cross the Virgin River at the Rockville Bridge. After one-eighth of a mile, the main road swings to the right. Continue straight on the dirt road another 1.5 miles to the trailhead. Small signs direct you to the Eagle Crags Trailhead. For more information contact St. George Field Office, Bureau of Land Management, 345 East Riverside Drive, St. George, UT 84790; (435) 688–3200; www.ut.blm.gov. *DeLorme: Utah Atlas & Gazetteer:* Page 17 D6. —*Originally contributed by Paul Boos*

P Rattlesnake Creek and Ashdown Gorge

This hike, from the northwest corner of Cedar Breaks National Monument down Rattlesnake Creek and Ashdown Gorge to Highway 14 east of Cedar City, is an exciting and rigorous backpack. The hike to Highway 14 requires a car shuttle, but in-and-out options are also possible from the trailhead. The route drops 3,400 feet in 9 miles and receives only occasional use (mostly during fall hunting seasons). It is not recommended for hikers with little map-reading experience. The trail is good only in isolated spots, and you must follow rock cairns and slashes on trees.

The Cedar Breaks area has a rich history. Early exploration began in 1851, when Mormons settled in Parowan and Cedar City. In 1905 the area was included as a part of the Sevier (now Dixie) National Forest, administered by the USDA Forest Service. It was established as a national monument on August 22, 1933, under the administration of the National Park Service.

The trailhead is on the northern boundary of Cedar Breaks National Monument. From U.S. Highway 89 at Panguitch, take Highway 143 southwest to Cedar Breaks National Monument. Immediately north of the monument boundary turn west onto a dirt road (signed RATTLESNAKE CREEK–ASHDOWN GORGE), then drive about a mile and park off the road. *DeLorme: Utah Atlas & Gazetteer:* Page 18 A1.

To complete the shuttle, leave a car at the dirt road that exits north off Highway 14 about 7 miles east of Cedar City. This road exits toward Last Chance Canyon at Martins Flat, then parallels the road and Coal Creek for about 1.5 miles. For more information contact Cedar City Ranger District, 1789 Wedgewood Lane, Cedar City, UT 84721; (435) 865–3200; www.fs.fed.us/dxnf; or Cedar Breaks National Monument, 2390 West Highway 56, Suite 11, Cedar City, UT 84720; (435) 586–9451; www.nps.gov/cebr. *DeLorme: Utah Atlas & Gazetteer:* Page 17 A6. —*Originally contributed by Nancy Jane Cushing*

Q Paria Canyon

Hiking through Paria Canyon has become increasingly popular with visitors to southern Utah and northern Arizona since the early 1970s. In 1969 Paria Canyon was designated as one of the first Bureau of Land Management (BLM) primitive areas in the country. The canyon became part of the Paria Canyon–Vermilion Cliffs Wilderness with the passage of the Arizona Wilderness Act of 1984. Paria Canyon has been written about in various books and magazines, including *Arizona Highways* and *National Geographic.* Adding to the popularity of the hike is the easy access to the trailheads and the fact that hikers can exit the canyon downstream at the Colorado River.

For about the first half of its length, the canyon cuts through the Navajo sandstone formation. The lower half cuts into progressively older formations, adding variety to the beauty of the canyon. This route begins in Utah at the White House Trailhead just south of U.S. Highway 89; it ends 38 miles downstream in Arizona at Lees Ferry. Because the hike follows the course of the Paria River, the route is a gradual descent. You lose only about 1,100 feet of elevation in 38 miles. A minimum of three days is recommended for the trip; four to six days would be preferable. A fee of $5.00 per person, per day, is charged.

The road to the trailhead exits south from US 89 near mile marker 21, about 44 miles east of Kanab and 30 miles west of Page, Arizona. The Paria Information Station—open March 15 through November 15, daily from 8:30 A.M. to 4:15 P.M.—is a few hundred yards off the highway. The trailhead is about 2 miles beyond. The gravel road to the trailhead should not be a problem for most cars. *DeLorme: Utah Atlas & Gazetteer:* Page 19 D5.

The hike ends on the Colorado River at Lees Ferry in Arizona. To spot a car here, take US 89 east from the White House Trailhead, cross the Colorado River, and continue on US 89 past Page, Arizona. About 23 miles beyond Page, turn right onto U.S. Highway 89A and drive north, recrossing the Colorado River. The road to Lees Ferry turns to the right on the west side of the river. The distance by road from the White House Trailhead to Lees Ferry is about 75 miles. For more information contact Kanab Field Office, Bureau of Land Management, 318 North 100 E., Kanab, UT 84741; (435) 644–4600; www.ut.blm.gov or www.az.blm.gov/paria.
—*Originally contributed by Rod Schipper*

R Navajo Point

Navajo Point on Fiftymile Mountain offers spectacular views of the Escalante Canyon, the San Juan arm of Lake Powell, and the north side of Navajo Mountain, southeast across the former channel of the Colorado River. Fiftymile Mountain, a major unroaded plateau known in early literature as Wild Horse Mesa, is surrounded by 1,000-foot cliffs and extremely rough canyons. It is part of a 146,000-acre Bureau of Land Management (BLM) wilderness study area within Grand Staircase–Escalante National Monument. The route along the top of Fiftymile Mountain is in Glen Canyon National Recreation Area. This is a demanding two- to three-day hike, recommended for those experienced in desert camping and travel. Solitude predominates on this hike, which is seldom used by visitors. Piñon, juniper, and open grass and sagebrush cover the top of the plateau, with aspen in isolated patches, usually at canyon heads. Archaeology in the area is significant because of the density of late Ancestral Puebloan occupation sites.

Drive east from Escalante on Highway 12 about 5 miles to Hole-in-the-Rock Road. Turn right and drive about 48 miles south to the second turnoff for Fiftymile Bench Road. Turn right and drive 4.7 miles up the steep and winding road (four-wheel drive is necessary at times) until it forks on top of Fiftymile Bench (the bench below Fiftymile Mountain). Turn left (south) at the fork and continue about 2.2 miles to another fork. Stay to the right here. About 100 feet beyond the fork, a trail is visible on the right heading west toward the Straight Cliffs. Park here to begin your hike to the top of Fiftymile Mountain. For more information contact Escalante Interagency Visitor Information Center, Box 225, Escalante, UT 84726; (435)

826–5499; www.ut.blm.gov/monument or www.nps.gov/glca. *DeLorme: Utah Atlas & Gazetteer:* Page 20 C2. —*Originally contributed by Bill Booker*

S Fable Valley

Fable Valley provides a gentle alternative to the steeply walled canyons of the Dark Canyon area just to the south. This open, shallow valley with its sagebrush, grass, and sloping sandstone walls makes for pleasant hiking. Once you're in the bottom, the trail is hard to follow at times, winding in and out of the wash, but it stays mostly on the benches above the streambed. Fable Valley is part of the Bureau of Land Management's 62,000-acre Dark Canyon Primitive Area. The trail begins just west of the Sweet Alice Hills on Dark Canyon Plateau.

To reach the trailhead, turn north off Highway 95 toward Natural Bridges National Monument. After about a mile on the Natural Bridges Road, turn right and follow the graded road up Little Maverick Point and then over Bears Ears Pass. About 2 miles north of the pass, turn right at the junction. Follow Forest Road 088 northeast past Arch Canyon Overlook. Turn left 2 miles farther and head north past the Notch and Duck Lake to the North Long Point Road (Forest Road 091). Turn left here and continue west. Six and a half miles west of the Trail Canyon Trailhead, at the junction of Lean-to Point and Fable Valley Pasture, a signpost marks an old road heading north into Fable Valley Canyon. Park here. For more information contact Monticello Field Office, Bureau of Land Management, P.O. Box 7, Monticello, UT 84535; (435) 587–1510; www.blm.gov/utah/monticello. *DeLorme: Utah Atlas & Gazetteer:* Page 30 D1. —*Originally contributed by the Monticello Ranger District*

T Grand Gulch

Grand Gulch is much more than a hike; it is a trip through 2,000 years of history. The Ancestral Puebloan civilization flourished here, and signs of these Natives' architectural skills are common as you hike along the creek, dwarfed by massive sandstone walls. The largest site in the canyon is Junction Ruins, 4 miles in at the junction of Kane and Grand Gulches. The Bureau of Land Management (BLM) established Grand Gulch as a primitive area in 1970. Since then the hike has been extremely popular. Grand Gulch has three main trailheads—Kane Gulch, Bullet Canyon, and Collins Spring. Most hikers enter at Kane Gulch, near the top of the canyon, hike for a day or two, and then retrace their steps. Grand Gulch joins Kane Gulch about 4 miles from the trailhead and then winds about 50 miles to the San Juan River. Bullet Canyon enters from the east about a third of the way down, and the drainage from Collins Spring enters from the northwest about two-thirds down the gulch. Ask the BLM for more information on these two additional trailheads. An excellent book on Grand Gulch, as well as other canyons in the area, is *Wind in the Rock* by Ann Zwinger.

To reach the Kane Gulch Trailhead, take Highway 261 off Highway 95 east of Natural Bridges National Monument and west of Blanding. Drive about 4 miles and turn right to the Kane Gulch Ranger Station. The station is usually open between March 1 and November 15. Get a backcountry permit here, as well as information on protecting the area. For more information contact Monticello Field Office, Bureau of Land Management, P.O. Box 7, Monticello, UT 84535; (435) 587–1510; www.blm.gov/utah/monticello. *DeLorme: Utah Atlas & Gazetteer:* Page 22 B1. —*Originally contributed by Fred Blackburn*

∪ Behind the Rocks

Few hikers realize that within sight of Moab's main street is one of the premier hiking spots around. As you drive through Moab, notice the 1,000-foot sandstone wall to the southwest. This wall guards a Bureau of Land Management (BLM) wilderness study area of more than 12,000 acres. The area, called Behind the Rocks, offers fascinating hiking among eroded sandstone fins. In fact, the name might be a bit misleading, because as you hike through Behind the Rocks, you feel like you're actually *in* the rocks. Or, as one hiker described the experience in comments to the BLM, it's as if you are "in between the slices of a loaf of fresh bread." Despite proximity to Moab, a strong case for wilderness has been made because of the solitude provided by the many sandstone fins. After the climb to the top, you'll feel totally isolated, even though Moab is but a few miles away. The Navajo sandstone fins are an eighth to a quarter mile long, a few hundred feet thick, and several hundred feet high. Once you get back among them, you'll find virtually unlimited opportunities for exploration. But be cautious—fin canyons often end in pour-offs that cannot be climbed without ropes, and it is relatively easy to become disoriented and lost in this maze of rock.

The easiest access to the area is via the Moab Rim Trail. Turn west off U.S. Highway 191 in Moab onto Kane Creek Boulevard. This road is located on the south end of town, about half a mile from Center Street. After going under the power lines that cross the Colorado River, travel about a mile. Look for a small turnoff on the left side of the road, just beyond the first cattle guard. It appears that the road goes nowhere, but if you look closely you'll see it running along the redrock ledge. After hiking for a short distance, you begin to see the rubber marks of the jeepers. The road becomes more obvious on top, and you come to a 700-foot overlook of Moab. The trail shortly enters the wilderness study area.

There's plenty of exploring from here. If you follow the jeep road southeast, you connect with the Hidden Valley Trail, which originates at Angel Rock Road, 3 miles south of Moab on US 191. This would make a great 6.5-mile shuttle hike. Another access along Kane Creek Boulevard is on the Pritchett Canyon jeep road, 3.1 miles from the power lines just outside Moab. After crossing private property and paying a $1.00 fee, you can hike up the jeep trail and then head north in among the fins. For more information contact Moab Field Office, Bureau of Land Management, 82 East Dogwood, Moab, UT 84532; (435) 259–2100; www.ut.blm.gov. *DeLorme: Utah Atlas & Gazetteer:* Page 30 A3. —*Originally contributed by Glen Lathrop*

The Art of Hiking

When standing nose to nose with a mountain lion, you're probably not too concerned with the issue of ethical behavior in the wild. No doubt you're just terrified. But let's be honest. How often are you nose to nose with a mountain lion? For most of us, a hike into the "wild" means loading up the SUV with expensive gear and driving to a toileted trailhead. Sure, you can mourn how civilized we've become—how GPS units have replaced natural instinct and Gore-Tex, true-grit—but the silly gadgets of civilization aside, we have plenty of reason to take pride in how we've matured. With survival now on the back burner, we've begun to reason—and it's about time—that we have a responsibility to protect, no longer just conquer, our wild places: that they, not we, are at risk. So please, do what you can. The following section will help you understand better what it means to "do what you can" while still making the most of your hiking experience. Anyone can take a hike, but hiking safely and well is an art requiring preparation and proper equipment.

Trail Etiquette

Zero impact. Always leave an area just like you found it—if not better than you found it. Avoid camping in fragile, alpine meadows and along the banks of streams and lakes. Use a camp stove versus building a wood fire. Pack up all of your trash and extra food. Bury human waste at least 100 feet from water sources under 6 to 8 inches of topsoil. Don't bathe with soap in a lake or stream—use prepackaged moistened towels to wipe off sweat and dirt, or bathe in the water without soap.

Stay on the trail. It's true, a path anywhere leads nowhere new, but purists will just have to get over it. Paths serve an important purpose; they limit impact on natural areas. Straying from a designated trail may seem innocent but it can cause damage to sensitive areas—damage that may take years to recover, if it can recover at all. Even simple shortcuts can be destructive. So, please, stay on the trail.

Leave no weeds. Noxious weeds tend to overtake other plants, which in turn affects animals and birds that depend on them for food. To minimize the spread of noxious weeds, hikers should regularly clean their boots, tents, packs, and hiking poles of mud and seeds. Also brush your dog to remove any weed seeds before heading off into a new area.

Keep your dog under control. You can buy a flexi-lead that allows your dog to go exploring along the trail, while allowing you the ability to reel him in should another hiker approach or should he decide to chase a rabbit. Always obey leash laws and be sure to bury your dog's waste or pack it in resealable plastic bags.

Respect other trail users. Often you're not the only one on the trail. With the rise in popularity of multiuse trails, you'll have to learn a new kind of respect, beyond the nod and "hello" approach you may be used to. First investigate whether you're on a multiuse trail, and assume the appropriate precautions. When you encounter motorized vehicles (ATVs, motorcycles, and 4WDs), be alert. Though they should always yield to the hiker, often they're going too fast or are too lost in the buzz of their engine to react to your presence. If you hear activity ahead, step off the trail just to be safe. Note that you're not likely to hear a mountain biker coming, so be prepared and know ahead of time whether you share the trail with them. Cyclists should always yield to hikers, but that's little comfort to the hiker. Be aware. When you approach horses or pack animals on the trail, always step quietly off the trail, preferably on the downhill side, and let them pass. If you're wearing a large backpack, it's often a good idea to sit down. To some animals, a hiker wearing a large backpack might appear threatening. Many national forests allow domesticated grazing, usually for sheep and cattle. Make sure your dog doesn't harass these animals, and respect ranchers' rights while you're enjoying yours.

Getting into Shape

Unless you want to be sore—and possibly have to shorten your trip or vacation—be sure to get in shape before a big hike. If you're terribly out of shape, start a walking program early, preferably eight weeks in advance. Start with a fifteen-minute walk during your lunch hour or after work and gradually increase your walking time to an hour. You should also increase your elevation gain. Walking briskly up hills really strengthens your leg muscles and gets your heart rate up. If you work in a storied office building, take the stairs instead of the elevator. If you prefer going to a gym, walk the treadmill or use a stair machine. You can further increase your strength and endurance by walking with a loaded backpack. Stationary exercises you might consider are squats, leg lifts, sit-ups, and push-ups. Other good ways to get in shape include biking, running, aerobics, and, of course, short hikes. Stretching before and after a hike keeps muscles flexible and helps avoid injuries.

Preparedness

It's been said that failing to plan means planning to fail. So do take the necessary time to plan your trip. Whether going on a short day hike or an extended backpack trip, always prepare for the worst. Simply remembering to pack a copy of the U.S. Army Survival Manual is not preparedness. Although it's not a bad idea if you plan on entering truly wild places, it's merely the tourniquet answer to a problem. You need to do your best to prevent the problem from arising in the first place. In order to survive—and to stay reasonably comfortable—you need to concern yourself with the basics: water, food, and shelter. Don't go on a hike without having these bases covered. And don't go on a hike expecting to find these items in the woods.

Water. Even in frigid conditions, you need at least two quarts of water a day to function efficiently. Add heat and taxing terrain and you can bump that figure up to one gallon. That's simply a base to work from—your metabolism and your level of conditioning can raise or lower that amount. Unless you know your level, assume that you need one gallon of water a day. Now, where do you plan on getting the water?

Preferably not from natural water sources. These sources can be loaded with intestinal disturbers, such as bacteria, viruses, and fertilizers. Giardia lamblia, the most common of these disturbers, is a protozoan parasite that lives part of its life cycle as a cyst in water sources. The parasite spreads when mammals defecate in water sources. Once ingested, Giardia can induce cramping, diarrhea, vomiting, and fatigue within two days to two weeks after ingestion. Giardiasis is treatable with prescription drugs. If you believe you've contracted giardiasis, see a doctor immediately.

Treating water. The best and easiest solution to avoid polluted water is to carry your water with you. Yet, depending on the nature of your hike and the duration, this may not be an option—one gallon of water weighs eight-and-a-half pounds. In that case, you'll need to look into treating water. Regardless of which method you choose, you should always carry some water with you in case of an emergency. Save this reserve until you absolutely need it.

There are three methods of treating water: boiling, chemical treatment, and filtering. If you boil water, it's recommended that you do so for ten to fifteen minutes. This is often impractical because you're forced to exhaust a great deal of your fuel supply. You can opt for chemical treatment, which will kill Giardia but will not take care of other chemical pollutants. Another drawback to chemical treatments is the unpleasant taste of the water after it's treated. You can remedy this by adding powdered drink mix to the water. Filters are the preferred method for treating water. Many filters remove Giardia, organic and inorganic contaminants, and don't leave an aftertaste. Water filters are far from perfect as they can easily become clogged or leak if a gasket wears out. It's always a good idea to carry a backup supply of chemical treatment tablets in case your filter decides to quit on you.

Food. If we're talking about survival, you can go days without food, as long as you have water. But we're also talking about comfort. Try to avoid foods that are high in sugar and fat like candy bars and potato chips. These food types are harder to digest and are low in nutritional value. Instead, bring along foods that are easy to pack, nutritious, and high in energy (e.g., bagels, nutrition bars, dehydrated fruit, gorp, and jerky). If you are on an overnight trip, easy-to-fix dinners include rice mixes with dehydrated potatoes, corn, pasta with cheese sauce, and soup mixes. For a tasty breakfast, you can fix hot oatmeal with brown sugar and reconstituted milk powder topped off with banana chips. If you like a hot drink in the morning, bring along herbal tea bags or hot chocolate. If you are a coffee junkie, you can purchase coffee that is packaged like tea bags. You can prepackage all of your meals in heavy-duty resealable plastic bags to keep food from spilling in your pack. These bags can be reused to pack out trash.

Shelter. The type of shelter you choose depends less on the conditions than on your tolerance for discomfort. Shelter comes in many forms—tent, tarp, lean-to, bivy sack, cabin, cave, etc. If you're camping in the desert, a bivy sack may suffice, but if you're above the treeline and a storm is approaching, a better choice is a three- or four-season tent. Tents are the logical and most popular choice for most backpackers as they're lightweight and packable—and you can rest assured that you always have shelter from the elements. Before you leave on your trip, anticipate what the weather and terrain will be like and plan for the type of shelter that will work best for your comfort level (see Equipment later in this section).

Finding a campsite. If there are established campsites, stick to those. If not, start looking for a campsite early—around 3:30 or 4:00 P.M. Stop at the first decent site you see. Depending on the area, it could be a long time before you find another suitable location. Pitch your camp in an area that's level. Make sure the area is at least 200 feet from fragile areas like lakeshores, meadows, and stream banks. And try to avoid areas thick in underbrush, as they can harbor insects and provide cover for approaching animals.

If you are camping in stormy, rainy weather, look for a rock outcrop or a shelter in the trees to keep the wind from blowing your tent all night. Be sure that you don't camp under trees with dead limbs that might break off on top of you. Also, try to find an area that has an absorbent surface, such as sandy soil or forest duff. This, in addition to camping on a surface with a slight angle, will provide better drainage. By all means, don't dig trenches to provide drainage around your tent—remember you're practicing zero-impact camping.

If you're in bear country, steer clear of creekbeds or animal paths. If you see any signs of a bear's presence (i.e., scat, footprints), relocate. You'll need to find a campsite near a tall tree where you can hang your food and other items that may attract bears such as deodorant, toothpaste, or soap. Carry a lightweight nylon rope with which to hang your food. As a rule, you should hang your food at least 20 feet from the ground and 5 feet away from the tree trunk. You can put food and other items in a waterproof stuff sack and tie one end of the rope to the stuff sack. To get the other end of the rope over the tree branch, tie a good size rock to it, and gently toss the rock over the tree branch. Pull the stuff sack up until it reaches the top of the branch and tie it off securely. Don't hang your food near your tent! If possible, hang your food at least 100 feet away from your campsite. Alternatives to hanging your food are bear-proof plastic tubes and metal bear boxes.

Lastly, think of comfort. Lie down on the ground where you intend to sleep and see if it's a good fit. For morning warmth (and a nice view to wake up to), have your tent face east.

First Aid

I know you're tough, but get 10 miles into the woods and develop a blister and you'll wish you had carried that first-aid kit. Face it, it's just plain good sense. Many companies produce lightweight, compact first-aid kits. Just make sure yours contains at least the following:

- adhesive bandages
- moleskin or duct tape
- various sterile gauze and dressings
- white surgical tape
- an Ace bandage
- an antihistamine
- aspirin
- Betadine solution
- a first-aid book
- antacid tablets

- tweezers
- scissors
- antibacterial wipes
- triple-antibiotic ointment
- plastic gloves
- sterile cotton tip applicators
- syrup of ipecac (to induce vomiting)
- thermometer
- wire splint

Here are a few tips for dealing with and hopefully preventing certain ailments.

Sunburn. Take along sunscreen or sun block, protective clothing, and a wide-brimmed hat. If you do get a sunburn, treat the area with aloe vera gel, and protect the area from further sun exposure. At higher elevations, the sun's radiation can be particularly damaging to skin. Remember that your eyes are vulnerable to this radiation as well. Sunglasses can be a good way to prevent headaches and permanent eye damage from the sun, especially in places where light-colored rock or patches of snow reflect light up in your face.

Blisters. Be prepared to take care of these hike-spoilers by carrying moleskin (a lightly padded adhesive), gauze and tape, or adhesive bandages. An effective way to apply moleskin is to cut out a circle of moleskin and remove the center—like a doughnut—and place it over the blistered area. Cutting the center out will reduce the pressure applied to the sensitive skin. Other products can help you combat blisters. Some are applied to suspicious hot spots before a blister forms to help decrease friction to that area, while others are applied to the blister after it has popped to help prevent further irritation.

Insect bites and stings. You can treat most insect bites and stings by applying hydrocortisone 1% cream topically and taking a pain medication such as ibuprofen or acetaminophen to reduce swelling. If you forgot to pack these items, a cold compress or a paste of mud and ashes can sometimes assuage the itching and discomfort. Remove any stingers by using tweezers or scraping the area with your fingernail or a knife blade. Don't pinch the area as you'll only spread the venom.

Some hikers are highly sensitive to bites and stings and may have a serious allergic reaction that can be life threatening. Symptoms of a serious allergic reaction can include wheezing, an asthmatic attack, and shock. The treatment for this severe type of reaction is epinephrine. If you know that you are sensitive to bites and stings, carry a pre-packaged kit of epinephrine, which can be obtained only by prescription from your doctor.

Ticks. Ticks can carry diseases such as Rocky Mountain spotted fever and Lyme disease. The best defense is, of course, prevention. If you know you're going to be hiking through an area littered with ticks, wear long pants and a long sleeved shirt. You can apply a permethrin repellent to your clothing and a Deet repellent to exposed skin. At the end of your hike, do a spot check for ticks (and insects in general). If you do find a tick, coat the insect with petroleum jelly or tree sap to cut off its air supply. The tick should release its hold, but if it doesn't, grab the head of the tick firmly—with a pair of tweezers if you have them—and gently pull it away from the skin with a twisting motion. Sometimes the mouth parts linger, embedded in your skin. If this happens, try to remove them with a disinfected needle. Clean the affected area with an antibacterial cleanser and then apply triple antibiotic ointment. Monitor the area for a few days. If irritation persists or a white spot develops, see a doctor for possible infection.

Poison ivy, oak, and sumac. These skin irritants can be found most anywhere in North America and come in the form of a bush or a vine, having leaflets in groups of three, five, seven, or nine. Learn how to spot the plants. The oil they secrete can cause an allergic reaction in the form of blisters, usually about twelve hours after exposure. The itchy rash can last from ten days to several weeks. The best defense against these irritants is to wear clothing that covers the arms, legs and torso. For summer, zip-off cargo pants come in handy. There are also nonprescription lotions you can apply to exposed skin that guard against the effects of poison ivy/oak/sumac and can be washed off with soap and water. If you think you were in contact with the plants, after hiking (or even on the trail during longer hikes) wash with soap and water. Taking a hot shower with soap after you return home from your hike will also help to remove any lingering oil from your skin. Should you contract a rash from any of these plants, use an antihistamine to reduce the itching. If the rash is localized, create a light bleach/water wash to dry up the area. If the rash has spread, either tough it out or see your doctor about getting a dose of cortisone (available both orally and by injection).

Snakebites. Snakebites are rare in North America. Unless startled or provoked, the majority of snakes will not bite. If you are wise to their habitats and keep a careful eye on the trail, you should be just fine. When stepping over logs, first step on the log, making sure you can see what's on the other side before stepping down. Though your chances of being struck are slim, it's wise to know what to do in the event you are.

If a *nonpoisonous* snake bites you, allow the wound to bleed a small amount and then cleanse the wounded area with a Betadine solution (10% povidone iodine).

Rinse the wound with clean water (preferably) or fresh urine (it might sound ugly, but it's sterile). Once the area is clean, cover it with triple antibiotic ointment and a clean bandage. Remember, most residual damage from snakebites, poisonous or otherwise, comes from infection, not the snake's venom. Keep the area as clean as possible and get medical attention immediately.

If you are bitten by a poisonous snake, remove the toxin with a suctioning device, found in a snakebite kit. If you do not have such a device, squeeze the wound—DO NOT use your mouth for suction, as the venom will enter your bloodstream through the vessels under the tongue and head straight for your heart. Then, clean the wound just as you would a nonpoisonous bite. Tie a clean band of cloth snuggly around the afflicted appendage, about an inch or so above the bite (or the rim of the swelling). This is NOT a tourniquet—you want to simply slow the blood flow, not cut it off. Loosen the band if numbness ensues. Remove the band for a minute and reapply a little higher every ten minutes.

If it is your friend who's been bitten, treat him or her for shock—make the person comfortable, have him or her lie down, elevate the legs, and keep him or her warm. Avoid applying anything cold to the bite wound. Immobilize the affected area and remove any constricting items such as rings, watches, or restrictive clothing—swelling may occur. Once your friend is stable and relatively calm, hike out to get help. The victim should get treatment within twelve hours, ideally, which usually consists of a tetanus shot, antivenin, and antibiotics.

If you are alone and struck by a poisonous snake, stay calm. Hysteria will only quicken the venom's spread. Follow the procedure above, and do your best to reach help. When hiking out, don't run—you'll only increase the flow of blood throughout your system. Instead, walk calmly.

Dehydration. Have you ever hiked in hot weather and had a roaring headache and felt fatigued after only a few miles? More than likely you were dehydrated. Symptoms of dehydration include fatigue, headache, and decreased coordination and judgment. When you are hiking, your body's rate of fluid loss depends on the outside temperature, humidity, altitude, and your activity level. On average, a hiker walking in warm weather will lose four liters of fluid a day. That fluid loss is easily replaced by normal consumption of liquids and food. However, if a hiker is walking briskly in hot, dry weather and hauling a heavy pack, he or she can lose one to three liters of water an hour. It's important to always carry plenty of water and to stop often and drink fluids regularly, even if you aren't thirsty.

Heat exhaustion is the result of a loss of large amounts of electrolytes and often occurs if a hiker is dehydrated and has been under heavy exertion. Common symptoms of heat exhaustion include cramping, exhaustion, fatigue, lightheadedness, and nausea. You can treat heat exhaustion by getting out of the sun and drinking an electrolyte solution made up of one teaspoon of salt and one tablespoon of sugar dissolved in a liter of water. Drink this solution slowly over a period of one hour.

Drinking plenty of fluids (preferably an electrolyte solution/sports drink) can prevent heat exhaustion. Avoid hiking during the hottest parts of the day, and wear breathable clothing, a wide-brimmed hat, and sunglasses.

Hypothermia is one of the biggest dangers in the backcountry, especially for day hikers in the summertime. That may sound strange, but imagine starting out on a hike in midsummer when it's sunny and 80 degrees out. You're clad in nylon shorts and a cotton T-shirt. About halfway through your hike, the sky begins to cloud up, and in the next hour a light drizzle begins to fall and the wind starts to pick up. Before you know it, you are soaking wet and shivering—the perfect recipe for hypothermia. More advanced signs include decreased coordination, slurred speech, and blurred vision. When a victim's temperature falls below 92 degrees, the blood pressure and pulse plummet, possibly leading to coma and death.

To avoid hypothermia, always bring a windproof/rainproof shell, a fleece jacket, tights made of a breathable, synthetic fiber, gloves, and hat when you are hiking in the mountains. Learn to adjust your clothing layers based on the temperature. If you are climbing uphill at a moderate pace you will stay warm, but when you stop for a break you'll become cold quickly, unless you add more layers of clothing.

If a hiker is showing advanced signs of hypothermia, dress him or her in dry clothes and make sure he or she is wearing a hat and gloves. Place the person in a sleeping bag in a tent or shelter that will protect him or her from the wind and other elements. Give the person warm fluids to drink and keep him awake.

Frostbite. When the mercury dips below 32 degrees, your extremities begin to chill. If a persistent chill attacks a localized area, say, your hands or your toes, the circulatory system reacts by cutting off blood flow to the affected area—the idea being to protect and preserve the body's overall temperature. And so it's death by attrition for the affected area. Ice crystals start to form from the water in the cells of the neglected tissue. Deprived of heat, nourishment, and now water, the tissue literally starves. This is frostbite.

Prevention is your best defense against this situation. Most prone to frostbite are your face, hands, and feet, so protect these areas well. Wool is the material of choice because it provides ample air space for insulation and draws moisture away from the skin. Synthetic fabrics, however, have recently made great strides in the cold weather clothing market. Do your research. A pair of light silk liners under your regular gloves is a good trick for keeping warm. They afford some additional warmth, but more importantly they'll allow you to remove your mitts for tedious work without exposing the skin.

If your feet or hands start to feel cold or numb due to the elements, warm them as quickly as possible. Place cold hands under your armpits or bury them in your crotch. If your feet are cold, change your socks. If there's plenty of room in your boots, add another pair of socks. Do remember, though, that constricting your feet in tight boots can restrict blood flow and actually make your feet colder more quickly. Your socks need to have breathing room if they're going to be effective.

Dead air provides insulation. If your face is cold, place your warm hands over your face, or simply wear a head stocking.

Should your skin go numb and start to appear white and waxy, chances are you've got or are developing frostbite. Don't try to thaw the area unless you can maintain the warmth. In other words, don't stop to warm up your frostbitten feet only to head back on the trail. You'll do more damage than good. Tests have shown that hikers who walked on thawed feet did more harm, and endured more pain, than hikers who left the affected areas alone. Do your best to get out of the cold entirely and seek medical attention—which usually consists of performing a rapid rewarming in water for twenty to thirty minutes.

The overall objective in preventing both hypothermia and frostbite is to keep the body's core warm. Protect key areas where heat escapes, like the top of the head, and maintain the proper nutrition level. Foods that are high in calories aid the body in producing heat. Never smoke or drink when you're in situations where the cold is threatening. By affecting blood flow, these activities ultimately cool the body's core temperature.

Altitude sickness (AMS). High lofty peaks, clear alpine lakes, and vast mountain views beckon hikers to the high country. But those who like to venture high may become victims of altitude sickness (also known as Acute Mountain Sickness—AMS). Altitude sickness is your body's reaction to insufficient oxygen in the blood due to decreased barometric pressure. While some hikers may feel lightheaded, nauseous, and experience shortness of breath at 7,000 feet, others may not experience these symptoms until they reach 10,000 feet or higher.

Slowing your ascent to high places and giving your body a chance to acclimatize to the higher elevations can prevent altitude sickness. For example, if you live at sea level and are planning a weeklong backpacking trip to elevations between 7,000 and 12,000 feet, start by staying below 7,000 feet for one night, then move to between 7,000 and 10,000 feet for another night or two. Avoid strenuous exertion and alcohol to give your body a chance to adjust to the new altitude. It's also important to eat light food and drink plenty of nonalcoholic fluids, preferably water. Loss of appetite at altitude is common, but you must eat!

Most hikers who experience mild to moderate AMS develop a headache and/or nausea, grow lethargic, and have problems sleeping. The treatment for AMS is simple: stop heading uphill. Keep eating and drinking water and take meds for the headache. You actually need to take more breaths at altitude than at sea level, so breathe a little faster without hyperventilating. If symptoms don't improve over twenty-four to forty-eight hours, descend. Once a victim descends about 2,000 to 3,000 feet, his signs will usually begin to diminish.

Severe AMS comes in two forms: High Altitude Pulmonary Edema (HAPE) and High Altitude Cerebral Edema (HACE). HAPE, an accumulation of fluid in the lungs, can occur above 8,000 feet. Symptoms include rapid heart rate, shortness of breath at rest, AMS symptoms, dry cough developing into a wet cough, gurgling sounds, flu-like or bronchitis symptoms, and lack of muscle coordination. HAPE is life threatening so descend immediately, at least 2,000 to 4,000 feet. HACE usually occurs above 12,000 feet but sometimes occurs above 10,000 feet. Symptoms are similar to HAPE but also include seizures, hallucinations, paralysis, and vision disturbances. Descend immediately—HACE is also life threatening.

Hantavirus Pulmonary Syndrome (HPS). Deer mice spread the virus that causes HPS, and humans contract it from breathing it in, usually when they've disturbed an area with dust and mice feces from nests or surfaces with mice droppings or urine. Exposure to large numbers of rodents and their feces or urine presents the greatest risk. As hikers, we sometimes enter old buildings, and often deer mice live in these places. We may not be around long enough to be exposed, but do be aware of this disease. About half the people who develop HPS die. Symptoms are flu-like and appear about two to three weeks after exposure. After initial symptoms, a dry cough and shortness of breath follow. Breathing is difficult. If you even think you might have HPS, see a doctor immediately!

Natural Hazards

Besides tripping over a rock or tree root on the trail, there are some real hazards to be aware of while hiking. Even if where you're hiking doesn't have the plethora of poisonous snakes and plants, insects, and grizzly bears found in other parts of the United States, there are a few weather conditions and predators you may need to take into account.

Lightning. Thunderstorms build over the mountains almost every day during the summer. Lightning is generated by thunderheads and can strike without warning, even several miles away from the nearest overhead cloud. The best rule of thumb is to start leaving exposed peaks, ridges, and canyon rims by about noon. This time can vary a little depending on storm buildup. Keep an eye on cloud formation and don't underestimate how fast a storm can build. The bigger they get, the more likely a thunderstorm will happen. Lightning takes the path of least resistance, so if you're the high point, it might choose you. Ducking under a rock overhang is dangerous as you form the shortest path between the rock and ground. If you dash below treeline, avoid standing under the only or the tallest tree. If you are caught above treeline, stay away from anything metal you might be carrying, Move down off the ridge slightly to a low, treeless point and squat until the storm passes. If you have an insulating pad, squat on it. Avoid having both your hands and feet touching the ground at once and never lay flat. If you hear a buzzing sound or feel your hair standing on end, move quickly as an electrical charge is building up.

Flash floods. On July 31, 1976, a torrential downpour dumped tons of water into the Big Thompson watershed near Estes Park, Colorado. Within hours, a wall of water moved down the narrow canyon killing 139 people and causing more than $30 million in property damage. The spooky thing about flash floods, especially in western canyons, is that they can appear out of nowhere from a storm many miles away. While hiking or driving in canyons, keep an eye on the weather. Always climb to safety if danger threatens. Flash floods usually subside quickly, so be patient and don't cross a swollen stream.

Bears. Most of the United States (outside of the Pacific Northwest and parts of the Northern Rockies) does not have a grizzly bear population, although some rumors exist about sightings where there should be none. Black bears are plentiful, however. Here are some tips in case you and a bear scare each other. Most of all, avoid scaring a bear. Watch for bear tracks (five toes) and droppings (sizable with leaves, partly digested berries, seeds, and/or animal fur). Talk or sing where visibility or hearing are limited. Keep a clean camp, hang food, and don't sleep in the clothes you wore while cooking. Be especially careful in spring to avoid getting between a mother and her cubs. In late summer and fall bears are busy eating berries and acorns to fatten up for winter, so be extra careful around berry bushes and oakbrush. If you do encounter a bear, move away slowly while facing the bear, talk softly, and avoid direct eye contact. Give the bear room to escape. Since bears are very curious, it might stand upright to get a better whiff of you, and it may even charge you to try to intimidate you. Try to stay calm. If a bear does attack you, fight back with anything you have handy. Unleashed dogs have been known to come running back to their owners with a bear close behind. Keep your dog on a leash or leave it at home.

Mountain lions. Mountain lions appear to be getting more comfortable around humans as long as deer (their favorite prey) are in an area with adequate cover. Usually elusive and quiet, lions rarely attack people. If you meet a lion, give it a chance to escape. Stay calm and talk firmly to it. Back away slowly while facing the lion. If you run, you'll only encourage the curious cat to chase you. Make yourself look large by opening a jacket, if you have one, or waving your hiking poles. If the lion behaves aggressively throw stones, sticks, or whatever you can while remaining tall. If a lion does attack, fight for your life with anything you can grab.

Moose. Because moose have very few natural predators, they don't fear humans like other animals. You might find moose in sagebrush and wetter areas of willow, aspen, and pine, or in beaver habitats. Mothers with calves, as well as bulls during mating season, can be particularly aggressive. If a moose threatens you, back away slowly and talk calmly to it. Keep your pets away from moose.

Other considerations. Hunting is a popular sport in the United States, especially during rifle season in October and November. Hiking is still enjoyable in those months in many areas, so just take a few precautions. First, learn when the different hunting seasons start and end in the area in which you'll be hiking. During this time frame, be sure to wear at least a blaze orange hat, and possibly put an orange vest over your pack. Don't be surprised to see hunters in camo outfits carrying bows or muzzleloading rifles around during their season. If you would feel more comfortable without hunters around, hike in national parks and monuments or state and local parks where hunting is not allowed.

Navigation

Whether you are going on a short hike in a familiar area or planning a weeklong backpack trip, you should always be equipped with the proper navigational equipment—at the very least a detailed map and a sturdy compass.

Maps. There are many different types of maps available to help you find your way on the trail. Easiest to find are Forest Service maps and BLM (Bureau of Land Management) maps. These maps tend to cover large areas, so be sure they are detailed enough for your particular trip. You can also obtain National Park maps as well as high quality maps from private companies and trail groups. These maps can be obtained either from outdoor stores or ranger stations.

U.S. Geological Survey topographic maps are particularly popular with hikers—especially serious backcountry hikers. These maps contain the standard map symbols such as roads, lakes, and rivers, as well as contour lines that show the details of the trail terrain like ridges, valleys, passes, and mountain peaks. The 7.5-minute series (1 inch on the map equals approximately 2/5 mile on the ground) provides the closest inspection available. USGS maps are available by mail (U.S. Geological Survey, Map Distribution Branch, P.O. Box 25286, Denver, CO 80225), or at mapping.usgs.gov/esic/to_order.html.

If you want to check out the high-tech world of maps, you can purchase topographic maps on CD-ROM. These software-mapping programs let you select a route on your computer, print it out, then take it with you on the trail. Some software mapping programs let you insert symbols and labels, download waypoints from a GPS unit, and export the maps to other software programs.

The art of map reading is a skill that you can develop by first practicing in an area you are familiar with. To begin, orient the map so the map is lined up in the correct direction (i.e. north on the map is lined up with true north). Next, familiarize yourself with the map symbols and try and match them up with terrain features around you such as a high ridge, mountain peak, river, or lake. If you are practicing with a USGS map, notice the contour lines. On gentler terrain these contour lines are spaced further apart, and on steeper terrain they are closer together. Pick a short loop trail, and stop frequently to check your position on the map. As you practice map reading, you'll learn how to anticipate a steep section on the trail or a good place to take a rest break, and so on.

Compasses. First off, the sun is not a substitute for a compass. So, what kind of compass should you have? Here are some characteristics you should look for: a rectangular base with detailed scales, a liquid-filled housing, protective housing, a sighting line on the mirror, luminous alignment and back-bearing arrows, a luminous north-seeking arrow, and a well-defined bezel ring.

You can learn compass basics by reading the detailed instructions included with your compass. If you want to fine-tune your compass skills, sign up for an orienteering class or purchase a book on compass reading. Once you've learned the basic skills of using a compass, remember to practice these skills before you head into the backcountry.

If you are a klutz at using a compass, you may be interested in checking out the technical wizardry of the GPS (Global Positioning System) device. The GPS was developed by the Pentagon and works off twenty-four NAVSTAR satellites, which were designed to guide missiles to their targets. A GPS device is a handheld unit that calculates your latitude and longitude with the easy press of a button. The Department of Defense used to scramble the satellite signals a bit to prevent civilians (and spies!) from getting extremely accurate readings, but that practice was discontinued in May 2000, and GPS units now provide nearly pinpoint accuracy (within 30 to 60 feet).

There are many different types of GPS units available and they range in price from $100 to $400. In general, all GPS units have a display screen and keypad where you input information. In addition to acting as a compass, the unit allows you to plot your route, easily retrace your path, track your traveling speed, find the mileage between waypoints, and calculate the total mileage of your route.

Before you purchase a GPS unit, keep in mind that these devices don't pick up signals indoors, in heavily wooded areas, on mountain peaks, or in deep valleys.

Pedometers. A pedometer is a small, clip-on unit with a digital display that calculates your hiking distance in miles or kilometers based on your walking stride. Some units also calculate the calories you burn and your total hiking time. Pedometers are available at most large outdoor stores and range in price from $20 to $40.

Trip Planning

Planning your hiking adventure begins with letting a friend or relative know your trip itinerary so they can call for help if you don't return at your scheduled time. Your next task is to make sure you are outfitted to experience the risks and rewards of the trail. This section highlights gear and clothing you may want to take with you to get the most out of your hike.

Day Hikes

- camera/film
- compass/GPS unit
- pedometer
- daypack
- first-aid kit
- food
- guidebook
- headlamp/flashlight with extra batteries and bulbs
- hat
- insect repellent
- knife/multipurpose tool
- map
- matches in waterproof container and fire starter
- fleece jacket
- rain gear
- space blanket
- sunglasses
- sunscreen
- swimsuit
- watch
- water
- water bottles/water hydration system

Overnight Trip

- backpack and waterproof rain cover
- backpacker's trowel
- bandanna
- bear repellent spray
- bear bell
- biodegradable soap
- pot scrubber
- collapsible water container (2–3 gallon capacity)
- clothing—extra wool socks, shirt and shorts
- cook set/utensils
- ditty bags to store gear
- extra plastic resealable bags
- gaiters
- garbage bag
- ground cloth
- journal/pen
- nylon rope to hang food
- long underwear
- permit (if required)
- rain jacket and pants
- sandals to wear around camp and to ford streams
- sleeping bag
- waterproof stuff sack
- sleeping pad
- small bath towel
- stove and fuel
- tent
- toiletry items
- water filter
- whistle

Equipment

With the outdoor market currently flooded with products, many of which are pure gimmickry, it seems impossible to both differentiate and choose. Do I really need a tropical-fish-lined collapsible shower? (No, you don't.) The only defense against the maddening quantity of items thrust in your face is to think practically—and to do so before you go shopping. The worst buys are impulsive buys. Since most name brands will differ only slightly in quality, it's best to know what you're looking for in terms of function. Buy only what you need. You will, don't forget, be carrying what you've bought on your back. Here are some things to keep in mind before you go shopping.

Clothes. Clothing is your armor against Mother Nature's little surprises. Hikers should be prepared for any possibility, especially when hiking in mountainous areas. Adequate rain protection and extra layers of clothing are a good idea. In summer, a wide-brimmed hat can help keep the sun at bay. In the winter months the first layer you'll want to wear is a "wicking" layer of long underwear that keeps perspiration away from your skin. Wear long underwear made from synthetic fibers that wick moisture away from the skin and draw it toward the next layer of clothing, where it then evaporates. Avoid wearing long underwear made of cotton as it is slow to dry and keeps moisture next to your skin.

The second layer you'll wear is the "insulating" layer. Aside from keeping you warm, this layer needs to "breathe" so you stay dry while hiking. A fabric that provides insulation and dries quickly is fleece. It's interesting to note that this one-of-a-kind fabric is made out of recycled plastic. Purchasing a zip-up jacket made of this material is highly recommended.

The last line of layering defense is the "shell" layer. You'll need some type of waterproof, windproof, breathable jacket that will fit over all of your other layers. It should have a large hood that fits over a hat. You'll also need a good pair of rain pants made from a similar waterproof, breathable fabric. Some Gore-Tex jackets cost as much as $500, but you should know that there are more affordable fabrics out there that work just as well.

Now that you've learned the basics of layering, you can't forget to protect your hands and face. In cold, windy, or rainy weather you'll need a hat made of wool or fleece and insulated, waterproof gloves that will keep your hands warm and toasty. As mentioned earlier, buying an additional pair of light silk liners to wear under your regular gloves is a good idea.

Footwear. If you have any extra money to spend on your trip, put that money into boots or trail shoes. Poor shoes will bring a hike to a halt faster than anything else. To avoid this annoyance, buy shoes that provide support and are lightweight and flexible. A lightweight hiking boot is better than a heavy, leather mountaineering boot for most day hikes and backpacking. Trail running shoes provide a little extra cushion and are made in a high-top style that many people wear for hiking. These running shoes are lighter, more flexible, and more breathable than hiking boots. If you know you'll be hiking in wet weather often, purchase boots or shoes with a Gore-Tex liner, which will help keep your feet dry.

When buying your boots, be sure to wear the same type of socks you'll be wearing on the trail. If the boots you're buying are for cold weather hiking, try the boots on while wearing two pairs of socks. Speaking of socks, a good cold weather sock combination is to wear a thinner sock made of wool or polypropylene covered by a heavier outer sock made of wool. The inner sock protects the foot from the rubbing effects of the outer sock and prevents blisters. Many outdoor stores have some type of ramp to simulate hiking uphill and downhill. Be sure to take advantage of this test, as toe-jamming boot fronts can be very painful and debilitating on the downhill trek.

Once you've purchased your footwear, be sure to break them in before you hit the trail. New footwear is often stiff and needs to be stretched and molded to your foot.

Hiking poles. Hiking poles help with balance, and more importantly take pressure off your knees. The ones with shock absorbers are easier on your elbows and knees. Some poles even come with a camera attachment to be used as a monopod. And heaven forbid you meet a mountain lion, bear, or unfriendly dog, the poles can make you look a lot bigger.

Backpacks. No matter what type of hiking you do you'll need a pack of some sort to carry the basic trail essentials. There are a variety of backpacks on the market, but let's first discuss what you intend to use it for. Day hikes or overnight trips?

If you plan on doing a day hike, a daypack should have some of the following characteristics: a padded hip belt that's at least 2 inches in diameter (avoid packs with only a small nylon piece of webbing for a hip belt); a chest strap (the chest strap helps stabilize the pack against your body); external pockets to carry water and other items that you want easy access to; an internal pocket to hold keys, a knife, a wallet, and other miscellaneous items; an external lashing system to hold a jacket; and a hydration pocket for carrying a hydration system (which consists of a water bladder with an attachable drinking hose).

For short hikes, some hikers like to use a fanny pack to store just a camera, food, a compass, a map, and other trail essentials. Most fanny packs have pockets for two water bottles and a padded hip belt.

If you intend to do an extended, overnight trip, there are multiple considerations. First off, you need to decide what kind of framed pack you want. There are two backpack types for backpacking: the internal frame and the external frame. An internal frame pack rests closer to your body, making it more stable and easier to balance when hiking over rough terrain. An external frame pack is just that, an aluminum frame attached to the exterior of the pack. An external frame pack is better for long backpack trips because it distributes the pack weight better and you can carry heavier loads. It's easier to pack, and your gear is more accessible. It also offers better back ventilation in hot weather.

The most critical measurement for fitting a pack is torso length. The pack needs to rest evenly on your hips without sagging. A good pack will come in two or three sizes and have straps and hip belts that are adjustable according to your body size and characteristics.

When you purchase a backpack, go to an outdoor store with salespeople who are knowledgeable in how to properly fit a pack. Once the pack is fitted for you, load the pack with the amount of weight you plan on taking on the trail. The weight of the pack should be distributed evenly and you should be able to swing your arms and walk briskly without feeling out of balance. Another good technique for evaluating a pack is to walk up and down stairs and make quick turns to the right and to the left to be sure the pack doesn't feel out of balance. Other features that are nice to have on a backpack include a removable day pack or fanny pack, external pockets for extra water, and extra lash points to attach a jacket or other items.

Sleeping bags and pads. Sleeping bags are rated by temperature. You can purchase a bag made of synthetic fiber, or you can buy a goose down bag. Goose down bags are more expensive, but they have a higher insulating capacity by weight and will keep their loft longer. You'll want to purchase a bag with a temperature rating that fits the time of year and conditions you are most likely to camp in. One caveat: The techno-standard for temperature ratings is far from perfect. Ratings vary from manufacturer to manufacturer, so to protect yourself you should purchase a bag rated 10 to 15 degrees below the temperature you expect to be camping in. Synthetic bags are more resistant to water than down bags, but many down bags are now made with a Gore-Tex shell that helps to repel water. Down bags are also more compressible than synthetic bags and take up less room in your pack, which is an important consideration if you are planning a multiday backpack trip. Features to look for in a sleeping bag include a mummy style bag, a hood you can cinch down around your head in cold weather, and draft tubes along the zippers that help keep heat in and drafts out.

You'll also want a sleeping pad to provide insulation and padding from the cold ground. There are different types of sleeping pads available, from the more expensive self-inflating air mattresses to the less expensive closed-cell foam pads. Self-inflating air mattresses are usually heavier than closed-cell foam mattresses and are prone to punctures.

Tents. The tent is your home away from home while on the trail. It provides protection from wind, snow, rain, and insects. A three-season tent is a good choice for backpacking and can range in price from $100 to $500. These lightweight and versatile tents provide protection in all types of weather, except heavy snowstorms or high winds, and range in weight from four to eight pounds. Look for a tent that's easy to set up and will easily fit two people with gear. Dome type tents usually offer more headroom and places to store gear. Other tent designs include a vestibule where you can store wet boots and backpacks. Some nice-to-have items in a tent include interior pockets to store small items and lashing points to hang a clothesline. Most three-season tents also come with stakes so you can secure the tent in high winds. Before you purchase a tent, set it up and take it down a few times to be sure it is easy to handle. Also, sit inside the tent and make sure it has enough room for you and your gear.

Cell phones. Many hikers are carrying their cell phones into the backcountry these days in case of emergency. That's fine and good, but please know that cell phone coverage is often poor to nonexistent in valleys, canyons, and thick forest. More importantly people have started to call for help because they're tired or lost. Let's go back to being prepared. You are responsible for yourself in the backcountry. Use your brain to avoid problems, and if you do encounter one, first use your brain to try to correct the situation. Only use your cell phone, if it works, in true emergencies.

Hiking with Children

Hiking with children isn't a matter of how many miles you can cover or how much elevation gain you make in a day; it's about seeing and experiencing nature through their eyes.

Kids like to explore and have fun. They like to stop and point out bugs and plants, look under rocks, jump in puddles, and throw sticks. If you're taking a toddler or young child on a hike, start with a trail that you're familiar with. Trails that have interesting things for kids, like piles of leaves to play in or a small stream to wade through during the summer, will make the hike much more enjoyable for them and will keep them from getting bored.

You can keep your child's attention if you have a strategy before starting on the trail. Using games is not only an effective way to keep a child's attention, it's also a great way to teach him or her about nature. Play hide and seek, where your child is the mouse and you are the hawk. Quiz children on the names of plants and animals. If your children are old enough, let them carry their own daypack filled with snacks and water. So that you are sure to go at their pace and not yours, let them lead the way. Playing follow the leader works particularly well when you have a group of children. Have each child take a turn at being the leader.

With children, a lot of clothing is key. The only thing predictable about weather is that it will change. Especially in mountainous areas, weather can change dramatically in a very short time. Always bring extra clothing for children, regardless of the season. In the winter, have your children wear wool socks, and warm layers such as long underwear, a fleece jacket and hat, wool mittens, and good rain gear. It's not a bad idea to have these along in late fall and early spring as well. Good footwear is also important. A sturdy pair of high top tennis shoes or lightweight hiking boots are the best bet for little ones. If you're hiking in the summer near a lake or stream, bring along a pair of old sneakers that your child can put on when he wants to go exploring in the water. Remember when you're near any type of water, always watch your child at all times. Also, keep a close eye on teething toddlers who may decide a rock or leaf of poison oak is an interesting item to put in their mouth.

From spring through fall, you'll want your kids to wear a wide-brimmed hat to keep their face, head, and ears protected from the hot sun. Also, make sure your children wear sunscreen at all times. Choose a brand without Paba—children have sensitive skin and may have an allergic reaction to sunscreen that contains Paba. If you are hiking with a child younger than six months, don't use sunscreen or insect repellent. Instead, be sure that their head, face, neck, and ears are protected from the sun with a wide- brimmed hat, and that all other skin exposed to the sun is protected with the appropriate clothing.

Remember that food is fun. Kids like snacks so it's important to bring a lot of munchies for the trail. Stopping often for snack breaks is a fun way to keep the trail interesting. Raisins, apples, granola bars, crackers and cheese, cereal, and trail mix all make great snacks. If your child is old enough to carry her own backpack, fill it with treats before you leave. If your kids don't like drinking water, you can bring boxes of fruit juice.

Avoid poorly designed child-carrying packs—you don't want to break your back carrying your child. Most child-carrying backpacks designed to hold a forty-pound child will contain a large carrying pocket to hold diapers and other items. Some have an optional rain/sun hood.

Hiking with Your Dog

Bringing your furry friend with you is always more fun than leaving him behind. Our canine pals make great trail buddies because they never complain and always make good company. Hiking with your dog can be a rewarding experience, especially if you plan ahead.

Getting your dog in shape. Before you plan outdoor adventures with your dog, make sure he's in shape for the trail. Getting your dog into shape takes the same discipline as getting yourself into shape, but luckily, your dog can get in shape with you. Take your dog with you on your daily runs or walks. If there is a park near your house, hit a tennis ball or play Frisbee with your dog.

Swimming is also an excellent way to get your dog into shape. If there is a lake or river near where you live and your dog likes the water, have him retrieve a tennis ball or stick. Gradually build your dog's stamina up over a two- to three-month period. A good rule of thumb is to assume that your dog will travel twice as far as you will on the trail. If you plan on doing a 5-mile hike, be sure your dog is in shape for a 10-mile hike.

Training your dog for the trail. Before you go on your first hiking adventure with your dog, be sure he has a firm grasp on the basics of canine etiquette and behavior. Make sure he can sit, lie down, stay, and come. One of the most important commands you can teach your canine pal is to "come" under any situation. It's easy for your friend's nose to lead him astray or possibly get lost. Another helpful command is the "get behind" command. When you're on a hiking trail that's narrow, you can have your dog follow behind you when other trail users approach. Nothing is more bothersome than an enthusiastic dog that runs back and forth on the trail and disrupts the peace of the trail for others. When you see other trail users approaching you on the trail, give them the right of way by quietly stepping off the trail and making your dog lie down and stay until they pass.

Equipment. The most critical pieces of equipment you can invest in for your dog are proper identification and a sturdy leash. Flexi-leads work well for hiking because they give your dog more freedom to explore but still leave you in control. Make sure your dog has identification that includes your name and address and a number for your veterinarian. Other forms of identification for your dog include a tattoo or a microchip. You should consult your veterinarian for more information on these last two options.

The next piece of equipment you'll want to consider is a pack for your dog. By no means should you hold all of your dog's essentials in your pack—let him carry his own gear! Dogs that are in good shape can carry 30 to 40 percent of their own weight.

Most packs are fitted by a dog's weight and girth measurement. Companies that make dog packs generally include guidelines to help you pick out the size that's right for your dog. Some characteristics to look for when purchasing a pack for your dog include a harness that contains two padded girth straps, a padded chest strap, leash attachments, removable saddle bags, internal water bladders, and external gear cords.

You can introduce your dog to the pack by first placing the empty pack on his back and letting him wear it around the yard. Keep an eye on him during this first introduction. He may decide to chew through the straps if you aren't watching him closely. Once he learns to treat the pack as an object of fun and not a foreign enemy, fill the pack evenly on both sides with a few ounces of dog food in resealable plastic bags. Have your dog wear his pack on your daily walks for a period of two to three weeks. Each week add a little more weight to the pack until your dog will accept carrying the maximum amount of weight he can carry.

You can also purchase collapsible water and dog food bowls for your dog. These bowls are lightweight and can easily be stashed into your pack or your dog's. If you are hiking on rocky terrain or in the snow, you can purchase footwear for your dog that will protect his feet from cuts and bruises.

Always carry plastic bags to remove feces from the trail. It is a courtesy to other trail users and helps protect local wildlife.

The following is a list of items to bring when you take your dog hiking: collapsible water bowls, a comb, a collar and a leash, dog food, plastic bags for feces, a dog pack, flea/tick powder, paw protection, water, and a first-aid kit that contains eye ointment, tweezers, scissors, stretchy foot wrap, gauze, antibacterial wash, sterile cotton tip applicators, antibiotic ointment, and cotton wrap.

First aid for your dog. Your dog is just as prone—if not more prone—to getting in trouble on the trail as you are, so be prepared. Here's a rundown of the more likely misfortunes that might befall your little friend.

Bees and wasps. If a bee or wasp stings your dog, remove the stinger with a pair of tweezers and place a mudpack or a cloth dipped in cold water over the affected area.

Porcupines. One good reason to keep your dog on a leash is to prevent it from getting a nose full of porcupine quills. You may be able to remove the quills with pliers, but a veterinarian is the best person to do this nasty job because most dogs need to be sedated.

Heat stroke. Avoid hiking with your dog in really hot weather. Dogs with heat stroke will pant excessively, lie down and refuse to get up, and become lethargic and disoriented. If your dog shows any of these signs on the trail, have him lie down in the shade. If you are near a stream, pour cool water over your dog's entire body to help bring his body temperature back to normal.

Heartworm. Dogs get heartworms from mosquitoes which carry the disease in the prime mosquito months of July and August. Giving your dog a monthly pill prescribed by your veterinarian easily prevents this condition.

Plant pitfalls. One of the biggest plant hazards for dogs on the trail are foxtails. Foxtails are pointed grass seed heads that bury themselves in your friend's fur, between his toes, and even get in his ear canal. If left unattended, these nasty seeds can work their way under the skin and cause abscesses and other problems. If you have a long-haired dog, consider trimming the hair between his toes and giving him a summer haircut to help prevent foxtails from attaching to his fur. After every hike, always look over your dog for these seeds—especially between his toes and his ears.

Other plant hazards include burrs, thorns, thistles, and poison oak. If you find any burrs or thistles on your dog, remove them as soon as possible before they become an unmanageable mat. Thorns can pierce a dog's foot and cause a great deal of pain. If you see that your dog is lame, stop and check his feet for thorns. Dogs are immune to poison oak but they can pick up the sticky, oily substance from the plant and transfer it to you.

Protect those paws. Be sure to keep your dog's nails trimmed so he avoids getting soft tissue or joint injuries. If your dog slows and refuses to go on, check to see that his paws aren't torn or worn. You can protect your dog's paws from trail hazards such as sharp gravel, foxtails, lava scree, and thorns by purchasing dog boots.

Sunburn. If your dog has light skin he is an easy target for sunburn on his nose and other exposed skin areas. You can apply a nontoxic sunscreen to exposed skin areas that will help protect him from overexposure to the sun.

Ticks and fleas. Ticks can easily give your dog Lyme disease, as well as other diseases. Before you hit the trail, treat your dog with a flea and tick spray or powder. You can also ask your veterinarian about a once-a-month pour-on treatment that repels fleas and ticks.

Mosquitoes and deer flies. These little flying machines can do a job on your dog's snout and ears. Best bet is to spray your dog with fly repellent for horses to discourage both pests.

Giardia. Dogs can get giardia, which results in diarrhea. It is usually not debilitating, but it's definitely messy. A vaccine against giardia is available.

Mushrooms. Make sure your dog doesn't sample mushrooms along the trail. They could be poisonous to him, but he doesn't know that.

When you are finally ready to hit the trail with your dog, keep in mind that national parks and many wilderness areas do not allow dogs on trails. Your best bet is to hike in national forests, BLM lands, and state parks. Always call ahead to see what the restrictions are.

Appendix A

Trail Finder

Best Hikes for Backpackers

51   Arch Canyon
48   Dark Canyon
26   Eastern Uintas Highline Trail
45   Egypt–Twentyfive Mile Wash
50   Fish Creek and Owl Creek Loop
33   Fish Lake Mountains
20   Four Lakes Basin
42   Hackberry Canyon
23   Kings Peak
40   Kolob Arch
7   Lone Peak Area via Lake Hardy
46   Main Moody Canyon
39   Pine Valley Mountains
24   Rock Creek
18   Round, Sand, and Fish Lakes
36   San Rafael River
44   Swett Canyon
41   Under-the-Rim Trail
47   Upheaval Dome
22   West Fork Blacks Fork

Best Hikes for Children and Beginning Hikers

13   Daniels Canyon Nature Trails
53   Marching Men and Tower Arch
52   Mule Canyon
54   Negro Bill Canyon
32   Skyline National Recreation Trail
16   Thornton Hollow
19   Three Divide Lakes

Best Hikes for Peak Baggers

3   Deseret Peak
4   Gobblers Knob
23   Kings Peak
2   Malans Peak
12   Mount Nebo
5   Mount Raymond
10   Mount Timpanogos via Aspen Grove Trail

30 Notch Peak
11 Santaquin Peak
 9 The Pfeifferhorn
31 Wah Wah Mountains

Best Hikes for Lake Lovers
34 Fish Creek Lake
20 Four Lakes Basin
23 Kings Peak
 6 Lake Blanche
 7 Lone Peak Area via Lake Hardy
 8 Red Pine Lakes
24 Rock Creek
18 Round, Sand, and Fish Lakes
21 Stillwater Drainage
19 Three Divide Lakes
22 West Fork Blacks Fork
25 Yellowstone Drainage

Best Hikes for Fishing
26 Eastern Uintas Highline Trail
35 Fish Creek
34 Fish Creek Lake
20 Four Lakes Basin
27 Jones Hole Creek
23 Kings Peak
 6 Lake Blanche
 8 Red Pine Lakes
24 Rock Creek
18 Round, Sand, and Fish Lakes
21 Stillwater Drainage
19 Three Divide Lakes
25 Yellowstone Drainage

Best Hikes for Wildlife Lovers
48 Dark Canyon
35 Fish Creek
27 Jones Hole Creek
46 Main Moody Canyon
53 Marching Men and Tower Arch
12 Mount Nebo
52 Mule Canyon
54 Negro Bill Canyon

8   Red Pine Lakes
24   Rock Creek
19   Three Divide Lakes
28   Tule Valley
31   Wah Wah Mountains
1   Wellsville Mountains
22   West Fork Blacks Fork
25   Yellowstone Drainage

Best Hikes for Wildflower Lovers
51   Arch Canyon
27   Jones Hole Creek
12   Mount Nebo
24   Rock Creek
18   Round, Sand, and Fish Lakes
1   Wellsville Mountains

Best Hikes for Canyon Lovers
51   Arch Canyon
49   Bridges Loop
48   Dark Canyon
45   Egypt–Twentyfive Mile Wash
50   Fish Creek and Owl Creek Loop
42   Hackberry Canyon
27   Jones Hole Creek
37   Lower Black Box
43   Lower Muley Twist Canyon
46   Main Moody Canyon
52   Mule Canyon
54   Negro Bill Canyon
36   San Rafael River
44   Swett Canyon
41   Under-the-Rim Trail
47   Upheaval Dome
38   Upper Black Box

Best Hikes for River Wading
45   Egypt–Twentyfive Mile Wash
50   Fish Creek and Owl Creek Loop
42   Hackberry Canyon
37   Lower Black Box
52   Mule Canyon
36   San Rafael River

44 Swett Canyon
38 Upper Black Box

Best Hikes for Geology Lovers
51 Arch Canyon
49 Bridges Loop
48 Dark Canyon
50 Fish Creek and Owl Creek Loop
42 Hackberry Canyon
27 Jones Hole Creek
40 Kolob Arch
 7 Lone Peak via Lake Hardy
43 Lower Muley Twist Canyon
46 Main Moody Canyon
53 Marching Men and Tower Arch
52 Mule Canyon
54 Negro Bill Canyon
36 San Rafael River
44 Swett Canyon
41 Under-the-Rim Trail
47 Upheaval Dome

Best Hikes for Archaeology Lovers
51 Arch Canyon
49 Bridges Loop
48 Dark Canyon
50 Fish Creek and Owl Creek Loop
27 Jones Hole Creek
52 Mule Canyon
28 Tule Valley

Appendix B

Local Conservation Organizations

High Uintas Preservation Council
P.O. Box 72
Hyrum, UT 84319
(435) 245–6747
www.hupc.org

Sierra Club, Utah Chapter
2120 South 1300 E., Suite 204
Salt Lake City, UT 84106
(801) 467–9297
utah.sierraclub.org

Southern Utah Wilderness Alliance
1471 South 1100 E.
Salt Lake City, UT 84105
(801) 486–3161
www.suwa.org

Utah Wilderness Coalition
P.O. Box 520974
Salt Lake City, UT 84152
(801) 486–2872
www.uwcoalition.org

Utah Wildlife Federation
P.O. Box 526367
Salt Lake City, UT 84152
(801) 487–1946
www.nwf.org/about/affiliates.cfm

Wasatch Mountain Club
1390 South 1100 E., Suite 103
Salt Lake City, UT 84105
(801) 463–9842
www.wasatchmountainclub.org

Appendix C

Federal and State Agencies

Public Lands Information Center
3285 East 3300 S.
Salt Lake City, UT 84109
(801) 466–6411

USDA Forest Service
www.fs.fed.us/r4

USDA Forest Service, Intermountain
Region
Union Station
2501 Wall Avenue
Ogden, UT 84401
(801) 625–5306
www.fs.fed.us/r4

Ashley National Forest
355 North Vernal Avenue
Vernal, UT 84078
(435) 789–1181
www.fs.fed.us/r4/ashley

Duchesne Ranger District
85 West Main
P.O. Box 981
Duchesne, UT 84021
(435) 738–2482

Flaming Gorge Ranger District
25 West Highway 43
P.O. Box 279
Manila, UT 84046
(435) 784–3445

Roosevelt Ranger District
650 West Highway 40
P.O. Box 127
Roosevelt, UT 84066
(435) 722–5018

Vernal Ranger District
355 North Vernal Avenue
Vernal, UT 84078
(435) 789–1181

Dixie National Forest
1789 Wedgewood Lane
Cedar City, UT 84720
(435) 865–3700
www.fs.fed.us/dxnf

Cedar City Ranger District
1789 Wedgewood Lane
Cedar City, UT 84720
(435) 865–3200

Escalante Ranger District
P.O. Box 246
Escalante, UT 84726
(435) 826–5400

Pine Valley Ranger District
196 East Tabernacle
St. George, UT 84770
(435) 688–3246

Powell Ranger District
P.O. Box 80
Panguitch, UT 84759
(435) 676–9300

Teasdale Ranger District
P.O. Box 90
Teasdale, UT 84773
(435) 425–9500

Fishlake National Forest
115 East 900 N.
Richfield, UT 84701
(435) 896–9233
www.fs.fed.us/r4/fishlake

Beaver Ranger District
575 South Main
P.O. Box E
Beaver, UT 84713
(435) 438–2436

Fillmore Ranger District
390 South Main
P.O. Box 265
Fillmore, UT 84631
(801) 743–5721

Loa Ranger District
138 South Main
P.O. Box 129
Loa, UT 84747
(435) 836–2811

Richfield Ranger District
115 East 900 N.
Richfield, UT 84701
(801) 896–9233

Manti-LaSal National Forest
599 West Price River Drive
Price, UT 84501
(435) 637–2817
www.fs.fed.us/r4/mantilasal

Farron Ranger District
115 West Canyon Road
P.O. Box 310
Ferron, UT 84523
(435) 384–2372

Moab Ranger District
2290 Southwest Resource Boulevard
P.O. Box 386
Moab, UT 84532
(435) 259–7155

Monticello Ranger District
496 East Central
P.O. Box 820
Monticello, UT 84535
(435) 587–2041

Price Ranger District
599 West Price River Drive
Price, UT 84501
(435) 637–2817

Sanpele Ranger District
540 North Main 32-14
Ephraim, UT 84627
(435) 283–4151

Uinta National Forest
88 West 100 N.
P.O. Box 1428
Provo, UT 84603
(801) 342–5100
www.fs.fed.us/r4/uinta

Heber Ranger District
2460 South Highway 40
P.O. Box 190
Heber City, UT 84032
(435) 654–0470

Pleasant Grove Ranger District
390 North 100 E.
Pleasant Grove, UT 84062
(801) 785–3563

Spanish Fork Ranger District
44 West 400 N.
Spanish Fork, UT 84660
(801) 798–3571

Spanish Fork Ranger District—Nephi
Office
635 North Main
Nephi, UT 84648
(435) 623–2735

Wasatch-Cache National Forest
8236 Federal Building
125 South State Street
Salt Lake City, UT 84138
(801) 524–3900
www.fs.fed.us/r4/wcnf

Evanston Ranger District
1565 Highway 150 S., Suite A
P.O. Box 1880
Evanston, WY 82930
(307) 789–3194

Kamas Ranger District
50 East Center Street
P.O. Box 68
Kamas, UT 84036
(435) 783–4338

Logan Ranger District
1500 East Highway 89
Logan, UT 84321
(435) 755–3620

Mountain View Ranger District
321 Highway 414 E.
P.O. Box 129
Mountain View, WY 82939
(307) 782–6555

Ogden Ranger District
507 25th Street
Odgen, UT 84403
(801) 625–5112

Salt Lake Ranger District
6944 South 3000 E.
Salt Lake City, UT 84121
(801) 733–2660

National Park Service
www.nps.gov

Arches National Park
P.O. Box 907
Moab, UT 84532
(435) 719–2299
www.nps.gov/arch

Bryce Canyon National Park
P.O. Box 17001
Bryce Canyon, UT 84717-0001

(435) 834–5322
www.nps.gov/brca

Canyonlands National Park
2282 Southwest Resource Boulevard
Moab, UT 84532
(435) 719–2313
www.nps.gov/cany

Capitol Reef National Park
HC 70 Box 15
Torrey, UT 84775-9602
(435) 425–3791
www.nps.gov/care

Cedar Breaks National Monument
2390 West Highway 56, Suite 11
Cedar City, UT 84720
(435) 586–9451
www.nps.gov/cebr

Dinosaur National Monument
4545 East Highway 40
Dinosaur, CO 81610
(970) 374–3000
www.nps.gov/dino

Glen Canyon National Recreation Area
P.O. Box 1507
Page, AZ 86040
(928) 608–6200
www.nps.gov/glca

Natural Bridges National Monument
HC 60 Box 1
Lake Powell, UT 84533
(435) 692–1234
www.nps.gov/nabr

Rainbow Bridge National Monument
P.O. Box 1507
Page, AZ 86040
(928) 608–6404
www.nps.gov/nabr

Timpanogos Cave National Monument
RR 3, Box 200
American Fork, UT 84003
(801) 756–5238
www.nps.gov/tica

Zion National Park
SR 9
Springdale, UT 84767
(435) 772–3256
www.nps.gov/zion

Bureau of Land Management (BLM)

Bureau of Land Management
Utah State Office
324 South State Street, Suite 301
P.O. Box 45155
Salt Lake City, UT 84145-0155
(801) 539–4001
www.ut.blm.gov

Cedar City Field Office
176 East D. L. Sargent Drive
Cedar City, UT 84720
(435) 586–2401

Escalante Interagency Visitor
Information Center
755 West Main Street
Escalante, UT 84726
(435) 826–5499

Fillmore Field Office
35 East 500 N.
P.O. Box 778
Fillmore, UT 84631
(435) 743–3100

Henry Mountains Field Office
P.O. Box 99
Hanksville, UT 84734
(435) 542–3461

Kanab Field Office
318 North 100 E.
Kanab, UT 84741
(435) 644–4600

Moab Field Office
82 East Dogwood
Moab, UT 84532
(435) 259–2100

Monticello Field Office
435 North Main Street
P.O. Box 7
Monticello, UT 84535
(435) 587–1500

Price Field Office
125 South 600 W.
P.O. Box 7004
Price, UT 84501
(435) 636–3600

Richfield Field Office
150 East 900 N.
Richfield, UT 84701
(435) 896–1500

Salt Lake Field Office
2370 South 2300 W.
Salt Lake City, UT 84119
(801) 977–4300

St. George Field Office
345 East Riverside Drive
St. George, UT 84790
(435) 688–3200

Vernal Field Office
170 South 500 E.
Vernal, UT 84078
(435) 781–4400

State Offices and Land Management Agencies

Governor's Office
East Office Building, Suite E220
State Capitol Complex
P.O. Box 142220
Salt Lake City, UT 84114
(801) 538–1000 or (800) 705–2464
www.utah.gov/governor

Utah Department of Natural Resources
1594 West North Temple
P.O. Box 145610
Salt Lake City, UT 84114-5610
(801) 538–7200
www.nr.utah.gov

Utah Division of Forestry, Fire & State
Lands
1594 West North Temple, Suite 3520
P.O. Box 145703
Salt Lake City, UT 84114
(801) 538–5555
www.nr.utah.gov/slf/slfhome.htm

Utah Division of Wildlife Resources
1594 West North Temple, Suite 2110
P.O. Box 146301
Salt Lake City, UT 84116
(801) 538–4700
www.wildlife.utah.gov

Utah Division of Parks and Recreation
1594 West North Temple, Suite 116
P.O. Box 146001
Salt Lake City, UT 84114
(801) 538–7220
www.stateparks.utah.gov

Appendix D

Finding Maps

Maps published by the United States Geological Survey (USGS), National Geographic Trails Illustrated, and the Utah Travel Council are recommended as supplements to those in this guide.

The USGS maps are detailed 7.5-minute quads and are available from many commercial outlets throughout the state. Topos and state map indexes are available directly from USGS Information Services, P.O. Box 25286, Denver, CO 80225; (888) ASK–USGS; http://store.usgs.gov. Older 15-minute quads are no longer published and may be permanently out of stock. You may also find the USGS 1:100,000 series useful as an overview of an area. These maps are based on 1980 aerial photos.

National Geographic Trails Illustrated, an excellent line of recreational maps published by National Geographic Maps, covers Utah's most popular backcountry destinations and all its national parks. Each map is based on photo reproductions of USGS topographic maps, which are then updated and customized on an annual or biennial basis. The waterproof maps are available at book, map, and outdoor specialty stores, or can be ordered directly from National Geographic Maps, P.O. Box 4357, Evergreen, CO 80437; (800) 962–1643; www.nationalgeographic.com/maps/trails.

The Utah Travel Council publishes a set of four multipurpose maps that are helpful in navigating to the trailhead, since they offer a broader picture of the area. They are available from the Utah Travel Council, P.O. Box 147420, Salt Lake City 84114; (801) 538–1030 or (800) 200–1160; www.utah.com.

Other map outlets:

- The USDA Forest Service publishes maps for each of the six national forests in the state. These maps are available at national forest and ranger district offices. Check also for more detailed maps at the district offices.

- The Bureau of Land Management offers useful maps for some popular hiking areas. Check with a district or resource area office before making your hike to see if maps are available.

- The National Park Service has maps—generally as part of a brochure—for each of the parks. Stop in at a ranger station on the way to the trailhead.

- The Utah Department of Natural Resources maintains an official outlet for USGS publications and maps as well as a variety of maps and books for recreational activities in Utah. Contact the Natural Resources Map & Bookstore at (888) UTAH–MAP; http://mapstore.utah.gov.

- The Utah Division of Wildlife Resources publishes *Lakes of the High Uintas,* a helpful series of booklets describing the fishing potential in most of the Uinta lakes. Maps are included. They are available from the Division of Wildlife Resources main office and from some regional offices, or from the Natural Resources Map & Bookstore (above).

About the Author

Bill Schneider has spent thirty-five years hiking trails all across America. He has written twenty-one books and many magazine articles about wildlife, outdoor recreation, and environmental issues, and he has taught classes on bicycling, backpacking, zero-impact camping, and hiking in bear country for the Yellowstone Institute, a nonprofit educational organization in Yellowstone National Park. In 2000 Bill retired from his position as president of Falcon Publishing, which is now part of The Globe Pequot Press and has grown into the premier publisher of outdoor recreation guidebooks with more than 800 titles in print. He lives in Helena, Montana, with his wife, Marnie, and works as a publishing consultant and freelance writer.

Books by Bill Schneider

Backpacking Tips (1998)

Bear Aware, A Quick Reference Bear Country Survival Guide (2004)

Best Backpacking Vacations Northern Rockies (2002)

Best Easy Day Hikes Absaroka-Beartooth Wilderness (2003)

Best Easy Day Hikes Canyonlands and Arches (2005)

Best Easy Day Hikes Grand Teton (2005)

Best Easy Day Hikes Yellowstone (2003)

Best Hikes on the Continental Divide (1988)

Hiking Canyonlands and Arches National Parks (2005)

Hiking Carlsbad Caverns and Guadalupe Mountains National Parks (2005)

Hiking Grand Teton National Park (2005)

Hiking Montana (2004)

Hiking the Absaroka-Beartooth Wilderness (2003)

Hiking Yellowstone National Park (2003)

Hiking Utah (2005)

The Dakota Image (1980)

The Flight of the Nez Perce (1988)

The Tree Giants (1988)

The Yellowstone River (1985)

Where the Grizzly Walks (2003)

Learn more about Bill Schneider's books at www.billschneider.net.